The State, Society, and Foreign Capital in India

Why are some states in India able to manage Foreign Direct Investment (FDI) better than other states by facilitating economic institutions? This book answers the question by examining the relationships between the state, society, and foreign capital in two select provincial states in India, namely, Tamil Nadu and Odisha. Not only at the central government but also in the two states, it was found that the ideas of key policymakers on the need for foreign capital as important financial resources critically influenced the institutional changes favouring FDI inflows in the process of industrial development. The year 1967 was a crucial turning point for Tamil Nadu and Odisha during which regional political parties won the state legislative assembly elections and had a chance to capitalise on citizenship politics. In both states, the financial difficulties of the 1970s helped state leaders consider foreign investments as significant financial resources. However, such ideas were implemented with a significant difference in the two states.

This book details the difference. It scrutinises the socio–political factors, such as ideas and interests of political actors in restructuring institutions, which shaped the disparate levels of FDI inflows into the states. It emphasises the causal role of differing state–society relations in the evolution of institutions facilitating and regulating FDI inflows in the two states. It also aims to explain the dissimilar patterns of such institutional change at the union and state levels.

Sojin Shin researches and teaches at the Institute of South Asian Studies at the National University of Singapore. Her research focuses on the political economy of development in South Asia. As a comparative political scientist and area specialist, she is particularly interested in the puzzles of uneven economic and political development in the states of India and the dynamics of regional politics in South Asia. She is currently visiting Seoul National University's Asia Center.

The State, Society, and Foreign Capital in India

Sojin Shin

CAMBRIDGE
UNIVERSITY PRESS

University Printing House, Cambridge CB2 8BS, United Kingdom

One Liberty Plaza, 20th Floor, New York, NY 10006, USA

477 Williamstown Road, Port Melbourne, vic 3207, Australia

314 to 321, 3rd Floor, Plot No.3, Splendor Forum, Jasola District Centre, New Delhi 110025, India

79 Anson Road, #06-04/06, Singapore 079906

Cambridge University Press is part of the University of Cambridge.

It furthers the University's mission by disseminating knowledge in the pursuit of education, learning and research at the highest international levels of excellence.

www.cambridge.org
Information on this title: www.cambridge.org/9781108425063

© Sojin Shin 2018

This publication is in copyright. Subject to statutory exception and to the provisions of relevant collective licensing agreements, no reproduction of any part may take place without the written permission of Cambridge University Press.

First published 2018

Printed in India by Thomson Press India Ltd.

A catalogue record for this publication is available from the British Library

ISBN 978-1-108-42506-3 Hardback

Cambridge University Press has no responsibility for the persistence or accuracy of URLs for external or third-party internet websites referred to in this publication, and does not guarantee that any content on such websites is, or will remain, accurate or appropriate.

For Swe Soe and Shian Shin

Contents

List of Tables, Figures, Illustrations, and Maps ix
Acknowledgements xi

1. Introduction 1
2. FDI Inflows in India: Ideas, Interests, and Institutional Change 23
3. FDI Inflows in Tamil Nadu: Inclusionary Ideas, Weakened Interests, and Incremental Institutional Change 50
4. Making FDI Work in Tamil Nadu 79
5. FDI Inflows in Odisha: Weakened Ideas, Strong Interests, and Unstable Institutional Change 106
6. Making FDI Work in Odisha? 133
7. Conclusion 154

Bibliography 165
Index 179

List of Tables, Figures, Illustrations, and Maps

Tables
1.1	FDI Equity Inflows to the Select States in India (April 2000–March 2017)	3
1.2	Select Demographic Indicators of Tamil Nadu and Odisha	18
1.3	Select Human Development Indices of Tamil Nadu and Odisha	19
1.4	Dropout from Schools, Unemployment, and Poverty of Tamil Nadu and Odisha	20
2.1	Foreign Reserves of Total External Debt in India (1975–91)	31
2.2	FDI Inflows to India and China (1991–2015)	36
2.3	FDI Equity Inflows to India, FIPB Route (1991–2017)	44
3.1	Share of Tamil Nadu in Central Assistance Extended to All States	58
3.2	Trends of Growth Rates in the Select States (1960–80)	63
3.3	Select Human Development Indices in Poverty and Health, Tamil Nadu and India	76
5.1	Permanent Debt in Odisha in the 1970s	114
5.2	Dropout from Schools, Unemployment, and Poverty of Tamil Nadu and Odisha	123
6.1	State–Business Relation Ranks among States in India, 1985–2005	138

Figures
1.1	Theoretical Areas of FDI Studies	7
1.2	Linkage between State–Society Relations and Institutional Changes	13
1.3	Linkage between Ideas, Interests, and Institutional Changes in State and Society	16
7.1	Inclusionary State–Society Relations, Strong State Capacity, and High Level of FDI Inflows in Tamil Nadu.	159
7.2	Exclusionary State–Society Relations, Weak State Capacity, and Low Level of FDI Inflows in Odisha.	160

Illustrations

4.1	HMI in Chennai (27–28 December 2011)	83
4.4	MI's FDI Project in Thervoy Kandigai (17 January and 12 February 2012)	98
4.5	Rehabilitation for the Displaced Dalit Villagers in Thervoy Kandigai (12 February 2012)	101
6.1	Villages and Villagers in Kujang Tehsil	141

Maps

4.1	Fieldwork Sites in Tamil Nadu	81
6.1	Fieldwork Sites in Odisha	134

Acknowledgements

This book is about the politics of Foreign Direct Investment in India and is the fruition of my doctoral work that I pursued at the National University of Singapore (NUS). It is based on my doctoral dissertation that received the best PhD thesis award by Singapore Indian Chamber of Commerce and Industry. Publication materials for the book have been updated through fieldwork for the past couple of years. NUS provided research scholarship, fieldwork grant, and conference funding, and T J Park Foundation in POSCO from South Korea offered Asia Fellowship. However, I would like to clarify that the Fellowship did not influence my case selection of POSCO in Odisha. Furthermore, I have never received any preferential treatment from POSCO during my field research.

It was possible to publish this book thanks to encouragement and support from my teachers, colleagues, friends, and family. For this, I would like to extend my gratitude to all the individuals and groups involved.

First of all, I deeply appreciate my academic mentors and good friends, Rahul Mukherji and Kurtuluş Gemici, for their steadfast support and encouragement. I am heavily indebted to them who have constantly stimulated me to enhance my academic prowess. I hope to repay part of the debt through this book.

I would like to express my sincere gratitude to Aseema Sinha, Sooyeon Kim, and Duvvuri Subbarao for their time and engagement with the manuscript. I also thank Rob Jenkins, Bhanoji Rao, John Harriss, Irfan Nooruddin, and the two anonymous reviewers for their comments on the book manuscript. I would like to extend my special thanks to Cambridge University Press editors, Anwesha Rana, Qudsiya Ahmed, and Anushruti Ganguly for their hard work and pushing me.

I am thankful to my friends and senior professionals who helped me in many ways during my fieldwork in India, Satish Rengarajan, S. S. Rengarajan Sundaram, Madhu Malathy Rengarajan, S. Narayan, Ashik Bonofer, M. Vijayabaskar, Andrew Wyatt, Bijayini Mohanty, Gobinda Ballava Dalai, Narutom, Avijit Panda, Antony Jacob, Shagufta Neyazi, Himanshu Jha, and Samyuel Park. I would extend my special thanks to villagers at Sriperumbudur and Thervoy Kandigai in Tamil Nadu and at Kujang and Kalinga Nagar in Odisha.

I am grateful to my colleagues in the Institute of South Asian Studies (ISAS) at NUS. I appreciate Ambassador Gopinath Pillai, Tan Tai Yong, Subrata Mitra, and Hernaikh Singh for their strong support of my work and academic activities at ISAS.

I have benefitted from the countless insightful seminars and conferences organised by the Institute. I would like to extend my thanks to Srikanth Thaliyakkattil, Amit Ranjan, Iftekhar Chowdhury, Rani Mullen, Sumit Ganguly, Dipinder Randhawa, and Riaz Hassan for their heated discussions of my research and cheerful encouragement. Also, I thank the faculty members in NUS including Jang-Sup Shin, Sea-Jin Chang, Gyanesh Kudaisya, Rajesh Rai, Maunaguru Sidharthan, and Subhasish Ray. I would like to send my special thanks to Taberez Neyazi, who has always been generous in providing constructive comments and encouragement for my work.

I extend thanks to my teachers, Soo-Jin Kim, Neera Chandhoke, and M. P. Singh, in my old schools, Ewha Womans University and the University of Delhi. I thank senior academics in Delhi, Indivar Kamtekar, Balveer Arora, A. N. Roy, and E. Sridharan. As a life member, I especially appreciate faculties and members of Indian Political Economy Association including V. Upadhyay, Kamal Kabra, Surinder Kumar, Ramana Murthy, Jayan Thomas, Reetika Khera, and many others who have always encouraged me with numerous positive comments and suggestions on my research. I apologise that I cannot enumerate all of their names for gratitude. However, I should mention Sarbeswar Sahoo who has always given me critical comments and useful sources for good research.

Also, I would like to highlight that questions and suggestions contributed by many academics from different institutes and international conventions have enabled me to enhance the book manuscript. I would like to thank academics in the Department of Political Science at SungKyunKwan University, International Relations and Peace Studies at Ritsumeikan Asia Pacific University, annual meetings of the Midwest Political Science Association, International Studies Association, and International Political Science Association. I am grateful to Seoul National University's Asia Center for providing me a visiting scholarship with study space where I am writing this page of acknowledgement. I thank faculty members and visiting academics across departments at Seoul National University for their engagement and animated discussions of my completed study. I also thank senior academics and professionals in South Korea, Yoon-Hwan Shin, Dae-Seung Hong, and Choongjae Cho. I am also grateful to faculties in various universities in Japan who have cheered for me in the publication process, Rohan D'Souza, Kazuya Nakamizo, Jonson Porteux, and Stephen Zurcher.

Last but not least, I reserve and express my deepest gratitude to my family, Moonja Youn, Hoasun Shin, Swe Swe Aung, Soe Min Than, Yeojin Yoon, and Kwancheol Shin. They have been my pillars of support at home by cheering me on and babysitting while I am away at work or on international conference trips. My special thanks to Tin Maung Maung Than for giving time and comments on the book manuscript. I am so lucky to have an established political scientist at home. Without their tremendous support and trust, my study could never see the light. In closing, I send my special gratitude and love to my buttress in life, Swe Soe and Shian Shin.

At Seoul National University, April 2018

1

Introduction

Empirical puzzles

On the evening of 18 March 2017, *The Economic Times* informed that POSCO, the world's fifth-largest steel producer from South Korea,[1] would drop its US$12 billion steel project in the eastern Indian state of Odisha.[2] After signing a Memorandum of Understanding (MOU) with the Government of Odisha in June 2005, it took as many as twelve years for POSCO to decide to cease its investment project. Odisha is one of the provincial states in India possessing abundant natural resources, such as iron-ore, bauxite, and many other minerals. Despite having heavy stock of natural resources, Odisha is, ironically, one of the economically most backward and the least industrialised states.[3] It was believed that the district of Jagatsinghpur, where POSCO's steel project was to take place, would transform like Rourkela, which became a wealthy and modernised city in Odisha through the establishment of the Rourkela Steel Plant built in the early years of post-colonial period.[4]

---

[1] 'Top Steel-producing Companies,' by World Steel Association, accessed 20 July 2017, www.worldsteel.org/steel-by-topic/statistics/top-producers.html.

[2] In fact, the Government of Odisha asked POSCO to pay pending dues of around 820 million Indian rupees for forest land diversion and others. While replying to its letter, POSCO made an official request to the Government of Odisha saying that it is not interested to take possession of the acquired land and pay the remaining amount. As of March 2017, POSCO acquired 1,700 acres in villages in Kujang near the Paradip port at the district of Jagatsinghpur in Odisha out of 2,700 acres of proposed land through the Government of Odisha.

*Orissa has been used instead of Odisha in this book for works published before 2010.

[3] As of July 2014, Odisha's per capita state domestic product was 66,552 Indian rupees (25th out of 30 states) and its per capita plan expenditure was 5,154 Indian rupees (23rd out of 30 states). See the NITI Aayog/Planning Commission for various data on state-wise socioeconomic indicators, accessed 4 August 2017, https://data.gov.in/catalog/major-socio-economic-indicators-states-india.

[4] The second modernisation of Rourkela steel plant began in 2015 with the support of Narendra Modi government at the union level. The first modernisation of Rourkela steel

POSCO's withdrawal from its steel project in Odisha was not shocking. POSCO had invested heavily in the project that eventually became one of the most controversial and highly politicised foreign investments in India. A variety of groups and organisations protested against POSCO in the past twelve years. While different groups of people were seeking to enhance their interests through the protests, which grew as big as a movement, villagers in Kujang got increasingly polarised. Political leaders, bureaucrats, foreign investors, and local citizens were entangled in POSCO's steel plan.

In fact, POSCO was not the only investor that had difficulties in carrying out a large-scale investment plan in the state. TATA Steel, the world's 10th largest steel producer based in India, also struggled for more than seven years in building its steel plant in Kalinga Nagar after signing an MOU with the Government of Odisha in 2004. Despite the struggle, TATA has managed to set it up.

What makes it difficult to materialise the large-scale investment projects in Odisha? Does the resource extractive nature of steel industry act as a barrier? If so, why did others struggle while the Rourkela steel project was viable? Does the timing of investments matter? If yes, how do we explain the subtle or substantial distinction between POSCO and TATA, a dropout and a survivor in the long and lagging investment process? Is the colour of money important as India's domestic investors seem to manage somehow to handle problems in the process while foreign investors fail? If so, how do we understand many other foreign investment plans that were undertaken successfully in other states of India?

Interestingly, POSCO's investment failure in Odisha seems to explain the low level of foreign investments to the state. Table 1.1 presents the accumulative Foreign Direct Investment (FDI) equity inflows that came into select states in India from April 2000 to March 2017.[5] According to the table, the cumulative FDI inflows in Maharashtra and Delhi during the period account for more than half of the total FDI inflows in India. Some states such as Tamil Nadu, Karnataka, and Gujarat have attracted a fairly large amount of FDI inflows. On the contrary, some northern and eastern states like West Bengal, Odisha, Bihar, and Jammu and Kashmir have struggled to attract foreign investors.

---

plant was pursued throughout the 1980s and the 1990s after the plant was built in 1964 by the Steel Authority of India, an India's Public Sector Undertaking. However, I would not discount adverse criticism of the Rourkela project that involved displacing a large number of local tribals in Odisha in the process of land acquisition.

[5] Organisation for Economic Co-operation and Development (OECD) defines Foreign Direct Investment as cross-border investment by a resident entity in one economy with the objective of obtaining a lasting interest in an enterprise resident in another economy.

Table 1.1: FDI Equity Inflows to the Select States in India (April 2000–March 2017)[6]

Group	RBI's Regional Office	States Mainly Covered	Cumulative Inflows (US$ in Million)	Percentage to Total Inflows
1	Mumbai	Maharashtra	102,283	31
	New Delhi	Delhi	68,037	20
2	Chennai	Tamil Nadu	23,760	7
	Bangalore	Karnataka	22,374	7
	Ahmedabad	Gujarat	16,652	5
	Hyderabad	Andhra Pradesh	13,766	4
3	Kolkata	West Bengal	3,985	1
	Bhubaneshwar	Odisha	416	0.1
	Patna	Bihar	103	0.03
	Jammu	Jammu & Kashmir	6	0
Total	-	-	331,991	100

Note: Group 1: $x > 10$; Group 2: $1 < x \leq 10$; Group 3: $x \leq 1$ [x= percentage to total inflows].
Source: DIPP, GOI.[7]

How have some states facilitated FDI inflows while others have struggled? Building upon the empirical evidence, this book addresses the regional variations of FDI inflows across states in India as a central question.

Theoretical puzzles

The differing level of state capacity at the subnational state level in generating economic growth has often been discussed in the discipline of India's political economy.[8] The puzzle of state-wise variations in the economic performance was

---

[6] One may find that the state-wise data on FDI inflows is not dealt with 'individual' states in India. Department of Industrial Policy & Promotion (DIPP) issues *FDI Fact Sheet* that presents the state-wise FDI statistics regularly by collecting data from various regional offices of the Reserve Bank of India across the country. However, it does not strictly classify individual states in the publication. For example, Delhi includes some part of Uttar Pradesh and Haryana, and Tamil Nadu covers Pondicherry. Neither DIPP nor RBI publishes the state-wise FDI statistics, though the DIPP's data presented is the most appropriate to compare states. I thank Vivek Aggarwal and Duvvuri Subbarao from RBI for their help in this matter.

[7] DIPP, Ministry of Commerce and Industry, Government of India (GOI), accessed 1 August 2017, http://dipp.nic.in/sites/default/files/FDI_FactSheet_January_March2017.pdf.

[8] See Rudolph and Rudolph (2001), 1542–43, for the discussion on a concept 'federal market economy' that captures the regional divergence in economic performance. The concept opened a scholarly discussion on the state-level analysis for India's economic growth.

examined thoroughly in Aseema Sinha's *A Divided Leviathan* and Atul Kohli's *Poverty Amid Plenty in the New India*.

Sinha (2005) explored the regional roots of developmental politics in India by comparing three select states – Gujarat, West Bengal, and Tamil Nadu. Sinha raised a question of differing levels of industrialisation in the three states and explored their developmental trajectories, paying attention to the pattern of industrial investment at the state level. An intriguing puzzle that Sinha asked was why Gujarat attracted a high level of domestic investment over time while West Bengal failed to capitalise on its initial strength as a capital-intensive state that structured a high level of industrialisation at the time of independence. Sinha paid particular attention to the regional variations in economic performance – Gujarat as a good performer, Tamil Nadu as a mediocre performer, and West Bengal as a bad performer – though her data set for the analysis was mainly focused on the pre-1991 economic reform period. Sinha suggested two variables in explaining the consequence of economic performance in the states, namely, vertical interactions and horizontal dimensions.

The vertical interactions, which are deeply associated with bureaucratic behaviours in the relationship between the central government and the state government, indicated that Gujarat built an integrated relationship with the central government through active bargaining and lobbying to provide an investment-friendly environment for the private sector. However, West Bengal had a confrontational relationship with the central government and Tamil Nadu's relationship with it was somewhat mixed between integration and conflict.

The horizontal dimensions are concerned with the regional institutional capacity and its linkage with the political incentives for local political leaders. It was found that Gujarat's institutional capacity was high while that of two other states was low. Gujarat pursued both the capital-intensive and labour-intensive industrialisation strategies so that it could fulfil key business sectors in general and get political support in the local elections. Meanwhile, West Bengal's left-wing government pushed a small and geographically limited industrial plan with the focus on Calcutta and gained political support from the agrarian sectors. It encouraged the anti-centre sentiment and enabled the left-wing government to rule the state for many years. However, Tamil Nadu's trajectory was quite mixed. It sought a strategy enhancing the public sector until the end of the 1960s when the regional political leaders could effectively lobby the central government. Then a regional Dravidian movement became very popular and it fuelled anti-centre sentiment from the 1970s to the mid-1980s. Changing their attitude again, however, the political leaders of Tamil Nadu tried to cooperate with the central government after the mid-1980s.

Kohli (2012) also paid attention to the regional diversities of states in India in reducing poverty and generating economic growth by comparing three select states – Uttar Pradesh, Gujarat, and West Bengal. Kohli's interests in the state-wise variations lay in looking at how the states had been governed and how they developed economies. Kohli suggested the differing 'political tendencies' of the three states in structuring state–society relationship that can generate economic growth.[9] Uttar Pradesh, a neo-patrimonial state, failed in both economic growth and distribution as its political elites appropriated power and public goods for personal gain or the benefits of narrow political communities. Meanwhile, West Bengal shaped a social–democratic politics in which political elites mobilised the low castes and classes. The populist politics and the left-wing party politics, which were more concerned about the improvement of living conditions of the poor rather than the large-scale investment projects, blocked economic growth in the state. However, Gujarat could achieve economic growth by developing its pro-business culture. Kohli observed that the politics in Gujarat was volatile with exclusionary characteristics despite a remarkable growth performance. Like that of the other developmental states in India, the politics in Gujarat was deeply associated with exclusionary nature, such as periodic riots and the killings of Muslims.[10]

If the suggestions from Sinha and Kohli are applicable to the area of foreign investments beyond the domestic investment activities in contributing to the state's economic growth, several socio–political variables, such as the centre–state relationship and the state's political structure need to be investigated in order to answer the empirical puzzles raised earlier for POSCO's investment failure in Odisha. What do the variables explain in a state's economic performance? How far can the variables travel to the realm of foreign investments? To what extent do the socio–political variables matter in facilitating foreign investments to states?

As such, POSCO's investment failure in Odisha and empirical puzzles invite our attention to the socio–political environment besides the market factors that can affect the process of FDI inflows.[11] Studying a linkage between the socio–political environment, which is a non-market variable, and FDI in host economies has been one of the three theoretical areas in FDI studies.

---

[9] Kohli highlights the 'political tendencies' of the states with the focus of political regime and governance structure as the source of regional diversities in economic development. I would rather emphasise the concept of 'state–society relationship' that reached the dissimilar consequences in the three states.

[10] Kohli (2012), 155. Maharashtra's politics is well-known as that of corruption and gangsters. Also, Haryana's feudal clan politics, Punjab's cronyism, and Andhra Pradesh's populism present how India's developmental states have the exclusionary nature.

[11] I define 'the process of FDI inflows' as the entire logistics of making investment projects materialised in host countries from the stage of firms' submitting investment proposals up to the point of their first production activities.

Figure 1.1 presents theoretical areas that FDI studies have explored. Area [A] deals with the impact of FDI inflows on economic growth in host countries, while Area [B] and Area [C] pay attention to the sources of FDI flows.

Area [A] addresses a question of whether FDI inflows contribute to economic growth in host countries.[12] On the one hand, it is believed that foreign presence can enhance the markets of host countries to equip higher competitiveness, efficiency, higher output, and higher growth.[13] Some found that FDI inflows are important for technology transfer, which contributes relatively more to growth than domestic investments do.[14] Also, the impact of FDI inflows on economic growth tends to have a positive correlation with the high level of human capital available in host countries. Further, FDI inflows are considered as a helpful financial resource compared to commercial loans in host economies. Many of the studies on the East Asian developmental states partly dealt with the subject in this manner, and demonstrated how foreign investments could be used for their industrial development in the process of building developmental states.[15]

On the other hand, some studies suggested that foreign capital does not matter for growth in non-industrial countries as even successful developing countries have limited absorptive capacity for foreign resources.[16] Further, relatively more fragile political and economic systems, exploitative nature of multinational corporations (MNCs), the emergence of the balance of payments crisis, and imperfectly competitive markets in host countries have usually been discussed as barriers that limit the positive impact of FDI inflows in developing countries.[17]

---

[12] See Borensztein et al. (1998); Bosworth et al. (1999); Cohen (2007); Grieco (1986); Prasad et al. (2007).

[13] Moran (1998).

[14] See Borensztein et al. (1998).

[15] See Haggard (1990); Krueger and Ito (2000); Shin (1996); Shin (2005); Wade (1990). Krueger and Ito recognised the benefits of FDI inflows in host countries; Haggard and Wade compared four differing developmental states' strategies in capitalising on foreign investments for their industrial development while Shin (2005) focused on a comparison between South Korea and Singapore. All of them agreed that FDI inflows were useful to the developmental states as an alternative form of foreign loans. They also presented how different industrial strategies (e.g., import-substituting to export-oriented projects for South Korea and Taiwan, entrepôt to export-oriented projects for Hong Kong and Singapore) helped them to promote growth.

[16] Prasad et al. (2007) argued that the financial markets of successful developing countries are underdeveloped or their economies are prone to overvaluation caused by rapid capital inflows, rapid consumption growth, and some combination of the factors.

[17] Cohen (2007).

Figure 1.1: Theoretical Areas of FDI Studies

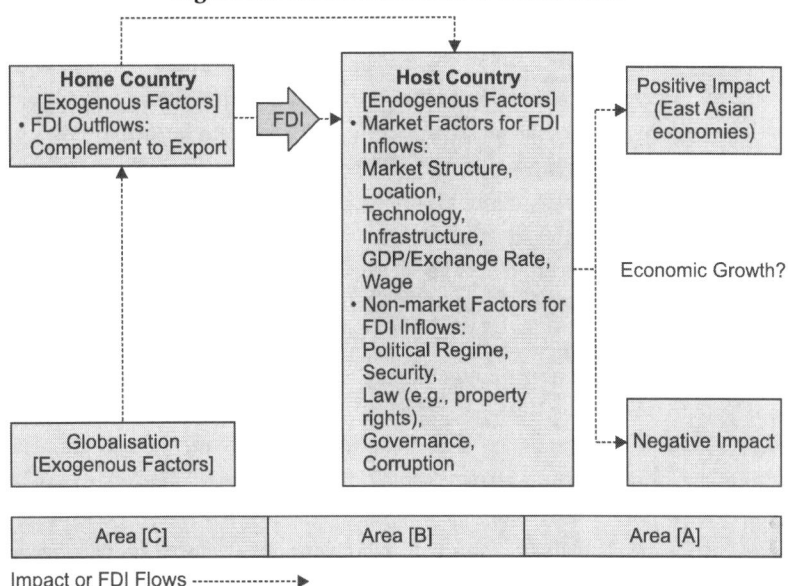

Source: Author based on various literature on FDI.

Area [B] is concerned about endogenous factors existing in host economies that would affect FDI flows to host countries, while Area [C] highlights the impact of globalisation and home country factors for FDI outflows.[18] Many of the studies in Area [B] have taken market factors and non-market factors as significant variables that influence the level of FDI flows to host economies. For example, scholars stressing the market factors argue that market structure, infrastructure, the location of investments, labour cost, and other macro-economic factors are influential in attracting FDI to host countries. On the contrary, some other studies highlight socio–political variables, such as political regime, security, institutional regulation, governance, and corruption.

From dependency theorists to industrial organisation theorists, scholars in different disciplines have discussed the significance of non-market factors in the literature of the politics of foreign capital in the industrial growth of host

---

[18] See Abramobitz (1986); Amsden (1990); Asiedu (2006); Bernard and Ravenhill (1995); Brunetti and Weder (1998); Bruton (1998); Busse and Hefeker (2007); Büthe and Milner (2008); Chang (2007); Cumings (1984); Encarnation and Wells (1986); Feng (2001); Gastanaga et al. (1998); Henisz (2000); Henisz and Williamson (1999); Keohane and Ooms (1975); Knack and Keefer (1995); Milner and Kubota (2005); Thun (2014); Vernon (1966); Wells (2007).

economies.[19] In a study of industrialisation patterns of countries in Latin America, Cardoso and Faletto (1979) stressed that Mexico could utilise foreign investments to improve agricultural productivity and accelerate development. They explained how a development alliance between the state and different sectors could broaden domestic economy in Argentina, Brazil, and Mexico. From a similar perspective emphasising the endogenous factors of foreign investment in host countries, Evans (1979) introduced a 'triple alliance' model which became a well-known concept in dependency theory studies. Drawing on the case of economic change in Brazil, Evans demonstrated how the state, domestic capital, and foreign capital had a strong tie for capital accumulation. Moreover, Evans showed how the three different actors having similar interests could make a coalition. For Evans, like Cardoso and Faletto, a non-market factor, which was the congenial interest of various groups in society, had a significant role in transforming the Brazilian economy. As other dependency theorists did, Cardoso and Faletto and Evans indicated the importance of structural constraints in host economies that limit the activities of foreign investors.

However, some scholars have argued that dependency theory may be inaccurate in analysing the patterns of FDI inflows due to constraints found in the process of global trade and investment. For example, Haggard (1989) studied the structural constraints of different sectors in the industry of Latin America by reviewing the relationship between foreign investment in host economies and MNCs. Haggard pointed out that the bargaining power of firms in the host countries needs to be carefully scrutinised as it is deeply related not only to available resources in host countries but also to negotiation skills and tactics between host countries and foreign firms. Haggard's finding was a notable achievement as it was a breakthrough in the development of analysing the power relationship between foreign investments host countries and MNCs. Furthermore, it is also worth noting in Haggard's study that such bargaining power and conflicts are substantially influenced by non-market factors, such as the political and societal structures in host economies. In another work, Haggard (1990) suggested that the pattern of FDI inflows is observable by examining not only the domestic industrial structures of host economies, such as sectors and firms, but also the institutional structures like property rights.

Some other studies in the literature of the political economy of industrial organisation, exploring the behaviours of MNCs, have also observed the socio–political hazards that can act as barriers in the process of FDI flows to host

---

[19] I have discussed elsewhere the significance of socio–political environment in host economies that affect the FDI performance with the particular focus on South Asia. See Shin (2016) for a literature review on the theories and practices of FDI flows to countries in South Asia.

economies. Henisz and Williamson (1999) examined how economic activity gets organised under different institutional regimes, particularly property rights regimes in FDI host countries, and suggested a transaction cost theory. The theory addresses the added complications surrounding the market entry mode choice between entering a given country using minority or majority equity control of MNCs relative to domestic firms in host economies.

Adding to the transaction cost theory, Henisz (2000) analysed whether the political hazards influence the decision of MNCs by testing the samples of overseas manufacturing operations. Henisz found that the MNCs encountered an increasing threat of opportunistic expropriation by governments in host countries when independent political problems increased through institutional changes and other financial constraints. In these circumstances, having partnerships in the host countries can act as a safeguard against the hazards. However, the potential risks that joint venture partners will manipulate the political systems for their benefit at the cost of MNCs will also grow when independent contractual hazards increase. Henisz argued that the contractual risks would outweigh the political dangers so that MNCs would prefer majority-owned plants rather than joint ventures.

Other socio–political factors mostly include government instability, policy uncertainty, and enforcement uncertainty.[20] First, government instability relates to the change of government through elections or other political events. The variable of government instability presents that institutional uncertainty in FDI inflows grows when the volatility of the government increases. It is concerned about frequent incumbency changes that may create FDI policy inconsistency between the old and the new government. Second, the variable of policy uncertainty indicates the volatility of institutional framework in the realm of FDI inflows. The frequency of changes in the constitution and the acts that may discourage or regulate FDI inflows could be a typical example. Foreign investors may avoid investment activities in such an uncertain environment. Third, the variable of enforcement uncertainty is deeply associated with judiciary and bureaucracy in FDI host countries that block foreign investors from having the confidence of pursuing their FDI projects. Any form of bureaucratic red tape, inefficiency, ignorance, corruption, and the low level of bureaucratic commitment can be included in this category.

As such, this book poses several theoretical questions that existing literature on the role of socio–political variables in the political economy of FDI has highlighted

---

[20] See Brunetti and Weder (1998), 516. Brunetti and Weder found that the variable of enforcement uncertainty has the largest effect on investments, though all political hazards they tested had the expected negative relations with aggregate investments. I would like to advance their clarification on the concepts of (political) institutional uncertainty variables herein, by applying possible hypotheses to the performance of implementing FDI projects in host economies.

by linking the aforementioned empirical puzzles: What do socio–political variables explain in the differing levels of FDI inflows to states in India? How do the factors of government instability, policy uncertainty, and enforcement difficulty matter in the process of FDI inflows to states in India? How do other socio–political factors like centre–state relations and political tendencies affect the consequences of FDI inflows to states in India?

Arguments

The ostensible reasons why POSCO could not succeed in its investment plan in Odisha were due to the failure of acquiring land and mineral right, which are market factors that can act as constraints in the process of FDI inflows in host countries. However, the actual barrier was the ability of the state that failed in negotiating with villagers affected by POSCO's steel plant project. The low level of state capacity was structured by extractive-industry-oriented state strategies towards industrialisation and executed by knowledge-lacked and inefficient bureaucracy. Such socio–political variables contributed to the little commitment of bureaucracy to implementing FDI projects in Odisha.

I advance an argument that the nature of the state–society relationship is significant from which the level of bureaucratic commitment stems for economic performance. In other words, this book primarily addresses socio–political factors that shaped the disparate levels of FDI inflows to states in India. In particular, it emphasises the causal role of differing state–society relations in the evolution of institutions facilitating and regulating FDI inflows in select states in India – Tamil Nadu and Odisha.

Not only at the central government but also in the two states, namely, Tamil Nadu and Odisha, it was found that the ideas of key policy-makers on the need for foreign capital as an important financial resource critically influenced the institutional changes favouring FDI inflows in the process of industrial development. It is worth noting that the year 1967 was a crucial turning point for Tamil Nadu and Odisha during which regional political parties won the state legislative assembly elections and had a chance to capitalise on citizenship politics. In both states, the financial difficulties of the 1970s helped state leaders consider foreign investments as a significant financial resource. However, such ideas were implemented with a significant difference in the two states.

In Tamil Nadu, which is defined as a developmental state in the book, state agencies playing roles to promote industrial development and inclusionary policies protecting the rights of marginalised citizens developed incrementally throughout the 1970s and 1980s. The state of Tamil Nadu was much better prepared than many other states for the institutional change favouring FDI inflows. The state's agencies and policies began seeking FDI inflows actively during the post-reform period after 1991.

The nature of inclusionary state–society relationship was a critical source for attracting a high level of FDI inflows in Tamil Nadu. The state had the power to selectively introduce market force in the manufacturing sector, especially in the automobile industry. In addition, it has acquired strategic necessities to make private investments as transformative projects. The strategic necessities have been realised through policies of social inclusion and ruling parties based on the support of broader strata of citizens including marginalised groups. The social integration was found in land reforms, public distribution, education, health services, and employment that state leaders were concerned about. It was significant that the nature of the developmental state helped Tamil Nadu accumulate substantial private capital for its industrial development. Such significant findings provided a causal link between the role of social inclusion and a higher level of FDI inflows to Tamil Nadu. Historical explanations about the lower caste base of the Dravidian parties also supported the link.

Through the economic reform in 1991, various policies were introduced to attract FDI actively in the state of Tamil Nadu, driven by the central government's liberalisation and inclusionary state–society relations. Similarly to the case of the centre, the 1991 reform brought further economic institutional change to Tamil Nadu. The economic institutions were reproduced and adapted after 1991 in a way that existing ideas on industrialisation and private investment strongly drove the institutional change favouring FDI. The muted interests from society in Tamil Nadu supported the change while the interest group against FDI inflows at the union level was quite strong. Therefore, ideas won over interests in the case of Tamil Nadu, and thereby, it made the institutional change incremental.

On the contrary, a new norm and a belief on foreign investments were realised in Odisha at a much later stage. Also, the neo-patrimonial nature of the state and high level of social conflict acted as barriers to FDI inflows in Odisha. Although Biju Patnaik, who served as the Minister of Steel and Mines at the union level and a Chief Minister of Odisha, conceived ideas favouring FDI inflows and industrial development in Odisha's steel industry in the early 1970s. His ideas failed to be materialised for several socio–political reasons, such as the failure of ruling parties in providing inclusionary schemes for citizens, frequent regime change, political conflicts between key state leaders and their factional politics, and rent-seeking bureaucrats that have allied with the upper-middle group of society. Despite a severe fiscal deficit in the 1970s, policy-makers did not capitalise on the private sector investment to overcome the economic crises. It was a stark difference between Tamil Nadu and Odisha.

In the case of Odisha, the recent renewal of institutions was promoted by societal demands forged by left-wing parties and marginalised citizens insisting inclusionary state–society relationship. The demands of society have stressed inclusionary schemes that need to be implemented especially for those who are displaced in the process of large-scale investments embarked on in the state.

The findings of linkage between the inclusionary nature of the state–society relationship and a high level of FDI inflows in Tamil Nadu and that between the exclusionary state–society relationship and a low level of FDI inflows in Odisha are new. The findings and arguments developed in this book present counter-evidence of what other scholars have argued in the political economy of private investment in India.[21]

Concepts and a Historical Institutionalist Approach

This book deals with several important concepts. First, *state* indicates rule makers, such as technocrats and political leaders. The rule makers are, for example, the Prime Minister, Ministers, Chief Ministers, and political leaders in political parties who participate in the decision-making process regarding FDI inflows both at the union and state levels in India. State also includes bureaucrats in government agencies or organisations. The bureaucrats are not always necessarily rule makers, but they can play a role as rule implementers because many of rules in the economic sphere are usually applied through them. State agencies that the bureaucrats belong are part of 'institutions' discussed in this book. For example, they are the Ministry of Finance, the Ministry of Commerce and Industry, and many other state organisations having important roles to promote large-scale investments like FDI projects, industrialisation, and private capital accumulation. Their primary function is to implement policies regarding FDI inflows and make investments transferable.

Second, *society* means by and large citizens, Indian domestic firms, and foreign companies; and all of them can be rule takers. Society discussed here consists of various interest groups that support or oppose FDI inflows. Although the study in this book sees the state as part of society, the various interest groups in society are, by definition, the third element that exists out of the state apparatus. Despite that, they can influence the decision-making process regarding FDI inflows by forcing their demands and interests upon the state. Therefore, state–society

---

[21] See Kohli (2012) and Murali (2017). Kohli has clearly demonstrated that India's developmental states have the exclusionary nature of political tendency (see aforementioned discussion and note 10). In her recent study, Murali argued that narrow class-based electoral coalitions, especially narrow-capitalist coalitions, are more favourable than others to growth-oriented policies in states in India. Murali highlighted that the joint presence of core groups with relatively wealthy profiles and business interests were most conducive to a growth-friendly policy framework. She pointed to identity politics that enabled the poor support such growth-friendly policy framework in economically advanced states in India.

relationship addressed in this book is focused on the relationship between rule makers, rule implementers in the state apparatus, and the various interest groups in society who are rule takers.

Third, *institutions* indicate policies and state agencies that are involved with FDI inflows.[22] Therefore, institutional changes favouring FDI inflows here mean the evolution of such policies and the functional and structural change of state agencies for promoting FDI inflows.[23] For example, monetary policies like the Foreign Exchange Management Act (FEMA), land reform policies for acquiring lands for investors, administrative reform policies like single window system, and various investment promotion boards and corporations run by governments at the union and the state levels of India are all included in the discussion.

Figure 1.2: Linkage between State–Society Relations and Institutional Changes

```
┌─────────────────────────────────────────────────────┐
│                      Society                         │
│          ┌──────────────────────────────┐           │
│   ┌─────▶│   Rule Makers in State       │◀─────┐   │
│   │      │ (Political Leaders, Technocrats)│      │   │
│   │      └──────────────────────────────┘      │   │
│   │                    ↓                        │   │
│   │      ┌──────────────────────────────┐      │   │
│   │  ┌──▶│     Rules as 'Regimes'       │◀──┐  │   │
│   │  │   └──────────────────────────────┘   │  │   │
│   │  │              ↓       ↑                │  │   │
│   │  │   ┌──────────────────────────────┐   │  │   │
│   │  │   │ Rule Implementers in State   │   │  │   │
│   │  │   │ (State Agencies, Bureaucracy)│   │  │   │
│   │  │   └──────────────────────────────┘   │  │   │
│   │  │              ↓                        │  │   │
│   └──┴── Rule Takers as Third Parties in Society ──┘   │
│          (Citizens, Domestic and Foreign Investors)   │
└─────────────────────────────────────────────────────┘
```

Influence ⟶

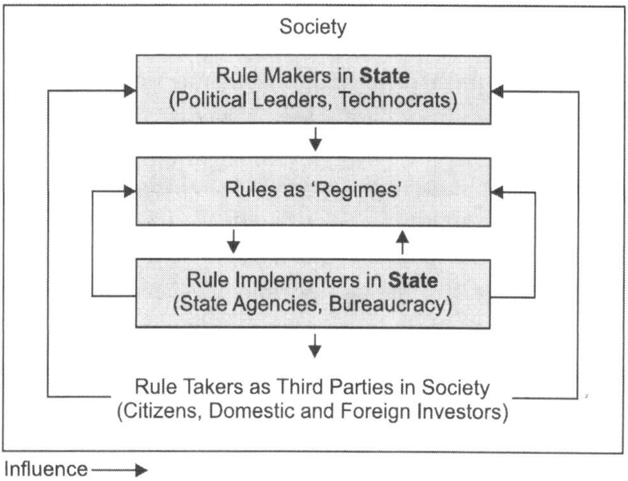

Note: Shaded parts are *institutions* discussed in this book.

Source: Author extended from Streeck and Thelen (2005), 13.

---

[22] See Streeck and Thelen (2005), 10–13. I would like to specify the term institutions used in this book, by agreeing with Streeck and Thelen's definition of institutions as obligatory regimes that reflect the certain ideational orientation of rule makers. I would stress that the concept *institution* differs from *policy* in this sense. In this book, *institution* as a broader notion includes certain policies and organisations or agencies playing a role to implement such policies. See also Greif and Laitin (2004), 635. Greif and Laitin consider that the concept of institutions includes rules, norms, and beliefs having a role of facilitating individuals to choose behaviour. Therefore, an economic institutional change would mean the change of such rules, norms, and beliefs in the economic sphere.

[23] For a discussion on whether organisations can be institutions, see Streeck and Thelen (2005), 12.

The linkage of state–society relations and institutional change implies that the patterned relationship between the state and society is fundamental in producing disparate results in economic institutional changes. Given that other conditions are equal, for example, the results of economic performance would be dissimilar according to whether the state is available to make investments transferable. Following the line of Skocpol (1985) and other political scientists,[24] I see that the state has the autonomy to structure and pursue goals which are not merely reflective of demands from various interest groups in society. Such autonomous state actions can 'attempt to reinforce the authority, political longevity, and social control of the state organisations whose incumbents generated the relevant policies or policy ideas'.[25] It also takes that the state is an autonomous actor although social actors can penetrate it.

Also, I take institutional continuity or discontinuity and institutional reproduction as a dynamic political process.[26] A theoretical contribution of this book is that the divergent paths of economic institutional changes are compared.

This book discusses the nature of states as an important source to decide the nature of the state–society relationship that influences the process and result of the institutional change. In comparative political economy studies looking at the process of industrial transformation, states have been classified based on the nature of the relationship with societies. In the studies, for example, developmental states pursue their goals for industrialisation through the efficient administrative organisations of the states, while neo-patrimonial states fail to carry out state goals due to several socio–political reasons.[27] Regarding the states' important

---

[24] Skocpol (1985), 3–43. See also Evans (1995).
[25] Skocpol (1985), 15.
[26] See Streeck and Thelen (2005).
[27] For developmental states in the context of East Asia, see Amsden (1989); Evans (1992); Evans et al. (1985); Kohli (2004); Leftwich (1995); Skocpol (1982); Wade (1999). After Chalmers Johnson conceptualised the term 'developmental state' in indicating the influential role of Ministry of International Trade and Industry (MITI) in the Japanese state in the 1960s for its industrial development and economic growth, others have used the concept in explaining the rapid growth of four states in East Asia in the 1970s and 1980s, namely, Singapore, Taiwan, Hong Kong, and South Korea. Amsden and Haggard discussed the strategies of developmental states for industrialisation by considering domestic socio–political factors significant to make such economic transition, while Evans focused on the relational power of political actors in a specific industrial sector – information technology. They have pointed to several common characteristics of developmental states to make such rapid growth such as the efficient, disciplined, and knowledgeable bureaucracy, states' close ties with industrialists, and states' intensive support of selected industries. In the contrary context, neo-patrimonial states have been explored by Evans and Kohli. Evans defined Zaire under Mobutu's regime that came to power in 1965 and ruled over 30 years as a predatory state

Introduction   15

roles of capital accumulation for growth and industrialisation, Evans (1995) clearly distinguished contrasting functions between the developmental states and the neo-patrimonial states by putting it.

> Those who control these (predatory) states plunder without any more regard for the welfare of the citizenry than a predator has for the welfare of its prey. Other (developmental) states foster long-term entrepreneurial perspectives among private elites by increasing incentives to engage in transformative investments and lowering the risks. [28]

A question is how one can analyse the linkage between such socio–political variables as an input and economic institutional changes as an output. In a historical institutionalist approach, comparative political scientists have often concerned not only with 'how institutions mediate and filter politics' but also with 'how the impact of institutions is itself mediated by the broader political context'.[29] This approach will be useful to examine the pattern of institutional changes favouring FDI inflows in India. I suggest two socio–political sources in this book to understand the institutional changes favouring FDI inflows in India: *ideas* and *interests*.

In fact, the idea–interest framework can coexist with the theoretical framework of state–society relations that was described above to explain economic institutional changes. It is because the policy ideas are generated by political leaders in the 'state' apparatus, while various interests in 'society' either support or oppose the state's pursuing ideas. Figure 1.3 presents the linkage between ideas, interests, and institutional changes that I will focus as an analytical tool to compare the state-wise variations in garnering FDI inflows. In the figure below, it can be seen that state apparatus generates and pursues ideas while society constitutes interests. The institutions are structured and implemented through interaction between rule makers and rule implementers in the state apparatus. Society can also partly participate in the process of rule-making or institutional change by pressurising political leaders by pursuing interests that can oppose the state's ideas.

To what extent do ideas and interests matter in structuring economic institutions? First, the ideational change of key policy-makers or state leaders is

---

where a small interest group captured all significant positions for decision-making in the state apparatus. Evans clearly showed that the rent-seeking state elites in Zaire impeded growth by undermining predictability of policies for private investments and producing distorted incentives. Similarly, Kohli found Nigeria in the colonial period under the British rule as a neo-patrimonial state where the state goals and tasks were undermined by personal and narrow group interests.

[28] Evans (1995), 44.
[29] Thelen (1992), 16.

crucial in structuring and restructuring institutions favouring FDI inflows. The role of ideas in transforming economic institutions has been discussed in many studies.[30] For example, Mukherji (2009) demonstrated how the ideational changes of technocrats at the Prime Minister's Office (PMO) in India could promote FDI inflows and the private sector participation in the telecommunication sector. In another research, Mukherji (2013) suggested that the economic changes of India follow a 'tipping point' model that highlights the ideas of key policy-makers and domestic politics in the process of economic changes. Mukherji argued that India's economic reform in 1991 was driven gradually and largely in an endogenous manner by the ideas and domestic politics even though there was some impact of exogenous shocks, by comparing the two balance of payments crises in 1966 and 1991.

Figure 1.3: Linkage between Ideas, Interests, and Institutional Changes in State and Society

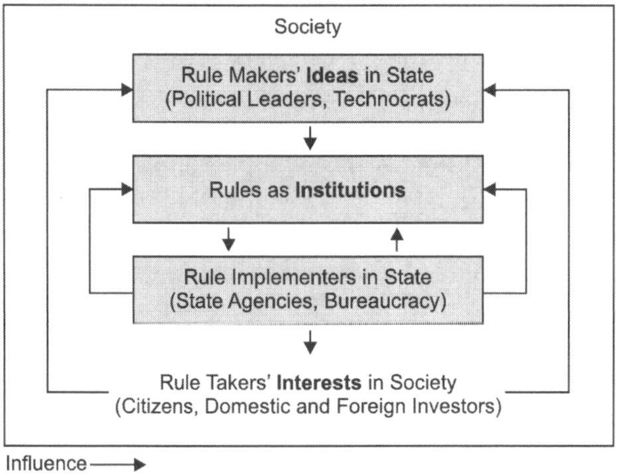

Society
- Rule Makers' **Ideas** in State (Political Leaders, Technocrats)
- Rules as **Institutions**
- Rule Implementers in State (State Agencies, Bureaucracy)
- Rule Takers' **Interests** in Society (Citizens, Domestic and Foreign Investors)

Influence ⟶

Note: Shaded parts are *institutions* discussed in this book (see also Figure 1.2).
Source: Author.

Second, the demands of different interest groups from society also matter in changing economic institutions. The various interest groups, who are either based on specific industrial sectors or social classes, also have significant roles in pressurising state leaders to structure and restructure institutions. For example, Milner (1988) showed why the MNCs of the United States and France in the manufacturing sector resisted the protectionist orientation of their states in the 1970s that resulted from the economic turmoil, while the firms in the 1920s

---

[30] See Blyth (2002); Mukherji (2009; 2013; 2014).

agreed to protection under the similar economic difficulties. Milner argued that it was because the interests of MNCs in developed countries were deeply tied to the international economy in the 1970s as compared with the 1920s; thereby the internationally oriented firms' preference for trade policies was anti-protectionist in the 1970s. Similarly, Cox (1996) explained the different interests of two business groups, namely, consumer electronics and automobiles and their differing preference towards Caribbean Basin Initiative and NAFTA. Cox demonstrated how the business groups were allied with differing political groups in the United States market after the 1970s when the Japanese firms were competitive in the country. The United States automobile business group having labour-intensive characteristics opposed an agreement with NAFTA, while the US companies in the electronics industry supported the Caribbean Basin Initiative. Both business groups built political alliances and lobbied the state for protecting their interests of activities from the regional trade agreements.

Taking ideas and interests as significant sources in economic institutional changes, this book details how different patterned relationships between the state and society have produced disparate results of economic performance and institutional variations in the realm of FDI inflows in the states of India.

Case Selection: Tamil Nadu and Odisha

Two provincial states in India, namely, Tamil Nadu and Odisha, are examined in this book. South Korean investments – Hyundai Motor Company's automobile plant project in Tamil Nadu and POSCO's steel project in Odisha – were taken as main case studies. South Korean big businesses have constituted considerable greenfield investments in Tamil Nadu and Odisha. The greenfield type of investment projects need lands for building factories to produce goods especially in the manufacturing sector in the states. As both states have tried to garner substantial FDI inflows from South Korea in the sector, a comparison between Tamil Nadu and Odisha is justifiable. The trend of growing trade and investment between India and South Korea explains that the select cases can be representative of substantive foreign investments to the manufacturing sector in the states. The comparison is justifiable because South Korean investments in India have focused on the manufacturing sector rather than the service and the information technology sectors.[31]

---

[31] See *The Export-Import Bank of Korea*, accessed 13 August 2017, FDI data, http://stats.koreaexim.go.kr/odisas.html. More than 80 per cent of total FDI from South Korea to India went to the manufacturing sector from 2000 to 2017. See also DIPP, 'FDI Synopsis

However, one may raise questions about the different nature of FDI inflows resulting from pre-existing economic conditions in Tamil Nadu and Odisha. For example, many of greenfield type of FDI projects embarked upon in Odisha are more likely to be natural resource-oriented than those in Tamil Nadu. However, the comparison in this book addresses *how states interact and negotiate with societies in the process of FDI inflows*, particularly in the land acquisition process that foreign investors have encountered substantial problems. Also, I would like to underline that industrially advanced states like Tamil Nadu have also struggled from social opposition sporadically against FDI projects. It means that better pre-existing economic conditions like industrial advancement do not necessarily produce high level of FDI inflows. What matters more is how the states tackle conflicts and challenges that occurred in the process of FDI inflows beyond certain economic conditions. Therefore, the different nature of FDI inflows resulting from pre-existing economic conditions would not be of much significance within the scope of this book. Tamil Nadu and Odisha will be good cases to compare and find causal linkage between socio–political factors and the success or failure of the management to garner FDI inflows.

Table 1.2 shows several demographic indicators of the two states. It indicates that the population of Tamil Nadu is distributed evenly in both rural and urban areas, while the rural population accounts for five times than that of the urban population in Odisha. In addition, Tamil Nadu has many lower caste groups, while Odisha takes a substantial number of tribal groups.

Table 1.2: Select Demographic Indicators of Tamil Nadu and Odisha

	Population						Scheduled Caste (SC) and Scheduled Tribe (ST) in Rural and Urban	
	Male (Million)	Female (Million)	Sex Ratio	Rural (Million)	Urban (Million)	As Per Cent of Total	SC	ST
Tamil Nadu	36.2	36	995	37.2	35.0	48.4	7.2	0.8
All India	623.7	586.5	940	833.1	377.1	31.2	NA	NA
Odisha	21.2	20.8	978	35.0	7.0	16.7	3.6	9.2

Source: Office of the Registrar General of India, Ministry of Home Affairs and Census of India 2011.

Table 1.3 presents select Human Development Indices (HDI) of the two states. Many of the indicators such as infant mortality, maternal mortality, and literacy rate in Odisha tend to lag behind Tamil Nadu.

---

on Country South Korea,' accessed 13 August 2017, http://dipp.nic.in/sites/default/files/fdi_synopsis_korea.pdf.

Table 1.3: Select Human Development Indices of Tamil Nadu and Odisha

	Human Development Index[a] (Rank)			Infant Mortality Rate[b]			Maternal Mortality Rate[c]	Literacy Rate[d] (Per cent)		
	1991	2001	2007–08	1971	1991	2010	2007–09	1991	2001	2011
Tamil Nadu	0.466 (14)	0.531 (3)	0.570 (8)	113	57	24	97	63	73	80
All India	0.381	0.472	0.467	129	80	47	212	52	65	74
Odisha	0.345 (28)	0.404 (11)	0.362 (22)	127	124	61	258	49	63	73

Notes: Infant Mortality Rate is the ratio of infant deaths to live births during the year multiplied by 1000; Maternal Mortality Rate is the number of maternal mortality in the age group 15–49 years per one lakh live birth; Literacy Rate estimated by the population aged seven years and above.

Sources: (a) India Human Development Report 2011; (b) and (c): Sample Registration System (www.censusindia.gov.in); (d) Registrar General of India for relevant years

Furthermore, it is worth noting that there are stark differences between the two states in the dropout rates from classes in upper primary and secondary schools and unemployment rates in both rural and urban areas, as seen in Table 1.4. This gap between the two states in education and employment could be correlated to the change of poverty ratio. For example, Tamil Nadu with a higher level of education among its residents could employ them in the industry, and this may have affected poverty reduction. On the other hand, the high rate of school dropouts in Odisha seems to be related to the failure in mobilising an educated work force in its industry. The notably high levels of rural and urban unemployment in Odisha are likely to explain why this state has shown poor performance when it comes to poverty alleviation over the last several decades. Odisha is economically far more backward than Tamil Nadu, even though Odisha has plentiful natural resources.[32]

The empirical observation implies the significance of industrialisation and the concerns of states for social welfare schemes that have a close relationship with economic growth in these states. It is also possible to see that social inclusion makes investments more likely by reducing protests at the time of land acquisition. In other words, the state could establish social inclusion to increase legitimacy which Migdal (2001) explained in his well-known work, *State in Society*. According to Migdal, 'legitimacy involves an acceptance of the state's rules of the game' and 'the acceptance of the symbolic order associated with the idea of the state as people's own

---

[32] Political economists often call it as 'resource curse' to describe regions having natural resource abundance yet poor economic growth.

system of meaning'.[33] This legitimacy is used by state leaders to increase societal compliance and thereby achieve state goals, because 'the strength of the idea of the state in an environment of conflict depends, in large part, on the social control the state organisation exercises'.[34] The causal link between social inclusion and state's legitimacy to pursue its goals for garnering FDI inflows is discussed in detail in the following chapters of this book with empirical evidence found on the ground.

Table 1.4: Dropout from Schools, Unemployment, and Poverty of Tamil Nadu and Odisha

	Dropout Rates from Classes 2010-11[a] (Per cent)			Unemployment Rates 2004-05[b] (Per cent)		Poverty Ratio[c] (Per cent)			Per Capita State Domestic Product at Current Prices 2013-14[d] (Indian Rupees)
	Primary	Upper Primary	Secondary	Rural	Urban	1983-84	1993-94	2004-05	
Tamil Nadu	-	8	25.9	1.2	3.5	Rural			112,664
						54	33	23	
						Urban			
						47	40	22	
All India	27	40.6	49.3	1.7	4.5	Rural			74,380
						46	37	28	
						Urban			
						41	32	26	
Odisha	7	55	64	6.7	13.4	Rural			52,559
						68	50	47	
						Urban			
						49	42	44	

Sources: (a) Ministry of Higher Education and Statistics of School Education 2010-11; (b) National Sample Survey Organisation (NSSO); (c) Planning Commission; (d) National Institution for Transforming India (NITI Aayog).

Organisation of Chapters

In Chapter 2, the pattern of institutional change favoring FDI inflows at the union level in India is discussed. The discussion examined how the ideas of policy-makers and various interests in society supporting or opposing foreign capital have influenced the economic institutional change favoring FDI inflows. It suggested

---

[33] Migdal (2001), 52.
[34] Ibid., same page.

three different periods of FDI regime change: anti-FDI (1969–75), selective FDI (1975–91), and pro-FDI (1991 onwards). Also, it explored how Foreign Investment Promotion Board, a significant state agency promoting FDI inflows, was used by policy-makers in the Ministry of Finance and the Ministry of Commerce and Industry as a means of their political tussle.

Discussions in Chapters 3 and 4 focus on the case of Tamil Nadu. In Chapter 3, the pattern of institutional change favouring FDI inflows in Tamil Nadu is explained. The ideas of policy-makers towards industrialisation and inclusion were consistently pursued by different ruling parties throughout the 1970s to the post-reform period. The social inclusion, especially found in land reforms, public distribution, education, health services, and employment, helped the state garner legitimacy in pursuing state goals for industrialisation. The discussion highlighted the nature of the developmental state that led Tamil Nadu to accumulate substantial private capital for its industrial development, thereby contribute to a high level of FDI inflows. Unlike the existing literature underlining some exclusionary nature in India's developmental states, the discussion in Chapter 3 emphasises an inclusionary nature of the state–society relationship in Tamil Nadu.

Chapter 4 presented how the tripartite alliance between the state, bureaucrats, and foreign capital contributed to the substantial growth of FDI inflows in Tamil Nadu by discussing fieldwork findings collated from foreign investments by Hyundai Motor India and Michelin India. Some interest groups opposing foreign capital sometimes protest against the state-led industrialisation process in Tamil Nadu, where foreign investors deliver large-scale investment projects. However, their interest was muted while the state provided substantial employment and education for citizens especially for the marginalised groups in society that are prone to ally with left-wing extremists for protests. India's domestic workers hired by foreign firms in the state not only seemed to be highly satisfied with their job, but also presented support of their companies, though they sometimes tried to bargain with foreign management through collective action for wage increase and promotion.

Chapters 5 and 6 proceed with discussions on Odisha. In Chapter 5, the pattern of institutional change favouring FDI inflows in Odisha is demonstrated. Compared to Tamil Nadu, the idea of policy-makers favouring FDI was materialised at a much later stage in Odisha. Biju Patnaik, former Chief Minister of Odisha and Minister of Steel and Mines in the Government of India, attempted to invite foreign investors to Odisha's steel industry in the 1970s. However, Patnaik's ideas on industrialisation and private and foreign investments promotion were challenged by several socio–political reasons: the failure of governance in capturing legitimacy from citizens, frequent regime change, and rent-seeking bureaucrats having close ties with the upper-middle group of society. Also, a societal structure that aggravated citizens polarised between coastal areas and hilly areas and social insecurity that was often caused by left-wing extremists also influenced on the state's bad performance in the economic spheres. The demand of society towards the state has been increasing for inclusionary socio–economic schemes. Such demand has been expressed mainly by the displaced citizens from the large-scale investments process in the state.

A discussion in Chapter 6 examines two large-scale steel plant projects by POSCO and TATA. It addressed the causal linkage between the exclusionary state–society relationship, weak state capacity, and a low level of FDI inflows in Odisha. Findings from fieldwork highlighted that citizens in the state were mobilised by left-wing parties and their alliance with extremists such as Naxalites and Maoists to oppose the state-led industrialisation. It was also found that the inefficient, ill-informed, and incoherent administrative organisation substantively blocked the state from intervening economic affairs. The discussion demonstrated the explanatory variables that led to the low level of FDI inflows in the state.

Finally, arguments and findings are summarised in Chapter 7. The concluding chapter also provides some limitations of this study and suggestions for future research.

2

FDI Inflows in India
Ideas, Interests, and Institutional Change

A 'tipping point' model of economic change for India ... highlights the explanatory importance of both home-grown ideas and politics. India's transition to globalisation and deregulation is a saga of a government promoting institutions that facilitated competitive markets within a democratic polity while powerful social actors opposed these changes.[1]

How do socio–political factors influence institutional changes favouring FDI inflows in India at the union level? Ideas and interests can affect institutional changes. Some scholars in India's political economy have argued that the economic orientation and ideas of key policy-makers are decisive of institutional changes.[2] However, others who take interests important have stressed the pluralist structure of society and various interest groups that influence institutional changes.[3] By taking two socio–political sources – *ideas* and *interests* significant in the economic institutional changes, I would discuss how the ideas of key policy-makers in the state apparatus and various interests in society have affected institutional changes at the union level in India in the realm of FDI inflows.[4] I conducted

---

[1] Mukherji (2013), 363.
[2] See Kothari (2009) and Frankel (2005). Both Kothari and Frankel believed that the ideas of policy-makers matter in structuring institutions. They demonstrated that Nehru's leadership and his vision of a socialist orientation and respect for cultural and linguistic heterogeneity had fundamental roles in the earliest stage of industrialisation as well as the process of nation-building in India.
[3] See Nayar (1971) and Bardhan (1984). Both Nayar and Bardhan paid attention to interest politics in their studies. They focused on indigenous business groups in India who were in a power struggle with political leaders to influence their viewpoints in economic reforms and industrialisation.
[4] Many scholars in India's political economy have discussed the economic reform of 1991. See Frankel (2005); Ganguly and Mukherji (2011); Kohli (1989); Mooij (2005); Mukherji (2007); Panagariya (2008); Tendulkar and Bhavani (2007). However, their studies did not focus on FDI as a main subject.

fieldwork in India from December 2011 to March 2012. I interviewed some of the political leaders, bureaucrats, and industrialists who had involved in the process of FDI inflows. Fieldwork findings present that the ideas of political leaders were competing between supporters and opponents of FDI. Also, the interests of different individuals and groups in society also varied towards FDI inflows.

Following a historical institutionalist approach that emphasises a role of political context in shaping an economic institutional change, this chapter explains the pattern of FDI inflows at the union level in India. I argue that the economic institutions favouring FDI inflows have gradually changed through an incremental FDI regime change from anti-FDI inflows (1969–75) to selective FDI inflows (1975–91) and further to pro-FDI inflows (1991 economic reform onwards). The discussion in this chapter proceeds following the periodisation. After that, the discussion focuses on the episodes of Foreign Investment Promotion Board (FIPB) relocation which was politically driven between key ministries having a role in promoting India's industrialisation.

Anti-FDI Inflows (1969–75)

India's industry was relatively open to foreign capital before 1969. Jawaharlal Nehru, who served as the first Prime Minister of India from August 1947 to May 1964, had a positive attitude towards foreign capital and foreign investments for India's industrialisation. Even though he pursued a strong socialist orientation with the focus of enhancing heavy industry through public ownership, Nehru recognised the need for foreign capital as a means of economic growth in India. He thought foreign capital could contribute to India's national interests, though the government needed to monitor and regulate it carefully.[5] During the Nehru government, the number of foreign companies was bigger than that of domestic businesses in India's industry.[6] Such positive atmosphere towards foreign capital remained until the early period of Indira Gandhi government. Indira Gandhi, who served as the Prime Minister of India after Nehru and Shastri, thought foreign capital, especially in the form of foreign aid, was beneficial to boost India's industry. The Indira Gandhi government even attempted to liberalise the trade and investment sectors in 1966 with the idea that foreign capital's participation in India's industry would contribute to economic growth in the country.[7]

However, the Indira Gandhi government initiated institutional arrangements with a socialist orientation in 1969. The Congress Party in which Indira Gandhi

---

[5] Panagariya (2008).
[6] See Kidron (1965) and Tomlinson (1978).
[7] Mukherji (2014), 63–107.

struggled with a Party's faction split and the government tried to mobilise the poor as a supporting base through a political and economic transition.[8] The state's approach to foreign private capital became more rigorous than in those of any other governments. Several institutions were arranged in the period for stringently regulating financial resources including foreign capital. First, domestic banks were nationalised in 1969. After that, the Quantitative Restrictions that restricted imports up to a limit on items that were sensitive to domestic industries were strengthened.[9] The socialist orientation of Indira Gandhi government influenced an attitude towards regulating foreign investments as well through the enactment of Foreign Exchange Regulation Act (FERA) in 1973.

Such institutional arrangements were the consequence of political struggles that Indira Gandhi had against her political opposition in political and economic instability.[10] Party members in Syndicate, an old and dominant group within the Congress Party, deemed they could manipulate Indira Gandhi for their political sake during the absence of a charismatic national leader in the party.[11] Indira Gandhi, however, was getting political support from the left-leaning leaders within the party, and her political inclination was against the Syndicate whose political and economic orientation was more right-leaning. The peak of political conflicts between Indira Gandhi and the Syndicate was the Faridabad Congress Party session in April 1969.[12] In the session, Indira Gandhi nominated V. V. Giri, leader of All India Trade Union Congress, as the new President of India against Neelam Sanjeeva Reddy, who was supported by the Syndicate and the majority of party members. Giri finally won the election with support from the left-wing parties, but the political conflicts that were aggravated during the session drove Congress Party to split in the same year. Despite such misfortune of Congress Party, Giri's victory helped Indira Gandhi remove her worries of being removed from the Prime Minister's Office (PMO). After the incident, Indira Gandhi aggressively pursued socialist goals in the economic agenda. The stringent schemes on import and foreign exchange need to be understood in this context.

A series of political and economic crises that occurred during this period encouraged Indira Gandhi to pursue socialist goals. First, the government was

---

[8] See Hewitt (2008), 9; Kaviraj (1986; 1699).

[9] Tendulkar and Bhavani (2007).

[10] For the political conflicts between Indira Gandhi and Syndicate, see Hewitt (2008), 81–82; Kaviraj (1986), Chapters 7 and 10; Mukherji (2007), 1–26; Nayar (2006), 107–34; Panagariya (2008), 50–51.

[11] Verghese (2010), 82. The absence of strong leaders in the Congress Party resulted from Nehru's death in 1964 and Shastri's death in 1966.

[12] Nayar (2006), 120–29; Mukherji (2007), 9.

struggling from economic instability especially due to the substantial cut of foreign aid from other countries. The United States suspended its financial support to India and Pakistan in 1965 during the Indo–Pakistan war.[13] Many policy-makers in the government realised the importance of an import-substituting industrialisation strategy with the focus of heavy industry for India's economic development. At the nascent stage of industrialisation, financial aid from abroad especially from the United States and international organisations, such as the International Monetary Fund (IMF) and the World Bank was crucial, since it was difficult for India to mobilise financial resources from domestic private capital that was not yet competitive in the global market. The difficulties caused by losing financial aid from abroad dealt a severe blow to India's economy in the Indira Gandhi government.[14]

The United States with pressure from international organisations forced the Indira Gandhi Government to enforce devaluation. In late March 1966, Indira Gandhi visited the United States to get food and foreign exchange.[15] During a meeting with the President of the United States, Indira Gandhi was forced to pursue liberalisation with the promise of continuous financial assistance from the United States. The Balance of Payments (BOP) status that was reaching a crisis point and the external pressure from the United States pushed Indira Gandhi to choose devaluation, but her attempt at liberalisation was short-lived.[16] Interestingly, Indira Gandhi purposefully kept key policy-makers out of the decision-making process when she decided on devaluation. B. G. Verghese, who had worked as the Prime Minister's press secretary under the Indira Gandhi government, observed the lack of coordination among the key policy-makers at that time.[17]

Domestic private capital and left-wing political parties like the Communist Party of India (Marxist) CPI(M) strongly opposed the devaluation policies. They opposed the liberalisation attempt with an idea of *swadeshi* [self-sufficiency]. Further, their interests were conflicting with devaluation because they not only had to compete with foreign private capital in India's industry but also had to buy expensive imports. Trade unions also opposed devaluation and increasing economic instability by organising *bandhs* [strikes] in many provincial states including Bihar, Kerala, Odisha, Uttar Pradesh, West Bengal, and some others. As a consequence of these *bandhs* and continuous political turmoil, Congress Party lost ninety-five

---

[13] Frank, (2001), 296.
[14] Ibid., 322–26.
[15] Malhotra (1989), 95.
[16] Mukherji (2000).
[17] See Verghese (2010), 87.

seats in many states in the fourth general election in February 1967.[18] A factional strife within Congress Party intensified through a party split in 1969, though it could remain in power.

In such uncertain political and economic environment, the Indira Gandhi government nationalised domestic banks in 1969. The bank nationalisation aimed at solidifying Indira Gandhi's political support from the poor and left-wing parties. The political motivation of why Indira Gandhi strongly supported the bank nationalisation was well described by I. G. Patel, who served as the Governor of the Reserve Bank of India (RBI) and had a close relationship with Indira Gandhi.[19] The Government established the Banking Department under the Ministry of Finance (MOF) to manage financial resources more efficiently and gave autonomy to the Department to supervise nationalised banks. Indira Gandhi used the new presence of the government organisation as a means of securing her political support from the poor. She thought that bank nationalisation could be a way to easily manipulate banking resources in economically hard times and food scarcity. According to Patel (2002), Indira Gandhi 'was heralded as the angel of the poor and she made *garibi hatao* [poverty alleviation]' after the bank nationalisation.[20]

However, the good image of Indira Gandhi was short-lived because the political and economic instability became worse after bank nationalisation. In the financial sector, Indira Gandhi's younger son, Sanjay, wasted millions of Indian rupees from several domestic banks and big businesses like the Birla in funding the Maruti car company, which he was involved with as a government project. A poor harvest and droughts threatened food scarcity, endangering Indira Gandhi's leadership. External factors like the oil shocks in 1973 and 1974 negatively affected India's economy by depressing agricultural production and generating inflationary pressure.[21] Corruption was pervasive among politicians and bureaucrats in the government both at the union and the state levels.[22]

Political instability peaked in 1975 when the Allahabad High Court charged Indira Gandhi with electoral corruption. Indira Gandhi was accused by Raj Narain, the Prime Minister's defeated opponent in the 1971 parliamentary election, of malpractice during the election campaign. However, she refused the conviction by insisting, 'There is a lot of talk about our government not being clean, but

---

[18] Frank (2001), 304.
[19] Patel (2002), 135–38.
[20] Ibid., 136. Patel pointed to the impact of political motivation that Indira Gandhi had in the incident, by putting it, 'It is remarkable how momentous decisions are made in the heat of political struggle'.
[21] Ahluwalia (1986).
[22] Kochanek (1987), 1290.

from our experience, the situation was very much worse when (opposition) parties were forming governments'.[23] Indira Gandhi's corruption charge encouraged her political opposition to call for her immediate resignation.

Like the bank nationalisation, the enactment of FERA was also a by-product of Indira Gandhi's political struggle through which she showed how to enforce disciplines for socialist goals. FERA was introduced in line with the Industrial Development and Regulation Act that was enacted in 1951 for regulating industrial investments and production. The FERA included various restrictions on the import and export of foreign currency, acquisition and holding of immovable property, and the establishment of business in India for 'the interests of the economic development of the country'.[24] It is noteworthy that the federal government of India had a monopolistic role in overall activities related to foreign currency through the enactment of FERA. For example, no individuals and state agencies could participate in any activities regarding foreign currency, except RBI, a national bank of India, which was designated as the only authorised foreign currency dealer by the government of India. The government of India restricted foreign equity shares in domestic companies in India up to 40 per cent and made RBI monitor the activities of firms strictly. Also, FERA was in favour of domestic companies when they needed to bargain with foreign firms in India's industry. The enactment of FERA enhanced the bargaining position of India's domestic firms, thereby competition among the Multinational Corporations (MNCs) in accessing the market escalated.[25]

Several key bureaucrats dealt with the issues of foreign exchange within RBI for strict monitoring. Some of them were L. K. Jha who served as the Governor of the RBI from 1967 to 1970, I. G. Patel who was the Governor of the RBI from 1977 to 1982, and Ashok Mitra who served as the Chief Economic Advisor in the Banking Department. Patel was especially trusted and was asked by Indira Gandhi to prepare the bill for nationalising domestic banks in 1969. As a well-known economist, Patel also worked in the Planning Commission, the MOF, and the United Nations Development Program. In his autobiography, Patel lively narrated his role in dealing with the major economic issues of the time.[26] According to Patel, the position of the Secretary of RBI had exclusive responsibility for the larger questions of monetary policy, management of government debt, and foreign exchange.

---

[23] BBC News, '1975: Gandhi Found Guilty of Corruption,' 12 June 1975, accessed 12 April 2012.

[24] Reserve Bank of India, 'Foreign Exchange Regulation Act, 1973,' accessed 16 August 2017, www.rbi.org.in/scripts/ECMUserView.aspx?CatID=12&Id=21.

[25] Encarnation and Wells (1986), 118.

[26] Patel (2002), 135–38.

FERA forced many firms in India's industry to limit the foreign shares in their companies. Firms retaining more than 40 per cent of foreign equity shares were discriminated under the FERA scheme. The companies had to either reduce foreign shares up to 40 per cent or sell the ownership to other Indian industrialists. The government of India retained such strict attitude towards foreign capital until the economic reform of 1991. India under the Indira Gandhi Government looked like the 'most comprehensively regulated market economy in the world'.[27] Rakesh Mohan, who was the Deputy Governor of RBI under both the Bharatiya Janata Party (BJP) and the Congress governments, also described the 1970s under Indira Gandhi's leadership as 'the dark age for the industrial economy'.[28]

The vigilant attitude of the government of India was also applied to the area of foreign collaboration. The government of India said, 'Care (had) to be taken to ensure that foreign collaboration is resorted to only for meeting a critical gap and does not inhibit the maximum utilisation of domestic know-how and services'.[29] The government of India further puts it:

> It (was) necessary to subject every proposal for foreign collaboration to fairly rigid tests; even [import of foreign know-how particularly in sophisticated industrial fields], it would be essential to make simultaneous efforts for the adaptation of such know-how through indigenous effort and to improve on it to avoid the need for future purchase.[30]

The government of India set up Foreign Investment Board (FIB) to identify fields where foreign collaboration was needed and streamline the procedure for review. Unlike today's FIPB in the MOF that promotes foreign investments, the main role of FIB in the Indira Gandhi government was to control and regulate foreign investments in India.

Selective FDI Inflows (1975–91)

Indira Gandhi attempted to mute political threats from her opposition group through the internal emergency of 1975. The Indira Gandhi government 'sought to open up channels to key sections of society – notably the middle classes and

---

[27] Tendulkar and Bhavani (2007), 23.
[28] *Outlook*, 'What if Indira Gandhi Hadn't Been PM?' 23 August 2004, accessed 22 April 2012.
[29] Government of India, *The 4th Five Year Plan* (New Delhi: Planning Commission, 1969), Chapter 14, accessed 28 April 2014, http://planningcommission.nic.in/plans/planrel/fiveyr/4th/4planch14.html.
[30] Ibid.

peasants – to enhance cooperation and collaboration with the state, as well as to ensure a more efficient form of resource extraction'.[31] The emergency was announced as a means of centralising and personalising Indira Gandhi's political power in the government.

Indira Gandhi also thought that an attempt to rearrange economic institutions would create a new atmosphere that may help to centralise her political power. The government of India tried to streamline the process of reviewing industrial license and strengthen bureaucratic efficiency in the process. After such attempts, the public sector managed to increase output. In 1976, the industrial production indicated a ten per cent increase over that of 1975.[32] Nayar (2006) also observed the economic transition around that time and argued that the year 1975 was the end of Hindu growth rate and the initiation of liberalisation in India's economy.[33]

Deregulation in the private sector significantly contributed to further growth in India's economy. The *Economic and Political Weekly* issued in 1976 states:

> Industrial licensing has been diluted through a series of relaxations and exemptions, the restrictions on large houses have been relaxed, and the anti-concentration provisions of the MRTP Act have been rendered virtually inoperative, import policy has been relaxed, a variety of generous subsidies and concessions have been extended to exports, foreign companies are being encouraged to expand under the liberal provisions of FERA ... In other words, major advances have been made in the direction of an open, free market, private enterprise economy ... Private businessmen, whether American or British, have sought to conceal their preferences even less.[34]

The economic transition of 1975 also influenced the area of foreign investments in India's industry. Interestingly, the Indira Gandhi government encouraged foreign capital to participate in the private sector and contribute to generating growth instead of the unproductive public sector, although the original aims of emergency were to pursue socialist goals.[35] The state was 'being reorganised to serve the interests of big – and foreign – capital more efficiently and, relative to other economic sectors and political interests, more exclusively'.[36]

A puzzle is why the Indira Gandhi government shifted the economic strategies from controlling both domestic and foreign capital towards dismantling industrial

---

[31] Hewitt (2008), 128.
[32] Ibid., 129.
[33] Nayar (2006). The economic transformation towards liberalisation was largely affected by intolerable inflation and difficulties of getting commercial loans from the IMF.
[34] Economic and Political Weekly (1976).
[35] Hewitt (2008), 130.
[36] Frank (1977), 473.

regulations and promoting the participation of foreign capital in the domestic industry? The strategies seemed to be affected by the interests of business groups who welcomed deregulation. At the same time, Indira Gandhi attempted to mobilise the business groups to centralise power in the government and make a wider societal collaboration. Indira Gandhi, however, failed to successfully mobilise the poor after the split who were the initial support base of her leadership.[37]

The Indira Gandhi government's attempt on deregulation and encouraging foreign capital's participation in India's industry contributed to an increase of the total foreign reserves. Table 2.1 presents the foreign exchange reserves of total external debt in India from 1975 to 1991. Foreign exchange reserves gradually grew from 1975 and reached over US$12 billion in 1980.

Table 2.1: Foreign Reserves of Total External Debt in India (1975-91)

Year	Current US$ Million*	Per cent of Total External Debt
1975	2,064	15
1976	3,729	26
1977	6,085	39
1978	8,316	50
1979	11,815	64
1980	12,010	57
1981	8,109	35
1982	8,242	30
1983	8,216	26
1984	8,536	25
1985	9,493	23
1986	10,480	22
1987	11,512	20
1988	9,186	15
1989	8,048	11
1990	5,637	7
1991	7,616	9

Note: *including gold.
Source: Based on the *World Bank Indicators*.

A puzzle in the pattern was that foreign reserves were steadily increasing even during the Janata Party government, which began in March 1977 and pursued a strong socialist orientation in the economic sphere. Interestingly, it did not result from the positive attitude of policy-makers towards foreign capital. At that time, Morarji Desai took over as the Prime Minister of India after Indira Gandhi. H.

---

[37] Hewitt (2008), 130.

M. Patel became the Finance Minister of India in the Morarji Desai government. Desai's leadership of getting support from the communist parties of India took a very cautious view to the growth of remittances. The Morarji Desai government did not use the readily available foreign exchange reserves although the overall economy had recovered in the areas of growth, inflation, and foreign exchange.[38] In fact, the chronic shortage of foreign currency that remained from the previous governments strongly affected key policy-makers in the Morarji Desai government to consider foreign reserves as a means of saving. Such attitude towards foreign reserves was contrary to that of East Asian countries like South Korea thinking that foreign reserves could be earned by export as well.

The Janata Party government under Morarji Desai's leadership and then Charan Singh's leadership attempted to rearrange economic institutions in many industrial sectors in the areas of import and export controls, tariffs, technology collaboration with foreign companies, and investment of Non-resident Indians (NRIs) in India's industry.[39] The attempt aimed to increase industrial participation from NRIs and the domestic private capital for industrial growth but not from foreign capital. Interestingly, even though key policy-makers in the Ministry of Commerce at that time considered foreign technology acquisitions significant, they did not arrange any institutions to promote foreign investments through which domestic companies could easily gain access to advanced foreign technology. The ideological base of the Janata Party that valued a self-reliant economy seems to have influenced it. Besides, a nationalist wave for a self-sufficient economy that was getting support from many groups in society affected some of the US-based MNCs, such as Coca-Cola, IBM, and PepsiCo, to be pulled out from India in 1977 due to severe societal protests against them.

When Indira Gandhi returned as the Prime Minister of India in 1980, the process of industrial deregulation accelerated. For business groups, the Monopolies and Restrictive Trade Practices (MRTP) Act was diluted and entry barriers to India's market were reduced. The Indira Gandhi government sought to simplify licensing procedures. Nonetheless, there were two limitations in the reform attempt. First, Indira Gandhi's attitude towards foreign capital did not change much while she supported the participation of the domestic private capital in industry. Second, despite the considerable streamlining of licensing procedures in industry, further improvements were needed 'in reducing the period of time taken for disposal of applications for the creation of new capacities, proposals for substantial expansion, and the production of new items'.[40]

---

[38] Joshi and Little (1994).
[39] Government of India (1978), 4.
[40] Government of India (1980).

The foreign reserves of the total external debt steadily decreased in the 1980s during the Congress Party governments led by Indira Gandhi and Rajiv Gandhi consecutively. The low level of capital formation, external pressures from rising oil prices, and the world recession in the early 1980s again influenced the government of India to resort to commercial borrowings.[41] However, key policy-makers in the government kept a distance from an idea that foreign investments would be a more helpful financial resource than commercial borrowings. Under pressure from economic crises to get financing from external resources, an idea favouring foreign investments in comparison with commercial loans finally developed in the Rajiv Gandhi government in the late-1980s. At a national conference organised by the Confederation of Engineering Industry [predecessor of current Confederation of Indian Industry (CII)], Rajiv Gandhi (1988) pointed out the benefits of using foreign investments as follows:

> Our policy towards foreign investment is clear. It is not an open-door policy. We permit foreign investment on our terms, in a wide range of sectors within certain percentages of foreign equity. These percentages can be relaxed in areas of high technology or where there is a special contribution to exports. This basic policy is sound and *does not need any change*. Yet the actual inflow of direct investment into our economy is minuscule compared to inflows into other developing countries. Foreign investment in the ASEAN countries is around 1,500 crore rupees per year. Foreign investment in socialist China is about 2,000 crore rupees per year. Foreign investment in India is only about 100 crore rupees. The external borrowing has expanded over the past several years, reflecting our growing needs and absorptive capability. But the flow of direct investment has remained very small. Yet *direct investment has some advantages over loans*. Loans have to be repaid whether investments are productive or not. Investment leads to outflows only after there is production and then too only when there is profit ... One reason for the low levels of direct foreign investment is that our efforts at streamlining procedures, which have yielded good results in the area of domestic industrial licenses, have not been effectively extended to foreign investment proposals. I was given many examples of such problems on my recent visit to Japan. There is need to expand procedural simplification and efficiency on this area also. *We can absorb a larger flow of foreign investment, with advantage to our economy, by speeding up procedures and removing unnecessary irritants* (emphases added).[42]

Two factors seem to have affected Rajiv Gandhi to support FDI inflows to India. First, Rajiv Gandhi's visit to Japan offered a chance to learn its experience for

---

[41] Joshi and Little (1994), 58–62; See also Ganguly and Mukherji (2011).
[42] Gandhi (1998).

development.⁴³ Through the experience, he confirmed his belief in the significance of technology and close ties between the state and industry for development. He knew that foreign investments are the easiest way for the domestic industry to access advanced technologies. Second, his positive attitude towards foreign capital was encouraged by the difficulties of handling external resources.⁴⁴ Their inspiration was in reality embodied to devise industrial strategies in India to make the state and industry more cooperative. Nonetheless, the Rajiv Gandhi government did not entirely open India's market to foreign investors. It was largely due to the strong lobby from the domestic capital and their assertion of protecting domestic industry against foreign capital.

India's external payments position was deteriorating, and the country had to resort to further commercial borrowings. The government of India attempted an economic institutional change especially in foreign trade policies through the Eighth Five-Year Plan to overcome financial difficulties.⁴⁵ The Janata Dal government led by V. P. Singh, who succeeded Rajiv Gandhi as the Prime Minister of India, pursued economic reforms. The government established new statutory organisations like the Securities and Exchange Board of India (SEBI) to regulate domestic capital markets more efficiently. The SEBI has played a major role in managing FDI proposals since then. According to the *Economic Survey 1990-91*, the economic conditions became worse in the consecutive government led by Chandra Shekar, who was in power as the Prime Minister of India beginning in November 1990. Yashwant Sinha, who served as the Finance Minister of India for the Chandra Shekar government, narrates in his autobiography that the government began to behave more responsibly than most of the people had expected by successfully negotiating with the IMF for financial assistance.⁴⁶ Sinha

---

⁴³ Interestingly, some other political leaders both at the union and the state levels also visited Japan for learning the East Asian development strategies in the 1980s. Their inspirations were in reality embodied to devise industrial strategies in India in a way to make the state and industry more cooperative. For example, M. G. R. who was the Chief Minister of Tamil Nadu at that time visited Japan with some of his party members including C. Ponnaiyan serving as the Finance Minister of Tamil Nadu in order to learn the East Asian industrial development. Interview with C. Ponnaiyan in Chennai on January 31, 2012. The strategies were presented in various government reports issued. For discussions on how India's political leaders thought of East Asia's developmental state model, see also Abegglen and Etori (1981); Mukherji (2014), Chapter 4; Sawhney (1985). In particular, Mukherji (2014) indicated that Chandrababu Naidu, who served as the Chief Minister of Andhra Pradesh from 1995 to 2004, was impressed by economic development models in East and Southeast Asia and convinced to promote investment projects in the state (152).

⁴⁴ Sawhney (1985).

⁴⁵ Singh (1990a; 1990b); Government of India (1991a).

⁴⁶ Sinha (2007), 6–7.

assessed that the financial deficit was the outcome of shortcomings in the macro-management of the past economy. Key policy-makers including Yashwant Sinha in the government of India thought that India had to share its economic concerns with the Parliament and the people so that the restoration of the economy could be achieved as a collective responsibility.[47]

Pro-FDI Inflows (After 1991)

The financial difficulties in the early 1990s were finally reflected in new economic policies in the area of foreign investments. Montek Singh Ahluwalia, who served as Commerce Secretary, confidentially submitted a new industrial policy paper titled 'Towards Restructuring Industrial, Trade and Fiscal Policies' to the PMO in 1990. The paper became the original design for economic reform that was implemented in 1991. It suggested the complete deregulation of the industrial sectors including foreign investments. For example, it proposed to increase the equity of foreign investors from 40 per cent to 51 per cent in domestic companies in many sectors. Through the policy change, foreign capital could actively participate in the process of industrialisation in India. Further, the *Budget 1991–92* also showed the need for foreign investments. In a budget speech, Manmohan Singh, who succeeded Yashwant Sinha as the Finance Minister, strongly supported FDI inflows to the domestic market.[48] Manmohan Singh believed that FDI inflows would provide access to capital and technology in the global market that could contribute to economic growth in India.

The imminent threat of the BOP crisis of 1991 and the consensus of key policy-makers for liberalisation led India's economy to open up to foreign capital. Since the extensive economic reform of 1991, the total FDI inflows have steadily increased. Table 2.2 shows the pattern of FDI inflows to India and China from 1991 to 2015. Interestingly, India has substantially increased FDI inflows as a per cent of gross fixed capital formation during the period. FDI inflows to India as a per cent of gross fixed capital formation sometimes have bigger than those to China especially for recent years. It means that FDI inflows in India have played an increasingly important role in capital formation over the past years. Through the reforms of 1991, foreign capital could participate in the process of industrialisation comparatively more easily than before by sharing up to 51 per cent of their equity in domestic companies of India in many sectors.[49]

---

[47] Singh (1990a), 12.
[48] Government of India (1991b), 5.
[49] Panagariya (2008), 199–200.

Table 2.2: FDI Inflows to India and China (1991–2015)

Year	FDI, Net Inflows (BOP, Current US$ Million)		FDI, Net Inflows (Percentage of GDP)		As a Percentage of Gross Fixed Capital Formation	
	India	China	India	China	India	China
1991	74	4,366	0.0	1.1	0.1	4.3
1992	277	11,156	0.1	2.6	0.4	8.4
1993	550	27,515	0.2	6.2	0.9	16.3
1994	973	33,787	0.3	6.0	1.3	16.9
1995	2,144	35,849	0.6	4.9	2.3	14.7
1996	2,426	40,180	0.6	4.7	2.5	14.3
1997	3,577	44,237	0.8	4.6	3.4	14.5
1998	2,635	43,751	0.6	4.3	2.5	12.6
1999	2,169	38,753	0.5	3.5	1.9	10.6
2000	3,584	42,095	0.8	3.5	3.2	10.4
2001	5,472	47,053	1.1	3.5	4.2	10.2
2002	5,626	53,073	1.1	3.6	4.3	10
2003	4,323	57,901	0.7	3.5	2.7	8.9
2004	5,771	68,117	0.8	3.5	2.7	8.6
2005	7,269	104,109	0.9	4.6	2.7	11.3
2006	20,029	124,082	2.1	4.5	6.4	11.3
2007	25,228	156,249	2.0	4.4	5.9	11.3
2008	43,406	171,534	3.5	3.7	10.5	9.3
2009	35,581	131,057	2.6	2.6	7.8	5.7
2010	27,397	243,703	1.6	4.0	4.9	8.9
2011	36,499	280,072	1.9	3.7	5.8	8.2
2012	23,996	241,214	1.3	2.8	3.9	6.2
2013	28,153	290,928	1.5	3.0	4.8	6.7
2014	34,577	268,097	1.7	2.6	5.5	5.7
2015	44,009	242,489	2.1	2.2	7.1	5.0

Source: The World Bank, *World Development Indicators* (various issues).[50]

When the plan for economic reform was informed in 1991, opinions diverged in the state and society. Many policy-makers strongly supported the so-called 'Montek Paper' that showed a comprehensive economic vision for both India's industry and international relations.[51] However, several key bureaucrats critically pointed out the feeble position of the state in pursuing the reforms against the power of vested

---

[50] World Bank's World Development Indicators, accessed 17 August 2017, http://databank.worldbank.org/data/reports.aspx?source=world-development-indicators#.

[51] Institute of Economic Growth Delhi (1990); Shastri (1997), 50.

interests, such as wealthy farmers, business groups, and trade unions. P. N. Dhar (1990), former Principal Secretary to the Prime Minister in the Indira Gandhi Government and Assistant Secretary-General of the United Nations, was one of them. He was concerned about the pervasive political fragmentation within political parties, which acted as a barrier to positive relationships with economic policies. Dhar made a critical comment on the state's pursuing reforms by putting it, 'in circumstances of political fragmentation economic policies are political weapons in power struggles rather than solutions to problems'.[52]

The power of vested interests in society and political fragmentation strongly disturbed the progress of economic reform of 1991. The first response from society to the reform plan rose in the big domestic businesses. Before the sanction of industrial policies, several dominant industry associations showed different opinions. The Associated Chambers of Commerce and Industry (ASSOCHAM) argued the need for a free flow of foreign investments while the Federation of Indian Chambers of Commerce and Industry (FICCI) held a reluctant view in increasing the equity of foreign investors. Unlike ASSOCHAM having a number of foreign firms as members, FICCI's principal members were indigenous business groups. It said, 'the final judgement on whether or not such investment is desirable should be left to the Indian entrepreneurs'.[53] FICCI again opposed foreign investments after a few years when the federal government of India under Vajpayee's leadership attempted economic reform in 1998, although its resisting attitude towards economic reform softened a little bit than before. It was mainly concerned about the structural changes of Indian business where foreign investors could more easily control companies once their equity increases. FICCI's conflicting interests and expectant competition with foreign investors had delayed the policy enactment.

Another example that shows how the interests of domestic businesses influenced the reform process, Bombay Club's '*swadeshi*' debates should not be missed. Bombay Club, India's big businesses community, led by Rahul Bajaj, Chairman and Managing Director of the Bajaj Auto, was unhappy with the increased competition with foreign capital as a consequence of the reforms.[54] With other indigenous firms in CII and FICCI, Bombay Club began insisting a level playing field for domestic companies against foreign firms. It resisted to economic reform more rigorously in late 1993 when the government of India could ease an immediate financial crisis. In an interview with a daily newspaper, Hari Shankar Singhania, one of

---

[52] Dhar (1990), 26.
[53] *The Hindu*, 'ASSOCHAM's Package of Economic Reforms,' 15 July 1991, accessed 6 April 2012.
[54] See Chibber (2003).

the Bombay Club members, argued that domestic businesses want 'a breathing space to catch up with other countries where industries were not hamstrung by a license-permit raj'.[55]

While Bombay Club opposed foreign investments by claiming continued tariff protection and internal reforms before opening the domestic market, competition for lobbying the Government of India to pursue their interests among business associations was getting more severe. FICCI, ASSOCHAM, and CII were the major business associations competing in the lobby.[56] By the 1980s, FICCI was recognised as the most influential business association, although there was a power struggle between the Calcutta and the Bombay group in the organisation. However, FICCI split in 1986 due to caste and family cleavage among members. After the incident, ASSOCHAM and CII emerged as powerful business associations.[57] The lobbying styles of the associations were also different. For example, CII sought professional and outward-looking strategies than the other two associations that were seeking close relationships with the principal ministers and bureaucrats.

Lobbying by domestic businesses to protect their business interests against foreign capital was considerable in the BJP-led National Democratic Alliance (NDA) Government under A. B. Vajpayee's leadership as the Prime Minister of India. When the Vajpayee government attempted to garner FDI through institutional arrangements in 1998 and 1999, Bombay Club opposed the state's idea towards opening the domestic market more widely to foreign capital.[58] The resisting voice of domestic big businesses was getting bigger because indigenous firms thought the ideological base of BJP, *swadeshi*, was not applied to the market's rule. P. Chidambaram (2007), who served as the Finance Minister of India at that time, showed his worry about the hostile attitude of Indian big businesses towards foreign capital in his autobiography, by putting it, 'Rahul Bajaj (and what survives of the Bombay Club) maintains that money has color; there is foreign money and there is Indian money, and the latter has to be preferred to the former'.[59]

Social activists who spoke for producers of small industries, farmers, artisans, and consumers, also opposed to the state's idea of opening the domestic market

---

[55] Chandra N. Mohan, 'The Swadeshi Fear of A Borderless World,' *The Times of India*, 27 January 1998, accessed 10 April 2012.

[56] See Kantha and Ray (2006).

[57] Kochanek (1995).

[58] The opposition from India's indigenous business groups to the state's idea towards further liberalisation perhaps influenced the Government of India to limit the activities of foreign investors to select sectors in India's industry. Nayar (2007) clearly presented that the BJP Government at that time framed policies to restrict FDI in some areas like in the consumer goods sector, even though it was not opposed to FDI inflows (210).

[59] Chidambaram (2007), 52.

to foreign capital. Social activists criticised domestic big businesses as well. From the eye of social activists and the poor in society, big companies looked to only seek their interests in the name of *swadeshi*. The negative attitude from society was often expressed through protests against the state and foreign capital and attempts to evict MNCs from India's market.

Interestingly, the protests have usually been involved with either left-wing political parties that seek political support by making alliances with the benefit losers of economic reforms or the extreme right-wing political organisations that aim to protect the interests of indigenous big businesses. In a couple of interviews, Prasenjit Bose, who was the convener of research unit in the CPI(M), explained fear that people on the ground feel when they are displaced in the process of FDI inflows, by putting it,

> There are two types of anti-FDI pictures from our (communist parties') perspective. First is a grass-root level resistance, which is protesting for people who are displaced from their resources and livelihood like land. Second is a sector-by-sector approach at the macro-economic policy level. We do not oppose the FDI inflows of every sector. We accept that we cannot avoid globalisation. So we consider the sensitivity of each sector (in opposing FDI inflows).[60]

Despite its compromise in understanding the influence of globalisation over India's market, the left-wing parties like CPI(M) have played a central role in opposing FDI inflows by organising its trade union and creating conflicts with the management of many foreign firms in India's industry. Fieldwork findings suggested that the communist parties deeply involved in frequent violence and female abuse in the process of mobilising protests against the state-led industrialisation. The ambiguous ideologies and identities among differing political organisations within the communist party, such as CPI, CPI(M), CPI(Maoist), and CPI(Marxist-Leninist) and their conflicts towards one other have not only intensified the level of violence but also adversely affected their original aim to support labour and displaced people from the process of FDI inflows.[61]

The Rashtriya Swayamsevak Sangh (RSS), a right-wing Hindu nationalist organisation, has also opposed globalisation and FDI inflows. The Swadeshi Jagran Manch (SJM) [self-reliance awareness front] that was set up in 1994 by the RSS has firmly resisted FDI inflows.[62] Its opposition activities were observed when Vajpayee was the Prime Minister of India. The SJM often alleged that it would conduct a social boycott of political leaders and bureaucrats who negotiated with

---

[60] Interview at the head office of CPI(M) in Delhi on 12 and 21 December 2011.
[61] See Bose (2010); Chakrabarty and Kujur (2010).
[62] Frankel (2005), 728–29.

the World Trade Organization and MNCs, by describing its opposition to MNCs as the 'second war of India's independence' using a slogan 'MNCs quit India; we won't accept globalisation'.[63] Likewise, the Vishwa Hindu Parishad, another right-wing Hindu nationalist organisation, strongly opposed foreign capital. For example, it campaigned against a McDonald's outlet on the grounds of 'cultural pollution' in Mumbai in 1998.

Society's strong protests against foreign investors can be found in many states in India today, even though economic institutions have shifted favourably towards FDI inflows. The anti-Special Economic Zone movements were organised in many states including Tamil Nadu and Maharashtra. A series of protests against POSCO at Jagatsinghpur in Odisha are broadly known. The strategies of protesters have been getting more complicated, as society's concerns about FDI inflows have been raised through questions in many terms, such as livelihood, security, and environment besides the idea of *swadeshi*. The protesters, ranging from political communities to non-government organisations, mobilise external supporters from abroad as well as local citizens who are directly affected by FDI projects. The different narratives about foreign investments from differing actors in India's society need to be understood.

It is significant that the Prime Minister's role reduced in the process of FDI approval during the pro-FDI inflow period. Instead, FDI approval required the discretionary support of the Chief Ministers in states for which the FDI plans are proposed. In an interview, V. S. Chauhan, formerly serving as the director of FIPB, explained why the Prime Minister's role diminished in the process of FDI inflows by putting it:

> When there is no policy, then the decision is taken at the highest level. When you clearly demarcate a policy, then you do not need to involve with the PM. You take the PM's approval only for the change of policy ... It should be seen as, the steering role of PMO (was needed) when there was no clearly articulated policy. Its implementation (however) has to be left to the administrative ministries.[64]

A question is why the significance of the role of provincial states has increased in the process of FDI inflows. The rate of FDI proposals that embarked through the automatic route in India accounts for 80 to 90 per cent of all the proposals.[65] The proposals then have to be guided by each provincial state for which FDI projects are proposed. In cases of FDI proposals that need to build plants for production

---

[63] Desai (1997).

[64] Interview at the Ministry of Finance (MOF) in North Block, Delhi on 21 March 2012.

[65] Interview with Ashish Kumar (Director of FDI Asia-Pacific Division) in the Department of Industrial Policy & Promotion (DIPP) in Udyog Bhawan, New Delhi on 15 March 2012.

– it is called a Greenfield type of FDI and is often found in the manufacturing sector, each state consults with the foreign investors in order to provide them necessities for their establishing the plants within the provincial state including land, electricity, water, and other infrastructure facilities.[66] At this stage, foreign investors have to obtain various clearances from either the central government or the related provincial state or both government bodies for proceeding to build the plants. The importance of cooperation between the central government and the states and the ongoing debate about the concept of economic federalism will be relevant in this context. At this stage, in fact, many foreign investors have faced difficulties in pursuing their FDI projects because of the multi-level and complicated steps to proceed in each provincial state despite the advantage of an automatic route that skips the approval process of FDI proposals.

Competition among the provincial states has intensified to present better performance than one another in approving more FDI projects.[67] Some of the Chief Ministers of India are well known as leaders who tried to garner FDI and utilise it as a financial resource for industrialisation. Chandrababu Naidu in Andhra Pradesh, Narendra Modi as former Chief Minister of Gujarat, J. Jayalalithaa as former Chief Minister of Tamil Nadu, and many others have attempted to promote FDI inflows. The liberal ideas of political leaders and learning from neighbouring states work as a driving force to deepen competition among states. As implied in the metaphorical word *bimaru* [sick], particularly used in indicating economically backward states, such as Bihar, Madhya Pradesh, Rajasthan, and Uttar Pradesh, such backward states have been attempting to escape from bad reputation by catching up with other economically advanced states. For the economically backward states, FDI inflows are considered as a means of catching up with the industries of other advanced states.

In a public lecture, Montek Singh Ahluwalia, who served as the Deputy Chairman of the Planning Commission from July 2004 to May 2014, also pointed out the different economic performances of states in India by putting it:

> The BIMAR(O)U states, Bihar, Madhya Pradesh, Rajasthan, UP, and Odisha, if you spell the bimaru, you should add 'o' for Odisha. Now look at these states ... Quite a few of them are catching up ... Each state has investment conferences, and images are created ... The other interesting thing is that states are actually changing the images (as investment friendly ones) ... The maintenance (to produce a good performance) is a very big problem ... this maintenance should be the job of all the state governments charged. The central government helps them to create capacities and the state governments maintain their capacities.[68]

---

[66] Government of India (2002).
[67] See FICCI (2012).
[68] Lecture in IIT Delhi on 3 March 2012. See also Ahluwalia (2000).

As discussed so far, the nature of institutional changes of FDI inflows at the union level of India is defined by largely endogenously driven socio–political factors, such as ideas, interests, and competition.

A gradual institutional change favouring FDI inflows at the union level in India supports a tipping point model for India's economic reforms that Mukherji (2013) suggested.[69] Mukherji highlighted the ideas of key policy-makers and domestic politics pushed to a 'tipping point' through which the economic institutional changes were made. By comparing the BOP crises in 1966 and 1991, Mukherji stressed that India's economic reform in 1991 was driven gradually and mostly endogenously by ideas and domestic politics, even though there was some influence from exogenous shocks. Likewise, the economic reform of 1991 played a critical role that accelerated the economic institutional changes to promote FDI inflows.

The subsequent part of this chapter will discuss how politics driven by ideas between two key ministries of the federal Government of India influenced to relocate FIPB, a critical state agency having a role in promoting FDI inflows, to one another.

FERA to FEMA and Politics behind FIPB Relocation

One of the most significant institutional arrangements in the area of FDI inflows in India was the enactment of the FERA in 1973, which was reconstituted in 1999 as the Foreign Exchange Management Act (FEMA).[70]

Unlike FERA, FEMA acknowledged some of the state agencies, such as the SEBI as participants in dealing with foreign currency in addition to RBI. The foreign currency-related works were subdivided to different organisations through the act. SEBI and RBI are mainly concerned with Foreign Institutional Investment and FDI inflows that do not need approval permission since they are reviewed under an automatic route.[71] Under the automatic route, foreign investors in various industrial sectors are allowed to embark on their business more easily than those in the other route.[72] Otherwise, the Secretariat for Industrial Assistance and the

---

[69] Mukherji (2013).

[70] Reserve Bank of India (2000).

[71] There are three categories – Wholly-Owned Subsidiary (WOS), Mergers and Acquisitions (M&A), and Joint Venture (JV) – of FDI flows to India. See Reserve Bank of India (2003).

[72] Interviews with Anupam Srivastava and Udit Srivastava in the 'Invest India', Joint Venture between the GOI and FICCI for FDI promotion, New Delhi in India on 5 March 2012. Despite such aims of the automatic route in easing the process of FDI inflows, many of the foreign investors have encountered difficulties in embarking their FDI projects in India.

FIPB examine proposals that are excluded from the automatic route. Thus, the role of the FIPB has become more significant in the approval and disapproval of proposals since the initiation of FEMA.

It is interesting to note that the competent authority of FIPB was transferred twice after the economic reform of 1991. The FIPB was initially constituted under the PMO during the reforms when Narasimha Rao was the Prime Minister of India and Manmohan Singh was the Finance Minister of India. However, it was transferred to the Department of Industrial Policy & Promotion (DIPP) under the Ministry of Commerce and Industry (MOCI) in 1996 and again relocated to the Department of Economic Affairs under the MOF in 2003. While FIPB was relocated twice, the lowest limit of total investment in proposals was revised upwards from 3 billion Indian Rupees to 6 billion Indian Rupees and from 6 billion Indian Rupees to 12 billion Indian Rupees, respectively.[73] The upward adjustment of total FDI limit meant that two key ministries of India, MOF and MOCI, have important roles in the approval process of FDI inflows. These key ministries have realised the significance of FDI inflows in India's industry.

Regarding the relocation of FIPB, V. S. Chauhan, former Director of FIPB said:

> In the 1990s when India was looking for FDI inflows, there was no clear policy; so the PMO was handling it. In 1996, FIPB was shifted to DIPP (under MOCI). The DIPP stands for Department of Industrial Policy & Promotion. Now it is talking about 'industry'. It was considering FDI as 'industry'. Then bureaucrats realised that the growth of FDI was based on the India's service sector, not the manufacturing sector. So, FDI inflows needed to be seen as 'finances' which could be housed for industry. Now it is more (related to) finance matter.[74]

Chauhan's point of view indicated that a significant reason for the second relocation of FIPB from MOCI to MOF was that FDI inflows were later considered as financial resources. It also meant that the pattern of FDI inflows in India was now more orientated towards the service sector. Since most of the FDI proposals in the manufacturing sector are under the review of the automatic route, FIPB is taking FDI proposals with a focus on the service industry.

It is not clear if the goal of relocating FIPB to MOF was achieved, since V. S. Chauhan indicated that there was a functional difference between the two ministries. Table 2.3 presents the total FDI equity inflows to India in the FIPB route from 1991 to 2017. The total FDI inflows in the FIPB route substantially

---

[73] Government of India (2010a).

[74] Interview with V. S. Chauhan in the Ministry of Finance at North Block in Delhi on 21 March 2012.

increased after the second relocation of FIPB in 2003. It supports the enhanced role of MOF as a promoter of FDI inflows. In fact, Chauhan indicated that FDI inflows are considered as increasingly critical financial resources, compared to the period when FIPB belonged to MOCI. However, it seems difficult to mention distinguishing differences between the two separate ministries regarding their primary goal in the process of FDI inflows as FDI promoters without further evidence.

Table 2.3: FDI Equity Inflows to India, FIPB Route (1991–2017)

Financial Year (April–March)	FDI Inflows: FIPB Route/ RBI's Automatic Route/ Acquisition Route (US$ Million)
1991–92	129
1992–93	315
1993–94	586
1994–95	1,314
1995–96	2,144
1996–97 (First relocation of FIPB)	2,821
1997–98	3,557
1998–99	2,462
1999–00	2,155
2000–01	2,339
2001–02	3,904
2002–03	2,574
2003–04 (Second relocation of FIPB)	2,197
2004–05	3,250
2005–06	5,540
2006–07	15,585
2007–08	24,573
2008–09	31,364
2009–10	25,606
2010–11	21,376
2011–12	34,833
2012–13	21,825
2013–14	24,299
2014–15	30,933*
2015–16	40,001*
2016–17	43,478*

Note: *Provisional.

Sources: Fact Sheet on Foreign Direct Inflows, DIPP, MOCI (GOI, various issues).

A question is why FIPB, a statutory agency dealing with FDI inflows, had to move to two powerful ministries structuring and implementing the state's industrialisation. I would argue that the FDI inflows were used for policy-makers in two key ministries as a means of political tussle. Ministers in both MOF and MOCI competed for governing FIPB since the one who holds FIPB was supposed to have greater autonomy in giving approval power. In other words, the overwhelming power of deciding approval shifted from the Prime Minister to an Industry Minister and again to a Finance Minister of India.

Political agendas between the key ministers in PMO, MOCI, and MOF were pursued over the issue of FIPB relocation.[75] The Janata Dal Government under Deve Gowda's leadership decided to transfer FIPB in July 1996. The government was led by the United Front coalition which received political support from CPI(M). Amar Nath Verma, the Principal Secretary in PMO, was serving as the chairman of FIPB for four years. However, Murasoli Maran, an influential Industry Minister, opined that Verma was inefficient for the position in dealing with a deadlock in approving FDI proposals. Maran was a critical and influential minister, who led the FIPB's transfer from PMO to MOCI.[76] Maran criticised poor governance in Verma's dealing with FDI proposals and promised to solve the bottleneck problems found in the process of FDI approval.[77] Maran, interestingly, pointed out a political feud between political leaders as a factor that led to poor governance. Political conflicts between Narasimha Rao serving as the Prime Minister and K. Karunakaran serving as an Industry Minister seemed severe. According to a source, Karunakaran had a verbal duel one day with Rao and then refused to attend a meeting of the Cabinet Committee on Foreign Investment under FIPB where FDI proposals were submitted and reviewed.[78]

Maran had not only a 'tough' trade minister image but also a powerful political background. His maternal uncle and political mentor was M. Karunanidhi who served as the Chief Minister of Tamil Nadu and President of Dravida Munnetra Kazhagam (DMK) party. Maran was well known as the person who suggested that DMK should make an alliance with BJP in 1999 for an electoral victory, even though DMK had several conflicting ideological issues with BJP. After the two

---

[75] For another discussion on the impact of bureaucratic politics in making institutions, see Halperin and Clapp (2006). Halperin and Clapp discussed how several departments in the Government of the United States having dissimilar interests influenced the decision-making process in the areas of national security and foreign policy.

[76] George Skaria, 'The All New FIPB the Board's Streamlined Processes Are Speeding Up FDI Clearance,' *Business Today*, 22 April 1996, accessed 22 April 2012.

[77] Ibid. The problems include the malfunctions of FIPB, politically 'feud-ridden' approach from the preceding minister, and procrastination in FDI approval process.

[78] Ibid.

parties were tied for a political alliance, Maran became an Industry Minister again from 1999 to 2002 in the BJP-led NDA coalition Government when Vajpayee was the Prime Minister. Maran's role was critical in building close relationships between the Central Government and his home state – Tamil Nadu.

Political feuds and personal inclinations in the process of FDI approval led to discordance between MOCI and MOF and frequent delays of the approval process. Vajpayee observed the political discordance and felt that FIPB needed to be carefully monitored by PMO.[79] Vajpayee thought that PMO could coordinate key decisions between MOCI and MOF. However, FIPB was relocated from MOCI to MOF in January 2003 during a Cabinet reshuffle.

Despite FIPB's move to MOF, Vajpayee's leadership seemed to pursue a greater autonomy to decide the fate of FDI proposals. According to Thakurta (2004), PMO made a resolute decision in dealing with the economic agenda because the NDA Government was receiving criticism from the public and within other government bodies.[80] Vajpayee made bold decisions pushing the economic agenda to accelerate liberalisation. S. Narayan, a former IAS officer who participated in the decision-making process for economic reforms in the Vajpayee Government, also mentioned, 'I found Vajpayee to be an intuitive liberaliser, and on a number of occasions that I took decisions to him, he was in favour of more open economy and less control solutions'.[81]

It is also worth noting that the initial influence of a *swadeshi* orientation in structuring economic rules on the NDA Government does not seem to be strong due to the inconsistency of ideas between the major political leaders.[82] For example, Yashwant Sinha serving as a Finance Minister initially had a rigid *swadeshi* orientation while Ramakrishna Hegde, who was the Commerce Minister, supported liberalisation. The key ministers often expressed inconsistent and divergent ideological approaches to economic issues. Also, some ministers occasionally changed their economic orientation. Yashwant Sinha, who was considered a *swadeshi* believer, one day defined *swadeshi* as 'a very modern and dynamic concept which meant being pro-India without being anti-foreign' in favour of foreign investors.[83] The way Sinha interpreted *swadeshi* confused people. Many people began criticising the incoherent economic orientation that the

---

[79] *The Economic Times*, 'Move Afoot to Bring FIPB under PMO,' 3 January 1999, accessed 25 April 2012.
[80] The confusing ideologies of the BJP-led NDA Government are explained well in Thakurta (2004).
[81] Informal email correspondence on 6 December 2013.
[82] Nayar (2007).
[83] Sinha (2007), 39–40.

NDA government sought. Regarding the frequently changed ideas from leaders, Chidambaram, who later succeeded Jaswant Singh as a Finance Minister from 2004 to 2008 in the Congress-led UPA coalition government, wrote:

> The NDA government is like a football team that kicks and passes the ball aimlessly while waiting for the referee's final whistle. No attempt is made to score a goal, the object being to prevent a self-goal or a goal against the NDA side.[84]

Some scholars in India's political economy have also discussed the politics of the NDA government. Nayar (2007) argued that BJP was seeking power by diluting its idea of economic nationalism or *swadeshi* as it was part of a larger coalition. The NDA government in 1998 and 1999 even withdrew its extreme ideological position and took a centric and moderate economic orientation. Unlike Nayar, who saw the ideological diversity as a source of political coalition building, Thakurta (2004) considered it a contradiction of political alliances. Thakurta pointed out that the confusing ideologies of political parties in the NDA coalition were the main source of ideational incoherence and indicated it was an 'illusion of consensus'.

Opposition to the unstable economic orientation of the government became stronger not only in society but also within the NDA government. Many interest groups and political leaders opposed Vajpayee's ideas to increase FDI inflows from the European Union and make India an 'investment destination'.[85] For example, Swaminathan Gurumurthy, an outspoken ideologue of Sangh Parivar, a Hindu nationalist organisation, expressed strong opposition to Vajpayee's economic orientation. Gurumurthy said:

> Foreign investment is unwelcome in the consumer sector, wholesale and retail, agriculture, coastal shipping, telecom, defence and sectors where there is large local demand. For instance, in sectors like iron, steel, petroleum, real estate and construction no foreign investments should be allowed ... We are asking (the NDA government) for total review of mindless globalisation, economic liberalisation and we are not opposing just one or two components of this economic policy. In the government and outside, many people are afraid of being labelled as anti-globalisation and anti-liberalisation as in the (19)50s, when people were not ready to be seen as anti-socialist.[86]

---

[84] Chidambaram (2007), 63.

[85] *The Hindu*, 'Vajpayee Seeks India as Investment Destination,' 28 June 2000, accessed 6 April 2012; see also *The Times of India*, 'VP Warns Vajpayee on FDI in Print,' 26 February 2002, accessed 6 April 2012; *The Hindustan Times*, 'Keep FDI Out of Consumer Sector,' 1 December 2002, accessed 22 April 2012.

[86] *The Hindu* (2000), ibid.

Nonetheless, Vajpayee often met opposition groups, both in the ultra-right-wing and the left-wing parties, to convince them.[87]

Like FIPB's first transfer, the second relocation of FIPB that occurred in 2003 was also deeply involved in political struggles between the major ministers of the NDA government. It is said that none except a few top-level ministers in the Government knew about the FIPB relocation plan. Jaswant Singh, who served as a Finance Minister after taking over from Yashwant Sinha in 2002, announced the plan after a brief meeting with Vajpayee.[88] Since MOF was expected to deal with foreign investment proposals after the decision, Jaswant Singh's power strengthened. On the contrary, Arun Jaitley, a newly appointed Industry Minister, was seen as a loser in the power struggle. After the plan was announced within the government, bureaucrats in MOCI and MOF were confused about their tasks. It happened because FIPB was taken away to MOF without any notice to the officials at DIPP in MOCI, so they were confused and unsure of FIPB relocation plan.[89]

The relocation of FIPB was not far from the 'tug-of-war between sensible policy and vested interests' within a power struggle between key ministries.[90] After FIPB's second transfer, Kamal Nath who served as an Industry Minister after Arun Jaitley planned to relocate FIPB again.[91] Kamal Nath wanted to bring FIPB back to Udyog Bhawan where MOCI was located. He did not want FIPB to stay with a new Finance Minister, P. Chidambaram. He prepared to shift FIPB back to his ministry, and even informally arranged a new chairman of the Board. However, Nath's attempt failed because the Cabinet did not decide in favour of MOCI. FIPB has belonged to MOF since then.

Conclusion

This chapter discussed the dynamic interaction between socio–political factors and institutional changes in the realm of FDI inflows in India at the union level.

The primary objective of the discussion was to understand the pattern of FDI inflows in India that has gradually evolved from the regime of anti-FDI inflows (1969–75) to that of selective FDI inflows (1975–91) and finally that of pro-FDI inflows (the economic reform of 1991 onwards). In the period of anti-FDI inflows,

---

[87] Panagariya (2007).
[88] *Business Standard*, 'FIPB Shifted to Finance Ministry,' 31 January 2003, accessed 11 April 2012.
[89] *The Indian Express*, 'Confusion Looms Large in FIPB After Transfer to Finmin,' 1 February 2003, accessed 22 April 2012.
[90] *The Economic Times*, 'You've Heard This Before,' 13 January 2004, accessed 25 April 2012.
[91] Shubham Mukherjee and Partha Ghosh, 'Kamal Nath Wants FIPB Under His Wing,' 28 May 2004, accessed 22 April 2012.

it was found that political struggles between Indira Gandhi and her opposition called as Syndicate within the Congress Party had a significant role in restructuring economic rules against foreign capital.

In the period of selective FDI inflows, the need for foreign investments began to be shared between policy-makers in the government, especially in particular areas where foreign technology was necessary for India's industry. In the gradual transformation, ideas of key policy-makers who recognised the advantages of FDI inflows compared to commercial borrowings had a significant role. However, lobbying and political interests from domestic business groups against FDI inflows hindered policy-makers from opening the domestic market widely to foreign capital.

Finally, a momentous attitudinal change from selective FDI inflows to pro-FDI inflows was driven by the imminent threat of a financial crisis and the consensus of key policy-makers for liberalisation. In the transition, intensified competition between domestic private capital and foreign capital in India's industry and between provincial states has given more attention to social concerns supporting marginalised groups in the process of FDI inflows.

Also, the final section of the discussion paid attention to FIPB's relocation to two important ministries, namely MOF and MOCI, which were politically motivated between key ministers to meet the aims of ideas towards liberalisation that the Prime Minister of India pursued.

3

FDI Inflows in Tamil Nadu
Inclusionary Ideas, Weakened Interests, and Incremental Institutional Change

The very success of the developmental state in structuring the accumulation of industrial capital has changed the nature of relations between capital and the state.[1]

Tamil Nadu is the most urbanised state in India with 48.45 per cent of its population living in urban areas.[2] The highest level of urbanisation is commensurate with the state's commitment to industrialisation. The state's aggressive land acquisition for industrialisation supports it. As of June in 2017, Tamil Nadu has the largest number of 36 operational Special Economic Zones (SEZs) among many provincial states in India.[3] Building SEZs primarily aims at promoting growth and productive capacity through a massive flow of foreign and domestic investment in the SEZs, particularly in infrastructure.[4] It is also expected to generate additional economic activities like the creation of employment opportunities. Such aims are clearly stipulated in the Tamil Nadu's Industrial Policy 2007, which promotes manufacturing capacity to meet global manufacturing competence.[5]

As such, the higher level of land acquisition in Tamil Nadu poses a question of 'how', particularly in its relations with socio–political facilitators, compared with

---

[1] Evans (1992), 165.

[2] The data is based on the ratio of population in urban areas to total population in Tamil Nadu measured for the Census 2011. Tamil Nadu is followed by Kerala (47.72%) and Maharashtra (45.23%). See the GOI (2011), accessed 28 September 2015, http://mospi.nic.in/mospi_new/upload/sel_socio_eco_stats_ind_2001_28oct11.pdf.

[3] Telangana (29), Maharashtra (28), and Karnataka (26) are following Tamil Nadu. See the GOI (2017), accessed 23 August 2017, www.sezindia.nic.in/writereaddata/pdf/StatewiseDistribution-SEZ.pdf .

[4] See the official website of Special Economic Zones in India run by the Government of India, accessed 28 September 2015, http://sezindia.nic.in/about-introduction.asp.

[5] See the Government of Tamil Nadu (GOTN), accessed 28 September 2015, www.tidco.com/images/industrialpolicy_e_2007.pdf.

other states that have struggled with land management for industrialisation. How do socio–political factors explain a high level of land acquisition that is coupled with intensive industrialisation in Tamil Nadu? This chapter attempts to answer the question by paying attention to the ideas of policy-makers on inclusive industrial schemes and societal structure presenting the upward mobility of low caste groups in the state. I argue that the state's commitment to making industries by aggressively making industrial lands has met the aspirations and needs of citizens favouring urbanisation, thereby contributing to industrial development. Also, the social inclusion, which has a significant role of managing social conflicts, could help the state garner legitimacy to pursue state goals for industrialisation.

This chapter considers the Madras legislative assembly election in 1967 as a critical event after which bipartisan rule began with two Dravidian regional parties, Dravida Munnetra Kazhagam (DMK) and All India Anna Dravida Munnetra Kazhagam (AIADMK). During the bipartisan rule, political elites could consistently pursue industrialisation with limited intervention from other parties. The leaders recognised FDI inflows as significant financial resources and advanced ideas favouring foreign capital. In addition, they have also implemented various schemes for social inclusion of the broader strata of citizens, such as land reforms, public distribution, education, health services, and employment in parallel with industrialisation. It is interesting that land reforms, in particular, seem to have helped state agencies acquire lands for industrial development and embark on FDI projects.

The findings from multiple instances of in-depth fieldwork present that such policies of social inclusion have played an important role in making citizens support the state in the pursuit of investments. Hence, the discussion in this chapter will trace the origin of ideational changes on foreign capital that the political elites developed and the inclusionary pattern of the state–society relations in Tamil Nadu. By doing so, it aims to explain how the inclusionary nature of the state–society relations in Tamil Nadu has resulted in a high level of FDI inflows.

The pattern of institutional change favouring FDI inflows in this state differs slightly from that of the central government. At the union level, the year 1975 was a turning point when economic strategies were shifted from control over both domestic and foreign capital towards industrial deregulation. However, a tipping point that brought a rapid change of the pattern of FDI inflows was the economic reform of 1991.[6] By contrast, the ideational orientation of key state leaders in

---

[6] For the concept of 'tipping point', see Capoccia and Keleman (2007). Capoccia and Keleman define it as 'a point at which the cumulative cause finally passes a threshold and leads to a rapid change in the outcome' (351).

Tamil Nadu favouring industrial investments in which foreign capital participated developed in the 1970s. It was because of owing to the positive role of multilateral organisations like the World Bank during industrialisation when political elites at the union level were deeply divided about the role of foreign capital.

Further, several state agencies of Tamil Nadu with an important role for industrialisation and urbanisation, which later became critical state authorities for promoting FDI inflows, were also founded in the 1970s. Such ideational consistency shared between state leaders support institutions favouring FDI inflows to be enhanced for decades. Tamil Nadu was thus better prepared than other provincial states in India to sustain the institutional stability.

This chapter consists of four parts. The first section reviews the literature on Tamil Nadu's political economy. It is followed by a discussion on the origin of ideas on the need for foreign capital that evolved in the 1970s. This section not only shows that the year 1967 was a key juncture in the political and economic transition of Tamil Nadu under the DMK's leadership but also explains why and how key political leaders of DMK conceived a positive attitude towards foreign capital in the 1970s while pursuing industrialisation. The discussion also will pay attention to the ideational development of state leaders on social inclusion, such as education and employment. Drawing attention to social inclusion in the discussion will help to understand how society's demand for industrialisation and employment creation encouraged foreign capital to participate in Tamil Nadu's industry. The following part will deal with the ideational evolution of key state elites in AIADMK, which was the ruling party in the 1980s in the state, on foreign capital and its usefulness in Tamil Nadu's industry. The last part of the chapter will present how the ideas favouring FDI inflows in the state and muted interests in society could bring substantial institutional change after the economic reforms of the central government in 1991.

Develompental State and Challenges to Local 'Strongmen' Perspective

Several studies that use a society-centred perspective have emphasised the influence of interest politics and societal structure on the transformation of Tamil Nadu's political economy. However, they have focused on the agrarian society of Tamil Nadu rather than its industrial setting. For example, Bouton (1985) challenged Barrington Moore's (1966) argument on the weakness of the modernising force in India's feudal society by closely examining the agricultural society of Thanjavur in Tamil Nadu. Bouton found that the agrarian societal structure of the district enhanced political forces that mobilise agrarian radicalism and communist strength through elections. Bouton pointed to the historical and ecological characteristics of the agrarian society as the sources that strengthen political forces. The factors taken into account were population growth, irrigated paddy region, price changes, labour wages, and landlord–tenant relations. Bouton showed how the factors mediated the impacts of political and economic modernisation in the region. According to Bouton, the landless labourer-dominant mode of production and high degree of stratification contributed little change to the agrarian society until the 1940s, even though capitalist and imperialist forces like the British trading post and the East India Company influenced societal transformation from the 18th century. Bouton's argument highlights the fact that the 1940s and 1950s held the potential for radical mobilisation due to persistent conflicts between large landlords and poor tenants and labourers.

However, some views slightly differ from Bouton. For example, Harriss-White (2003) argued that the intermediate classes of Indian society, namely, the capitalist class, local agricultural elites, and state officials, are the key actors that have structured political and economic institutions in Tamil Nadu. Similarly, Harriss (2006) and Harriss et al. (2010) explored the societal structure of Tamil Nadu by arguing that a caste system plays an important role in class relations in the state especially in the production process of an agricultural society where the local landlords class still holds great power. Their point of view supports a perspective on the influential role of local 'strongmen' in Indian society that has been discussed by many scholars.[7] They observe that the landed classes – mostly upper castes – or the local agricultural elites, in other words, have played significant roles not only in bargaining with bureaucrats to distribute the benefits of agricultural growth but also in participating in political activities through political parties and mobilisation. Further, the landed classes have pressurised policy-makers to structure economic institutions in favour of their interests at the local village level.

The industrial setting of Tamil Nadu, on the contrary, challenges the view of local strongmen. The next chapter in this book will discuss the counterevidence in detail by examining two FDI projects embarked on the state at the village level. In the process of FDI inflows to the state, for example, the roles of foreign investors are substantial not only in mediating social conflicts between different caste and religious groups in their firms but also in transforming the agrarian society into an industrial one. They have played significant roles in creating jobs and contributing to economic growth through the export of their production in the state. To achieve the two critical aims of employment and economic growth, state elites in Tamil Nadu have encouraged foreign investors to participate in industrial activities.

---

[7] See Bardhan (1984), Migdal (1988), Moore (1966), Rudra (1989), Vanaik (1990), Varshney (1995) for discussions on the role of local strongmen.

Several works with a state-centred approach have paid attention to the influence of political actors on changes in political institutions in Tamil Nadu. For example, Subramanian (1999 and 2002) showed how the successful mobilisation by political leaders in the Dravidian parties evolved and contributed to social pluralism in the state. By explaining changes in power relations largely between DMK, AIADMK, and Congress Party, Subramanian argued that the process of mobilisation by regional Dravidian parties created an inclusionary political arena because they addressed the intermediate and marginalised groups. For Subramanian, three components, namely, leadership flexibility, cadre autonomy, and supporter autonomy, were critical in reinforcing the organisational pluralism of the parties.

In fact, Subramanian's argument on the social pluralism contributed by regional parties could be strongly supported by Lakshman (2011). In a study of the role of caste politics in policy-making, Lakshman argued that a tendency for fragmented caste politics in the Dravidian parties has made pro-poor policy orientations sustainable in Tamil Nadu. Lakshman emphasised the organisational pluralism in DMK and the personal charisma of leaders in AIADMK as decisive factors that contributed to the Dravidian parties' allocating greater resources to the poor. Wyatt (2010) also paid attention to the political leaders in Tamil Nadu, who have affected changes in the party system at the state level, by calling the leaders 'political entrepreneurs' who have individual motivations in political participation. Wyatt argued that the political entrepreneurs formed the pattern of party competition by strategically selecting cleavages, such as ethnicity and caste that they want to emphasise when mobilising electorates.

In a similar fashion, Saraswathi (1995) showed how the ideas of state leaders in Tamil Nadu were influential in shaping clientelist relations between the leaders and citizens at the grassroots level. She traced the ideas of the political party, governance, welfare, and other significant agendas in the politics of Tamil Nadu by using the concept of 'linkage politics' to indicate the clientelist relations. Saraswathi argued that the Dravidian regional parties were successful in linking with *makkal* [people] on the grounds of both ideology and party organisation. These are based on notions of social inclusion that embrace the marginalised groups in society by making them feel 'kinship' or 'family' through political participation. Saraswathi's view ties in with those of Subramanian and Lakshman emphasising the inclusionary ideas of political leaders in the Dravidian parties.

On the other hand, Mitra (2006) and Vaasanthi (2006) saw that not only the strategies of the Dravidian parties were merely on the basis of populism and nepotism but also the attention-seeking politicians of the state failed to produce efficient governance. Mitra's work addresses corruption and the nepotistic orientation of political leaders in Tamil Nadu rather than the positive impacts of their mass mobilisation.

Inclusionary State–Society Relations and Investment-Friendly Institutional Arrangements in the 1970s

Backward group-based Dravidian party organisation and inclusionary ideas

The discussion here pays attention to the year 1967 when the idea favouring foreign capital has gradually evolved in Tamil Nadu. It challenges a view that the year 1967 was the initiation of the decline of economic growth in the industrial trajectory of Tamil Nadu that continued until the economic reform of the central government in 1991. Sinha (2005) insisted that the state of Tamil Nadu in this period neglected growth-oriented industrial policies and the DMK government merely asserted cultural populism by failing to connect welfare schemes with the economic growth of the state. As a significant factor that contributed to the failure of industrial growth, Sinha pointed to the political conflicts between DMK and Congress Party. It is true that the election victory of DMK under Annadurai's leadership in 1967 involved in frequent political conflicts with Congress Party both at the union and the state levels. The political conflicts became more severe in the 1970s when Congress Party was in power under Indira Gandhi's leadership at the union level. However, Sinha's substantial contradiction overlooks the ideas of DMK leaders on industrialisation and the detailed institutional arrangements that were implemented for industrial growth.

I found, on the contrary, that the frequent conflicts with the central government and the financial deficit at the union level influenced policy-makers of Tamil Nadu to promote foreign capital for its industrialisation and economic growth, even though the socialist orientation was strong in economic planning especially under Annadurai's leadership when DMK came to power in 1967. The financial support to this state from international organisations, such as International Monetary Fund and the World Bank in the process of urbanisation also greatly helped state leaders take a positive position about foreign capital.[8] The discussion in this part pays attention to the 1970s when ideas favouring foreign capital began to evolve, even though the ideas developed considerably in the 1980s.

Indian National Congress ruled in Tamil Nadu until the election of 1967. During this time, political leaders in the Congress Party, such as K. Kamaraj, who served as the Chief Minister of the state, tried to build a broader support base with not only the upper castes and landlord elites but also the marginalised groups. However, Congress Party was weaker than DMK in garnering electoral support from marginalised groups in particular. Tamil Nadu Congress Committee (TNCC) was thus conscious of the growing power of DMK and its ethnic

---

[8] Interview with T. K. S. Elangovan, DMK's spokesperson, at the head office of DMK in Chennai on 24 January 2012.

mobilisation through the 1950s and 1960s. Kamaraj knew it and worried about the weaker organisation of TNCC compared with that of the DMK. He asserted the need to strengthen the party organisation by interacting closely with more villagers and younger citizens. Also, he tried to pursue his ideas on the education of villagers that aimed at agricultural growth.[9] His ideas, however, failed to develop due to factionalism within Congress Party, as well as the strategies of DMK that led the party to win the election in 1967.

The factors that helped DMK gain broader support from the society have to do with its interest in social inclusion. The political leaders of DMK embodied the ideas of social inclusion in various policies by using other concepts, such as social justice, economic and social development, equality, and welfare. For example, social justice, which is 'the right of the weak, aged, destitute, powerless, women and children, and other underprivileged persons to the protection of the state against the ruthless competition of life', has been a key concept.[10] Saraswathi (1995) traced the origin of such idea to the year 1915 or 1916 when the South Indian Liberal Federation, known as Justice Party or Dravidar Kazhagam (DK), deployed its political movement against British colonialism. She argued that the idea of *sama neethi* [equal justice], which was raised for the successful self-respect movement in DK by E. V. Ramasamy, who is well-known as Periyar, was later developed into *samooka neethi* [social justice] by DMK when it came to power in 1967. The idea of social justice has been implemented by DMK leaders, particularly in providing citizens among marginalised groups access to vocational education and job applications. Through these inclusionary ideas, citizens could obtain benefits like other forward castes and classes of the state in the process of industrialisation.[11] For example, after the 1967 election, DMK leaders initiated a Public Distribution System (PDS) that was considered as a major instrument to ensure food security for the poor in society. According to Venkatsubramanian (2006), DMK leaders believed that food policy was a central issue for the government. The leaders committed to maintaining the price of rice below a certain level, monitoring the functions of the PDS, and enhancing the related policy implementation.

---

[9] GOTN (1956 and 1960).
[10] Saraswathi (1995), 122. See also Sen (2000).
[11] Chandra (2004), for example, clearly showed that DMK's success in mobilising electorates is quite high because its 'competitive organisational structure was able to represent a broad spectrum of elites and so capture the vote of the largest percentage of its target ethnic category' (28). In addition, Chandra's discussion implies that the success of mobilising electorates for ethnic parties like DMK would be higher when their patronage relations with the electorates aim to distribute the benefits of such relations to the electorates in the broad spectrum. See also Wyatt (2013).

As one of the strategies that DMK made for the election in 1967, the party first emphasised Periyar's philosophy of the self-respect movement and greater concern for citizens in marginalised groups in society.[12] C. N. Annadurai, the first Chief Minister of Tamil Nadu from DMK party, who was affectionately called *anna* [elder brother], *arignar* [learned], or *kalaignar* [artist] by his supporters, rooted DMK's founding ideas in Periyar's philosophy.[13] To achieve the goal of social justice in distributing power and economic benefits to the marginalised groups, Annadurai thought that socialism was a desirable orientation.[14] Other key leaders in the party have also continuously embraced the inclusionary idea. M. Karunanidhi, who served as the Chief Minister of Tamil Nadu several times, has also once said:

> I became a true disciple of Thanthai Periyar and then the affectionate younger brother of Arignar Anna and eventually a kin of the Tamil people dedicating myself to work for their betterment. ... In my whole life I have only one thought foremost in my mind, day in and day out, that is the right of the people belonging to the Scheduled Castes and Scheduled Tribes, Backward Classes and Most Backward Classes to live with dignity.[15]

Second, the inclusionary ideas stimulated a kinship or family feeling among DMK members.[16] This family feeling greatly helped DMK build strong organisations at the village level.[17]

Third, DMK party organisation seemed more democratic and stronger than others that party functionaries could provide active linkages between the government and citizens at the grassroots. In contrast, TNCC struggled with factional politics that finally led to the party split at the union level in 1969. The growth of bogus membership and internal factionalism within the TNCC hindered Kamaraj from delivering his ideas to the grassroots.[18]

---

[12] Barnett (1976).

[13] Informal discussions with Veeramani, president of Dravidar Kazhagam founded by Periyar, at the National University of Singapore on 17 November 2011 and at Periyar Maniammai University in Chennai on 10 January 2012. Interview with T. K. S. Elangovan in Chennai on 24 January 2012, *op. cit*. For Anna and Periyar's contribution to the Dravidian movement, see Ponnuswami (1982) and R. Kannan, 'Anna: Commoner Extraordinary,' *The Hindu*, 15 September 2008, accessed 2 March 2013.

[14] GOTN (1971).

[15] GOTN (1998).

[16] Saraswathi (1995), 54.

[17] Compared to the grassroot-oriented strategies of DMK to secure votes, AIADMK and Congress parties used more top-down approaches that depended on central leadership and alliance partners.

[18] Saraswathi (1995), 63.

Fourth, the key leaders of DMK also seemed to put greater weight on distributing public goods and rehabilitating displaced people from natural or industrial disasters as well as refugees from Burma and Ceylon.[19] The inclusionary characteristics successfully blocked marginalised and minority groups from being mobilised by opposition parties, such as the communist parties and the Congress Party.

Combative centre–state relations and financial difficulties in Tamil Nadu

The political conflicts between Congress Party and DMK became more intense in the 1970s. Saraswathi (1995) observed the political attack of Congress Party from both the union and the state levels towards DMK. She wrote:

> Having lost the governmental authority, Tamil Nadu Congress launched a campaign against DMK in the early 1970s charging interference in day-to-day administration and wrongful use of the official machinery for the private purpose … The new Congress supported the old Congress in criticising the growing politics in the administration of the DMK government.[20]

Such political conflicts between DMK and Congress Party were extended to financial matters. Although the budget deficit at the central government in the early 1970s was influenced by worldwide inflation,[21] V. R. Nedunchezhiyan who served as the Finance Minister of Tamil Nadu in the 1980s in AIADMK government pointed out that the substantial curtailing of financial assistance from the central government towards Tamil Nadu was not simply because of the its poor finances. As can be seen in Table 3.1, the gradual decrease in the share for Tamil Nadu from central assistance from the 1950s supports the view.[22]

Table 3.1: Share of Tamil Nadu in Central Assistance Extended to All States

Five-Year Plan	Share (Per Cent)
First Five-Year Plan (1951–56)	10.8
Second Five-Year Plan (1956–61)	9.0
Third Five-Year Plan (1961–66)	7.4
Annual Plans (1966–69)	6.8
Fourth Five-Year Plan (1969–74)	5.5
Fifth Five-Year Plan (1974–78)	4.1

Source: GOTN (1980), 40.

---

[19] GOI (1972), 33.
[20] Saraswathi (1995), 21.
[21] GOTN (1975).
[22] GOTN (1980).

It is worth noting that the centre–state relations are believed to be a critical factor that affects economic institutional changes in the provincial states of India. Aseema Sinha's (2005) *A Divided Leviathan* discusses this thesis by closely looking at the number of industrial licenses approved and the level of public sector investment allotted by the central government. Sinha argued that the centre–state relations were influential on the dissimilar levels of development among states in India with a limited data set for select states from 1955 to 1966. Likewise, this chapter underlines the significance of the centre–state relations in affecting policy-makers at the state level in restructuring economic institutions particularly during the pre-reform period before 1991.

The state of Tamil Nadu suffered from a decrease in financial assistance from the central government especially during the mid-1970s when drought aggravated agricultural and industrial output. The financial difficulties led policy-makers not only to reduce plan investments but also to seriously consider open market loans and borrowings from commercial banks to secure financial resources.[23] The former Finance Minister of Tamil Nadu in the AIADMK government who served from 2001 to 2006, C. Ponnaiyan, was one of those who observed the intense conflicts between the central government and the state at that time. In an interview, Ponnaiyan said:

> Our state was in hard times in the 1970s. When the Congress government reduced the central aid to our state, Indira Gandhi pointed out that 'your state (Tamil Nadu) is wealthier than others'. But our state in the 1970s was not industrialised much like today; our industry was heavily depending on the agricultural sector. And 85 per cent of farmers were marginalised in a sense that they had a very small size of land, less than five acres each, for farming.[24]

However, the key political leaders in Tamil Nadu seemed quite confident at that point about dealing with the financial deficit. It is not obvious how much they depended on open market loans and commercial borrowings. However, it is clear that the Government of Tamil Nadu not only utilised external financial aid from international organisations but also encouraged exports to get out of its financial difficulties. There was, in fact, a significant financial crisis in Tamil Nadu in 1962 due to the heavy pressure on foreign exchange reserves at the union level and an agricultural setback at the state level. The stock market also turned bearish after July 1962.[25] The quick recovery from the crisis by utilising external financial assistance and improving export performance gave policy-makers the confidence

---

[23] GOTN (1973; 1975).
[24] Interview in Chennai on 31 January 2012.
[25] GOTN (1963).

to overcome another financial deficit in the mid-1970s, and their experience helped to accumulate foreign capital. Although foreign capital participated substantially in Tamil Nadu's industry in the post-reform period after 1991 in the form of direct investment, it played a large role in assisting the state pursue industrialisation and urbanisation projects in the 1970s and 1980s.[26]

Since the political leaders of Tamil Nadu in the 1970s had at least a positive standpoint towards the role of foreign capital in Tamil Nadu's industry when many state leaders at the union level opposed it, the institutional change favouring FDI inflows to the state has to be interpreted more carefully.

The uncooperative attitude of the central government towards Tamil Nadu was also observed in the legislative process. In the Budget Speech delivered in 1975, Karunanidhi, the Chief Minister of Tamil Nadu at that time, mentioned:

> Many of the decisions taken by the central government with the objective of controlling inflation are not popular or palatable to the people. It is, therefore, desirable that the central government should consult the state governments who are in close contact with the people before understanding such measures. I have repeatedly emphasised that the central government should convene a conference of Chief Ministers to freely and frankly discuss the economic situation in the country and the various measures that need to be pursued. It is a matter for regret that the central government has not only not responded to this suggestion, but even the National Development Council which should be convened periodically has not met in the last 15 months.[27]

Such combative relationship between Tamil Nadu and the central government had a substantially negative influence on the price of commodities and agricultural development in Tamil Nadu. For example, the Fifth Five-Year Plan of the state reports:

> Delay in action at the union level in regard to procurement of essential inputs like cotton, crude oil, fertilisers, and pesticides had an inevitable impact on production and on prices; again, the delay of nearly two years in the approval of the process for production of fertilisers at Tuticorin led to continuing shortage of this vital commodity; some power schemes which should have been sanctioned years ago were still awaiting central decisions.[28]

---

[26] The World Bank's project and cooperation for eradicating slums in Madras is representative.

[27] See GOTN (1975), 2–3. The uncooperative attitude of the central government was often observed at that time. Another report issued by the Government of Tamil Nadu also shows a delayed decision by the central government on the Salem Steel project that was supposed to be set up in this state under the coordination of the central government. See also GOTN (1971), 12.

[28] GOTN (1973), iv.

Emergence of state agencies for industrial development in the DMK government and participation of multilateral organisations in the 1970s

Both political and financial non-cooperation from the central government encouraged the political leaders of DMK not only to argue its state independence or decentralisation of decision-making but also to secure financial resources itself. The leaders strongly argued for the enhancement of statutory power in pursuing industrialisation without waiting for delayed replies from the central government.[29] At the same time, they tried to secure financial resources from urban landowners in the state and several multilateral organisations. For example, they levied increased taxes on urban landowners for their land ownership.[30] They received financial assistance from UNICEF to build more than 10,000 tube-wells in several villages to provide a protected drinking water supply.[31] The World Bank also helped the state pursue urbanisation projects at that time. In an interview, G. Dattatri, former Chief of the Chennai Metropolitan Development Authority that led the urbanisation projects, emphasised the significance of the external financial assistance in overcoming financial crises and pursuing the urbanisation process in the state.[32]

It is highly significant in that the DMK government in the 1970s showed greater initiative in transforming its economy by establishing state agencies for industrialisation and pursuing urbanisation projects. For example, state agencies, such as Tamil Nadu Small Industries Development Corporation Limited (SIDCO) and State Industries Promotion Corporation of Tamil Nadu (SIPCOT) were set up to promote industrial development. The organisations, interestingly, later played important roles in supporting various FDI projects in the state especially after the economic reforms of the central government in 1991. SIDCO was incorporated in 1970 'with the specific objective of playing a catalytic role in the promotion and development of micro and small industries',[33] while SIPCOT was established

---

[29] The terms 'decentralisation' and 'state independence' often appear in various issues of the Budget Speech in Tamil Nadu. The term 'state autonomy', which is applied to state–society relations for indicating state capacity to structure and pursue policies over vested interest groups in society, has been in fact used to indicate state independence within the relations between the central government and provincial states in various documents issued by the state of Tamil Nadu.

[30] The land reforms were aggressively implemented in this regard.

[31] See GOTN (1971), 16. According to the document, Tamil Nadu received the assistance at a cost of 32 million Indian rupees by the year 1971 for five years.

[32] Interview at his residence in Chennai on 26 January 2012.

[33] For its objectives, see the official website of SIDCO, accessed 23 February 2013, www.sidco.tn.nic.in/rti.pdf.

in 1971 to encourage the participation of big businesses and the private sector.[34] SIPCOT has built, developed, maintained, and managed industrial complexes and SEZs in twelve districts of the state since then, by acquiring lands for domestic and foreign investors.[35] The Tamil Nadu Industrial Development Corporation (TIDCO) also began to actively operate in the 1970s after it was founded in 1965. TIDCO has been supporting large- and medium-scale industries by cooperating with the activities of SIPCOT.

The DMK Government under Karunanidhi's leadership strongly supported the enhancement of the state agencies. In the Budget Speech in 1975, Karunanidhi, the Chief Minister of Tamil Nadu at that time, appreciated their performance as follows:

> In the last four years, TIDCO has initiated 37 projects which are designed to cover the gaps in our industrial structure in petrochemicals, pharmaceuticals, chemicals, engineering, and other industries. ... The SIDCO will take up a program for the construction of 100 industrial sheds at a total cost of one crore rupees in 1975-76. A provision of 2 million Indian rupees as margin money has been made for this purpose in the Budget. ... The SIPCOT has sanctioned assistance to the tune of 98 million Indian rupees under various schemes and has canalised a total investment of 730 million Indian rupees with a direct employment potential for over 12,800 persons.[36]

Table 3.2 presents the trends of growth rates in select states in India from 1960 to 1980. Tamil Nadu showed a gradual increase in its growth rate during the period. The steady increase in the growth rate of the state, its growth in the 1970s in particular, needs to be understood in the context of the industrialisation that both DMK and AIADMK leaders pursued. The evidence supports what Kohli (2012) classified as a developmental state in his work on the state variations of economic growth in India.[37] It is because the incremental economic growth of Tamil Nadu has been substantially contributed by the private sector in industry through a close tie with the state.

In parallel with pursuing industrialisation, various social service programs for urbanisation were introduced. For the eradication of slums, the Tamil Nadu Slums Areas Act was enacted in 1971, and the outlay on the scheme was gradually

---

[34] GOTN (1971), 11.
[35] See the official website of SIPCOT, accessed 23 February 2013, www.sipcot.com/about_sipcot.html.
[36] GOTN (1975), 12–13.
[37] Kohli did not include the state of Tamil Nadu in the category of 'developmental state' for which he introduced the states of Gujarat and Maharashtra.

raised because of the significance of the project.[38] Furthermore, this scheme was attempted in parallel with creating employment for the slum dwellers.[39] For efficient progress, the statutory Slum Clearance Board was also set up in 1975.[40] Kurien and James (1975) observed the rapid increase in the urban population from the 1960s to the 1970s in Tamil Nadu as a consequence of such efforts. By highlighting the urbanisation process as an important economic change, they found that some cities in the state, such as Madras, Thanjavur, Coimbatore, and Chingleput showed rapid growth in the urban population. Kurien and James underlined that not only geographical factors but also the ideas of policy-makers favouring urbanisation strongly contributed to such growth.

Table 3.2: Trends of Growth Rates in the Select States (1960–80)

States	Net State Domestic Product (NSDP)		Net State Domestic Product (NSDP) per Capita	
	1960–61 to 1969–70	1970–71 to 1979–80	1960–61 to 1969–70	1970–71 to 1979–80
Karnataka	3.4	4.3	1.2	1.8
Delhi	5.1	6.2	0.7	1.7
Tamil Nadu	2.1	3.4	0.1	1.6
All-India	3.0	3.6	0.8	1.2
Andhra Pradesh	1.5	3.2	-0.4	1.1
West Bengal	2.5	2.9	0.02	0.7
Odisha	9.7	2.3	7.3	0.3

Notes:
1. States are organised by their rank in rates of growth of per capita NSDP from 1970–71 to 1979–80.
2. Since the deflators used to estimate the NSDP for Odisha in the period have discrepancies, the stated growth rates are non-comparable.

Source: Central Statistical Organisation; cited in GOI (2002), 35.

In the processes of industrialisation and urbanisation, the ideas of political leaders on social inclusion were again reflected in areas, such as land distribution, employment, and enhancement of vocational education. For example, many parts of forestlands were distributed to the landless poor from 1967 during the process of securing lands for industrialisation.[41] Through this land distribution, small

---

[38] See GOTN (1979), 19. According to the document, the outlay was increased to 30 million Indian rupees in 1971–72 from 7.5 million Indian rupees in 1969–70.
[39] De Wit (1997).
[40] Saraswathi (1995), 120.
[41] GOTN (1971), 20–21.

landholders benefitted while urban landowners, especially those who lived in the city of Madras, had to pay increased taxes.[42] Kosalram (1973) observed the revolutionary characteristics of the land reforms led by the DMK Government at that time. He highlighted that the Land Ceiling Act of 1961 was modified in 1971 and amended five times after that, by saying,

> The Government of Tamil Nadu shows the progress made in the assignment of surplus land. It has persuaded the landlords to offer concessions to the times.[43]

S. Chandrasekaran, an official working with J. Chandrakumar, Director of the land reforms department in the Government of Tamil Nadu, also agreed with the perspective that the 1970s was a critical period in terms of land reforms in the state. As he put it:

> The land reforms amendment in 1972 reflected the ideas of political leaders in Tamil Nadu on the utilisation of lands for industrial development. Lots of surplus lands were not only assigned to the poor but also commercialised with the purpose of selling to the private investors in the industry. Also, any public trust having aims to establish educational institutes or hospitals could easily purchase the land through the land reforms amendment.[44]

The inclusionary idea of political leaders was also pursued by offering employment and vocational education to citizens. The leaders in the DMK Government thought that 'a good government by definition cannot ignore the need for plans for mitigating the problem of unemployment', as Karunanidhi mentioned.[45] They considered the employment issue seriously by linking with poverty reduction.[46] The DMK government extended various employment programmes, such as the Apprentice Teacher Scheme and Industrial Training Institutes through the 1970s.[47] The concerns of political leaders on employment are frequently witnessed in various government reports. The State Planning Commission of Tamil Nadu, for example, estimated unemployment shortly and proposed various programmes towards 'full' employment.[48] In fact, the State Planning Commission revealed its concerns about the lack of employment in Tamil Nadu's industry. It estimated that the total unemployment would go up

---

[42] GOTN (1971), 29. Small landholders were exempted from the tax increase.
[43] Kosalram (1973), 13.
[44] Interview at the GOTN in Chennai on 21 November 2012.
[45] Kosalram (1973), 21.
[46] GOTN (1974), 14.
[47] Kosalram (1973), 22–23.
[48] GOTN (1974), 13–14.

to 21.2 million in 1983–84 from 5.2 million in 1973–74 and suggested that the education sector and some of the heavy industries should absorb the labour force.[49]

Such ideas on social inclusion seem to have been considerably encouraged by the demands of society. The strong support of the state in the education sector and political culture that encouraged political participation helped citizens not only support it in accelerating industrialisation but also demand their rights. For example, Srinivasan (2010) showed how the demands of citizens through active political participation contributed to improved performance of the PDS in the state. Through a study on The National Rural Employment Guarantee in a village of Tamil Nadu, Srinivasan found that marginalised groups and the poor in the state had become more influential in making demands to it for their well-being and development.

Coherent Ideas on Inclusion and Ideational Development for FDI Inflows in the AIADMK Government in the 1980s

MGR's leadership in social inclusion

The ideas of industrialisation and social inclusion were consistently pursued by M. G. Ramachandran (MGR) in the AIADMK government, which came to power after the state legislative assembly election in 1977. As one of the charismatic leaders of the state, M. G. R. led the AIADMK government from 1977 to 1988. Even though he was a Malayalee from the state of Kerala, his film fans who became his strong political supporters greatly helped him become the leader of the newly established Dravidian party and later the Chief Minister of Tamil Nadu. One important reason why M. G. R. received strong support from society in the state where the Tamil ethnic identity is significant was because his AIADMK party respected the ideas of Periyar and Annadurai. After it had split from DMK, AIADMK maintained a strong image as an ethnically based Dravidian party by following the ideas of Annadurai on Periyar's social justice and Tamilness. About Annadurai's idea on good governance, Nedunchezhiyan, who served as the Finance Minister of Tamil Nadu at that time, mentioned:

> Anna once remarked, 'What is the test of a good government? Like light to a lamp, like abundant yield to farmland, the prosperity, and peace of the people of the country are the real test of a good government'. Inspired by this ideal of bringing peace and prosperity to the people of Tamil Nadu, this government has endeavored to draw up and implement various schemes for their welfare.[50]

---

[49] Ibid., 14.
[50] GOTN (1980), 41.

Similar to Annadurai and Karunanidhi's leadership in the DMK government, M. G. R.'s leadership paid greater attention to the economic betterment, education, healthcare, and employment of citizens in the marginalised groups of society. For the AIADMK government in the 1980s, the state's independence from the central government in terms of both politics and economy was necessary for achieving the inclusionary aims that the DMK government had asserted in the past. Its assertion of state independence from the centre substantially resulted from the continuous non-cooperation of it in financial and legislative matters. Despite the fact, the AIADMK government gained confidence in dealing with the financial matters by learning from the preceding DMK government. The political leaders of the AIADMK government were able to overcome several financial crises and natural disasters through assistance from foreign capital. For example, by pointing to the catastrophic impact of the drought that occurred at that time, Nedunchezhiyan highlighted the timely and efficient actions of the AIADMK government in repairing the economic damage from the impact. He remarked:

> Government is also confident that such a situation will not arise in the coming months either, as a well worked out drought relief programme ensuring water, food supplies, and employment opportunities will continue to be implemented.[51]

In addition, the AIADMK government implemented massive welfare programmes for school children, villagers, and weaker sections of the society.[52] For example, the Chief Minister's Nutritious Noon-Meal Scheme began to benefit poor children in 1982. Other integrated nutrition and healthcare programmes were added in the mid-1980s. To school children up to Standard VIII, free uniforms and textbooks were given. For their education, the political leaders of the state strongly felt that the 'education system required a reorientation to fulfil its primary purpose of creating manpower, equipped to be absorbed in the labour market; education should provide the necessary skills for boys and girls so that they could find suitable vocations or self-employment'.[53] Also, the leaders were concerned with bonded labour and slum dwellers, which they highlighted in the 'Twenty-Point Programme' that aimed at getting the first rank regarding all-India performance from 1982 to 1985. State agencies, such as the Tamil Nadu Backward Classes Economic Development Corporation were also founded in the 1980s to enhance the welfare of backward classes in the state. Another observation by Goyal (2006) supports the superior performance of Tamil Nadu in human development.

---

[51] GOTN (1981), 3.
[52] GOTN (1986).
[53] GOTN (1984), 40.

Goyal showed the progress of the state not only in increasing the rate of schooling in rural areas but also in enhancing healthcare services compared to the state of Karnataka. Goyal argued that such improvement stems from the pro-poor nature of Tamil Nadu politics with political participation from the lower classes and castes.

Furthermore, M. G. R.'s leadership offered various rehabilitation packages not only to citizens displaced by natural disasters, such as frequent floods and drought but also to refugees from Sri Lanka. For recovery from damage caused by floods in 1985 and 1986, the AIADMK government provided flood relief to the displaced people with partial assistance from the central government.[54] Despite the frequent occurrences of such natural calamities, the state has spent substantial amounts for immediate recovery from disasters.[55] In addition, it established various refugee camps for the increasing refugee population that migrated to Tamil Nadu for safety.[56] M. G. R., in particular, among the political leaders of the state had a close relationship with the Sri Lankan Tamil militants (e.g., Liberation Tigers of Tamil Eelam [LTTE]), who were deeply linked to the refugees.[57] Such inclusionary approaches by the state effectively mobilised the minority groups of society, although its continuous support of Tamil militants aggravated political relations with the Congress government at the union level after LTTE's assassination of Rajiv Gandhi in 1991.

To efficiently pursue various inclusionary welfare programmes and industrialisation schemes, the need for administration reforms was emphasised during the AIADMK government. The administrative reforms in the AIADMK government in the 1980s were along the same lines as the DMK government in the 1970s in asserting enhanced state independence within India's federal structure. The political leaders of the AIADMK government thought 'a strong centre and prosperous states is a prerequisite for efficient administration', and 'the federal principle' is a 'method of dividing powers so that the central and regional governments ... should be independent of the other'.[58] The strategies of the AIADMK government in pursuing the reforms differed from those of DMK. It attempted to centralise power, whereas DMK encouraged self-government at the village level. For example, the reforms of DMK government that again came to power in 1989 highlighted the modernisation of *taluk* level [sub-district level,

---

[54] GOTN (1986).

[55] Interview with K. Deenabandu, Principal Secretary of the Department of Rehabilitation in the Government of Tamil Nadu, in Chennai on 21 November 2012.

[56] GOTN (1986), 4.

[57] For the close relationship between the AIADMK government in the 1980s and the Sri Lankan groups of Tamil militants, see Subramanian (1999).

[58] Goyal (2006), 6.

understood as *Tehsil* in other parts of India] administration in order to encourage the participation of citizens at the local village level.[59]

Need for foreign technology in Tamil Nadu's industry

The political leaders in Tamil Nadu in the 1980s encouraged the participation of the private sector for industrialisation. In contrast to Annadurai's socialist orientation in Tamil Nadu's economy, M. G. R. showed a stronger belief in the positive role of the private sector in the industry. Ponnaiyan, who was M. G. R.'s lawyer as well as an AIADMK leader at that time, described his trip to Japan with M. G. R. in an interview.[60] Recollecting the seventeen-day journey to Japan in 1982, he said:

> He (M. G. R.) and some other political leaders including me visited Japan to see its economic development and advanced technology in the industry. We got impressed so much when we saw them.

After the Japan visit, M. G. R.'s beliefs about the roles of the private sector, its close relations with the state, and the greater importance of technology became much stronger. Their inspirations were, in practice, embodied to devise industrial strategies in the state so as to make the state and industry more cooperative.[61] Learning from the Japanese experiences substantially influenced the political leaders of the state in promoting technological institutes and foreign technology.[62]

The need for foreign technology helped the leaders encourage the participation of foreign capital in Tamil Nadu's industry. For example, a high-technology project to promote small-scale industries was assisted by Japanese technology.[63] The project was pursued in various sectors, such as drugs and pharmaceuticals, medical electronic equipment, garments, food processing, and automobile components. Karunanidhi, who came to power again as the Chief Minister of Tamil Nadu in

---

[59] GOTN (1989).

[60] Interview on 31 January 2012, *op. cit.*

[61] Sinha (2005) observed that the strong tie between the state and the private sector was a significant factor that contributed to the successful economic reforms in public services in the case of Gujarat in India. In her case study on the reform process in the port, infrastructure policies, and the education sector, she argued that the commitment and abilities of Chief Ministers and senior bureaucrats and close state–private capital relations played powerful roles in the successful reforms in Gujarat. See also Chand (2010), Chapter 4.

[62] See also Abegglen and Etori (1981); Sawhney (1985).

[63] GOTN (1989).

1989, clearly pointed out the need for foreign capital in the industries of the state for two reasons. As he put it in the Budget Speech 1989–90:

> Although Tamil Nadu is advanced in the development of small scale industries, hundreds of small-scale units in our state are sick on account of financial and technological problems.[64]

To learn advanced technology and secure financial resources, the state gradually promoted foreign capital. Such needs for foreign capital were reflected in the institutional change favouring FDI inflows in the post-reform period after 1991.

In the promotion of foreign capital, the role of Non-Resident Indians (NRIs) was also important in facilitating the pro-FDI orientation of the political leaders in the state. The leaders were strongly convinced that their aim of creating jobs could be helped by actively promoting the participation of NRIs in Tamil Nadu's industry. The AIADMK government under M. G. R.'s leadership took 'a number of steps to attract investment by NRIs by encouraging them to set up industries in Tamil Nadu; this work was attended to by the international cell of SIPCOT; full use was also made of the Indian investment centres available abroad'.[65] The state further extended credit facilities to provide investors with the necessary infrastructure and utilised the services of consultants based abroad to ease their investment in Tamil Nadu's industry.[66]

Continuous financial assistance from international organisations like the World Bank also influenced the political leaders of the state to support foreign capital. The state of Tamil Nadu in the 1980s continued to get substantial financial assistance from the World Bank to pursue urbanisation projects. Through the assistance, several cities in the state including Madras, Salem, Tuticorin, Tirunelveli, Erode, Coimbatore, Tiruchy, Madurai, Tiruppur, and Vellore were benefitted.[67] Interestingly, the leaders of the state distributed the financial assistance equally to several cities in various districts rather than focusing on only a few cities. The consequences of this effort can be currently observed in several parts of Tamil Nadu. Not only Chennai, which is the capital of the state, but also several other cities in different districts have specialised industries. For example, the manufacturing sector is strong in Coimbatore, the textile sector is strong in Erode, and the IT sector is strong in Chennai.

---

[64] GOTN (1989), 19–20.
[65] GOTN (1984), 12.
[66] GOTN (1989), 26.
[67] Ibid., same page.

Consistent Ideas, Muted Interests, and Institutional Development Favouring FDI Inflows after 1991

Incremental institutional change favouring FDI inflows

Ideas favouring industrialisation and social inclusion have been continuously pursued by both AIADMK and DMK governments that have come to power alternately in Tamil Nadu since the economic reform of the central government in 1991. The ideas are clearly reflected in various schemes to promote industrial growth in the joint and private sectors, benefits to small and medium industries (SMIs), expansion of engineering colleges, and the number of polytechnic teachers, foreign capital for urbanisation, land reforms, and welfare of marginalised groups in society.[68] In the process of accelerating industrialisation, ideas favouring FDI inflows were greatly stimulated by the economic reform implemented at the central government in 1991. T. K. S. Elangovan, who served as DMK's spokesperson, also said the impact of the economic reform on states in India:

> The economic reform in 1991 was a watershed for promoting foreign investment. Now that the central government already set up the policy, the rest of things (performances) are state government responsibilities.[69]

A question is how the state of Tamil Nadu has performed in garnering a high level of FDI inflows. First, the political leaders of the state aggressively pursued land reforms after the central government's economic reform to develop industry through foreign investment and enhance distribution of its reform benefits to the poor. The Tamil Nadu Land Reforms (Amendment) Bill was enacted in 1991 and aimed to retrieve *benami* [illegal] lands and distribute them to the landless poor.[70] The political leaders of the state thought that the speedy execution of land reforms was critical for securing more lands for industrialisation and strengthening its economy. S. Muthumani, who served as a member of the Rajya Sabha from AIADMK from 1992 to 1998, mentioned:

> *Purachi thalaivi* (revolutionary leader, indicating Jayalalithaa) has taken this commendable step to retrieve *benami* lands from illegal holdings and to distribute them to the landless poor in the true spirit of land to the tiller.[71]

---

[68] GOTN (1991).
[69] Interview in Chennai on 24 January 2012, *op. cit.*
[70] GOI (1994).
[71] GOI (1994), 375.

Such forceful land reforms benefitted citizens not only in cities but also in rural areas. Lindberg et al. (2014) also showed the positive effects of such land reforms in the rural area of Tamil Nadu.[72] Through a case study of six villages in the Kaveri delta in Tiruchirappalli district of the state, Lindberg et al. highlighted that land reforms and industrialisation have contributed to the increase in total income and more equal distribution of assets and income in the villages.

Land reforms helped the state of Tamil Nadu promote FDI inflows. In the process of land reforms, the Tamil Nadu Urban Land Bill was amended in 1992 to increase the tax on landowners in urban areas. The Acquisition of Lands for Industrial Purposes Act was also enacted in 1997 in the context of the revision of the Industrial Act in 1997 that reflected ideas on the utilisation of lands for industrial growth. Such Acts considerably helped the state enhance the roles of SIPCOT to acquire lands for industrial purposes especially in urban areas. Jatindranath Swain, Principal Secretary of the land administration department in the Government of Tamil Nadu, also agreed with the perspective.[73] Supported by such institutional arrangements, SIPCOT was able to actively allocate lands to foreign investors who entered the market in the state.

SIPCOT has closely cooperated with TIDCO, which is another state agency that attracts joint ventures, to establish various industrial complexes and SEZs in several districts of the state. M. Velmurgan, an Executive Vice-Chairman of the Industrial Guidance and Export Promotion Bureau (GUIDANCE) in TIDCO who has participated in promoting FDI inflows for the past twenty-two years, pointed to the strong support from the state government and the coherent ideas of political leaders from different ruling parties as the most important factor that has boosted FDI inflows.[74] He said:

> The government support is very important to promote FDI inflows. Many important factors such as skilled labour, wage cost, infrastructure, labour and management relations, land availability for good location, and others need government support. The commitment of the government to creating relevant policies and incentives is necessary. In the system of democracy, the government (ruling party) keeps changing. An election keeps coming and after five years the government changes. But, industrial development plan needs 40 or 50 years, it does not respect this change of governments. The successful government should keep the promises of the previous government in pursuing such investment projects continuously. This is business, not politics (for economic growth). ... Both the DMK and the AIADMK governments consider these investment projects as

---

[72] Informal discussions with Lindberg in New Delhi on 14 December 2011.
[73] Interview at GOTN in Chennai on 21 November 2012.
[74] Interview at TIDCO on 2 February 2012.

significant in for industry, so successive government (regardless of party identity) has honoured such industrial promises of previous government … In addition, both governments have tried not to create any social displacement in the process (of FDI inflows) through financial and infrastructural compensation (for citizens).

He also mentioned that a project facility committee within TIDCO had held regular weekly meetings to force the implementation of policies regarding FDI inflows, and a three-tier monitoring system within TIDCO has also efficiently operated to attract FDI projects.

However, the process of land acquisition has sometimes been followed by protests from anti-capital groups in the society. Interestingly, such protests organised in Tamil Nadu were mainly pursued by left-wing political parties, such as CPI(M) rather than social organisations of citizens.[75] The left-wing political parties have not been successful in mobilising people either in the urban or the rural areas of the state because the various inclusionary schemes had effectively prevented them from being mobilised by the communist parties. As what CPI(M) did in the state of West Bengal as a ruling party,[76] the Dravidian parties rather than left-wing parties have successfully distributed the benefits of economic growth to its citizens.

In short, left-wing political parties have failed to convince the citizens of Tamil Nadu about the need for equal distribution or social justice because they have been strongly asserted by the Dravidian parties in the state. Consequently, conflicts between the citizens and the state have been quite muted in Tamil Nadu. In an interview, A. Soundararajan, a member of the legislative assembly in Chennai from CPI(M) who supported its trade union (CITU) activities for several decades, said:

> See, even in trade union movements, we cannot deploy it alone (because of our weak strength especially in the state). We have to ally with major parties like DMK or AIADMK. … Even if we are in an alliance with the major parties, we do not agree with the ruling party on many issues such as industry and labour.[77]

His remarks would indicate the similarity of ideas between DMK and AIADMK on industrial and labour issues even if the parties were to forge an alliance with the communist parties during election periods.

Not only the political leaders of AIADMK but also the leaders of DMK considered the automobile industry as an important manufacturing sector in

---

[75] *The Hindu*, 'Centre Urges to Increase EPF Interest,' 21 August 2004, 'Call to Stop Outsourcing Jobs,' 5 December 2007, accessed 2 March 2013.

[76] See Kohli (2012).

[77] Interview at Soundararajan's CPI(M) office in Chennai on 12 January 2012.

which they could promote FDI inflows for economic growth. In an interview, T. K. S. Elangovan said:

> Most of FDI projects were initially invited by our DMK government in the early- and the mid-1990s. Many foreign investors could enter especially in the automobile industry in Tamil Nadu at that time ... Tamil Nadu has good connectivity, airport, and ports for the foreign investors. For promoting FDI inflows, labour availability must be there; market must be there; infrastructure like power should be there; lands must be available; and power (for pursuing such investment projects) must be devolved (on the state government).[78]

In fact, Hyundai Motor, a South Korean automobile company, entered the market in the state in 1998 by establishing Hyundai Motor India when DMK party was in power, while Ford, an automobile firm from the United States, joined the industry in 1996 when AIADMK was ruling.[79] The ideas of political leaders played a major role in supporting the automobile industry. They considered the exit of labour force from the primary sector to the secondary and tertiary sectors necessary because the policy-makers observed the potential of such sectors in alleviating poverty since the largest number of citizens below the poverty line lived in rural areas.[80]

The increasing dependence on loans from international organisations and commercial banks due to the financial crisis at the union level was also influential in making the political leaders of the state promote FDI inflows. The lack of financial assistance from the centre to the state was a big challenge for decades, the state's burden in securing financial resources finally got heavier after the economic reform of the central government in 1991.[81] According to the *Budget 1993–94 of Tamil Nadu*:

> The centre is able to access structural adjustment loans from the World Bank and special funds from the International Monetary Fund, whereas the states have no such facility. No significant measures relating to the improvement of the states' finances have been implemented. ... The centre is now also suggesting that in the liberalised situation it is the states which should actively promote new investment.

---

[78] Interview in Chennai on 24 January 2012, *op. cit.*

[79] See also Kennedy (2004). DMK opposed AIADMK's support for Ford's FDI project when AIADMK was ruling. However, DMK pursued the Memorandum of Understanding with Hyundai Motor India when it came to power. This episode again supports the view that both DMK and AIADMK parties have consistently supported FDI projects with a positive attitude towards foreign capital when they were ruling.

[80] GOTN (1997).

[81] See Rudolph and Rudolph (2001).

... In the matter of plan revenue grants, Tamil Nadu got a raw deal. Overall, the state (of Tamil Nadu) has been left in an extremely vulnerable position. The Tenth Finance Commission would have to take note of the resulting serious imbalances in Tamil Nadu's finances and recommend appropriate reliefs.[82]

In such financial difficulties, FDI inflows were useful capital that could contribute to the creation of jobs and the growth of exports. The AIADMK government in 1993 when Jayalalitha was the Chief Minister of Tamil Nadu explicitly welcomed FDI inflows for the reasons. The Finance Minister of the state at that time mentioned:

> As part of the outward leaning strategy, we shall welcome FDI. It is for this reason we have chosen to promote actively the Indo–Singapore Trade Corridor at Madras. A detailed feasibility report has been prepared. An expert team visited Singapore recently. A high-level team headed by Ministers from Singapore has also visited Madras and held a detailed dialogue with the Chief Minister. The World Bank has also promised support. It will be our endeavour to establish the new corridor in the shortest possible time. ... We have established GUIDANCE as an agency to escort new investment in the state. A core group of secretaries to a government headed by the Chief Secretary will be constituted to further simplify procedures and set out the framework for one-step clearances.[83]

Such pro-FDI orientation has incrementally led the state leaders to restructure and reproduce institutions favouring FDI inflows. The state agencies of Tamil Nadu that were originally designed to promote industrialisation and urbanisation began to attract FDI inflows. Significantly, the state agencies could evolve through the 1970s to post-reform period gradually. In the incremental change, the inclusionary state–society relations played critical roles. The inclusionary pattern of the state–society relations enabled institutions to be reproduced in a way of enhancing the ideational pursuit of key political leaders on industrial development, urbanisation, and pro-FDI inflows in Tamil Nadu.

State's dual strategies for muting conflicting interests in society

The state also effectively intervened to mute conflicting interests, even if there were some contrasting interests in society in the process of FDI inflows, especially in the land acquisition process. First, it has deployed dual strategies of power and persuasion. The state has not only used its power to control the police force and

---

[82] GOTN (1993), 4–7.
[83] GOTN (1993), 22–24.

the media during the process of land acquisition, but it has also used persuasion to make protest groups support the state-led large-scale investment projects by promising them both financial compensation and inclusionary schemes, such as job offers and technical training. In other words, the strategies and inclusionary schemes of the state have had a synergistic effect in muting conflicting interests in society. The strategies are also observed in labour disputes in foreign companies as discussed in the next chapter.

The synergy between the dual strategies and inclusionary policies has frequently been observed in the process of FDI inflows. Before embarking on the land acquisition process for a project, the political leaders of Tamil Nadu especially emphasised employment opportunities to its citizens. The state leaders paid great attention to employment opportunities in manufacturing sectors, such as the automobile industry, which are both labour-intensive and capital-intensive. For example, one of the largest FDI projects in Tamil Nadu embarked on by Hyundai Motor India was expected to create a substantial number of jobs when the DMK government invited it. Also, both the DMK and AIADMK governments have coherently sought the synergy. Key state leaders in the two Dravidian regional parties have considered employment and exports as the most significant conditions when inviting foreign investors for large-scale investment projects.

Importantly, the inclusionary pattern is also observed in the minor industries of the state. Tamil Nadu has continuously been concerned not only with SMIs but also with primary industries, such as the agricultural sector and fisheries, even though it has greatly encouraged the participation of big businesses and foreign investors in the process of industrialisation. Such tendency demonstrates the continuous concerns of the state about the citizens of minor industries. To encourage the participation of SMIs in industry, it urged the central government and the Reserve Bank of India to lower interest rates further and ensured prompt payments by state public sector undertakings to the SMIs.[84] In addition, the state supported the activities of state agencies, such as the Small Industries Production Promotion Organisation for assisting the industries and secured financial assistance from the World Bank to establish new venture capital funds.[85] To promote agricultural growth through improved electricity supply, the state gave the Tamil Nadu Electricity Board a substantial cash subsidy and loans with a partial interest waiver.[86] The state, in addition, launched various programs to improve fish seed production for the growth of fisheries.[87]

---

[84] Ibid., 24.
[85] GOTN (1993), 25.
[86] Ibid., 27.
[87] Ibid., 20.

Such efforts by the state in implementing inclusionary ideas and schemes have come to fruition in the area of human development. The recent study on human development in India by the Institute of Applied Manpower Research under the Planning Commission finds that Tamil Nadu has substantially improved its human development status 'through appropriate policies that address the needs of the marginalised communities', even though the societal structure of Tamil Nadu in terms of caste composition is similar to that in Bihar and Uttar Pradesh which show a lower performance in improving the human development.[88] Table 3.3 shows select human development indices in poverty and health for Tamil Nadu and India. It presents that not only the poverty ratio in Tamil Nadu but also indices in the health sector, such as child mortality rate and maternal mortality rate are much lower than those for India. The good performance was also beneficial to marginalised groups in society like the lower caste citizens, as can be seen in the table. Santosh Mehrotra, the team leader of the research group of human development, highlighted, 'Tamil Nadu has shown the best performance especially in the area of public health and education for the last ten years'.[89] The improvement in human development provides clear evidence of a consistent ideational pursuit of social inclusion by state leaders in different ruling parties.

Table 3.3: Select Human Development Indices in Poverty and Health, Tamil Nadu and India

	Incidence of Poverty[a] (Per cent)	*Incidence of Poverty by Social Group, 2004–05[b] (Per cent)*		*Under-Five Mortality Rate, 2005–06[c] (Per cent)*		*Percentage of Underweight Children (0–5 Years), 2005–06[d] (Per cent)*		*Maternal Mortality Rate, 2010[e]*
		Rural SC	*Rural ST*	*All*	*SCs*	*All*	*SCs*	
Tamil Nadu	22.9	31.2	32.1	35.5	48.3	29.8	40.2	97
India	28.3	36.8	47.3	74.3	88.1	42.5	47.9	212

Note: Maternal Mortality Rate is the number of maternal deaths in the age group 15–49 years per one lakh live births. SC means Scheduled Caste and ST stands for Scheduled Tribe.

Sources: (a, b, c, d) Gandhi (2012), 82–84; (e) Sample Registration System (www.censusindia.gov.in), accessed on 27 January 2014.

---

[88] GOTN (2012), 4, accessed 18 September 2012, www.pratirodh.com/pdf/human_development_report2011.pdf.

[89] Seminar on India Human Development Report 2011 in New Delhi on 17 September 2012.

Conclusion

This chapter discussed how the state of Tamil Nadu promoted FDI inflows. Given that the ideas of key policy-makers favouring FDI inflows and social inclusion worked to protect the rights of citizens in the process of FDI inflows, the discussion traced the origins of the ideas and explained how the inclusionary nature of state–society relations contributed to the higher level of FDI inflows in the state. By citing historical evidence through various documents that support the ideas of social inclusion including an emphasis on social justice, economic and social development, equality, and welfare through education and employment, I argued that such inclusionary ideas helped citizens support the state's large-scale investment projects including FDI inflows. It was found that state leaders incorporated their inclusionary ideas in social welfare schemes in the process of industrialisation. Land reforms particularly have not only benefited the landless poor but also considerably helped state agencies secure lands for industrial purposes in the process. This may not happen to other provincial states in India like Odisha where the landlord class is powerful. As a critical factor in support of the ideas, the ideological base of the Dravidian ruling parties, which favours the lower castes and classes, was highlighted. It is worth underlining the central argument of this chapter that the bipartisan concern of social inclusion effectively prevented citizens from being mobilised by opposition parties like communist parties. The citizens did not need to support protests against the state's large-scale investment projects including FDI inflows, as they have been the primary beneficiaries of industrialisation. This point will be further explained in the next chapter.

The ideational evolution favouring FDI inflows in the case of Tamil Nadu needs to be understood in parallel with an understanding of the process of industrialisation and the inclusionary pattern of state–society relations. Influenced by the idea of social inclusion suggested by Periyar in the mid-1910s during the self-respect movement, the state leaders implemented various inclusionary schemes. They were actively implemented from 1967 when Dravidian regional parties came to power and formed stable bipartisan politics on the basis of broader political support from society that transcended class and caste cleavages. It was also found that coherent ideas about industrialisation, as a means of boosting Tamil Nadu's economy and reducing poverty, developed among the key policy-makers after 1967. The combative centre–state relationship forced the political leaders of Tamil Nadu to pursue their ideas because the lack of financial assistance from the central government was a critical challenge. The argument stressed in this chapter was that a 'tipping point' model of FDI inflows in Tamil Nadu originated in the ideational development of key state leaders who considered industrialisation and social inclusion as the most significant tasks for the state to achieve. It stressed that the economic reform of the central government towards liberalisation in 1991 was a threshold and led Tamil Nadu to promote FDI inflows more aggressively than before.

4

Making FDI Work in Tamil Nadu

The village in India ... has in recent decades seen profound changes. The twin shackles that once decided matters for India's villagers, caste and agriculture, no longer exercise their vigorous hold. While a break in caste rigidities has fostered greater fluidity in occupational choices, agricultural stagnation has ensured the constant march, in increasing numbers, of employable people in the villages towards urban areas.[1]

This chapter presents how the state and society of Tamil Nadu encourage FDI projects at the local village level. Data collected from two locations in the field where Hyundai Motor India (HMI hereafter) and Michelin India (MI hereafter) embarked on FDI projects strongly support the argument underlined in the previous chapter – the inclusionary nature of state–society relations has helped Tamil Nadu make FDI inflows work. The state of Tamil Nadu has provided inclusionary schemes like substantial compensation to citizens who lose their livelihood in the process of FDI inflows. As discussed in detail in the previous chapter, the ideas of social inclusion have been pursued for the broader strata of citizens through many different forms including land reforms and various rehabilitation packages. Land reforms, in particular, have been considerably helpful for the state agencies to acquire lands for an industrial purpose.

On the basis of the case study of two FDI projects carried out in the manufacturing sector in two different districts of Tamil Nadu, this chapter aims to understand the close relationship between the state, society, and foreign capital that are involved in the process of FDI inflows in Tamil Nadu. The two cases examined are HMI in the district of Kanchipuram and MI in the district of Thiruvallur (Map 4.1).

Data were collected during a four-month stay in Chennai and Delhi from December 2011 to March 2012 and a short revisit to the cities in August 2013. Intensive interviews were conducted with different groups of people including political leaders, bureaucrats, social activists, villagers, Indian domestic

---

[1] Gupta (2005), 751.

industrialists, and foreign investors through several visits to the two manufacturing factories of HMI and the construction site of MI. On the basis of fieldwork findings, I suggest that the process of FDI inflows in the state of Tamil Nadu has been tacitly but aggressively pursued by a tripartite alliance between the state, bureaucrats, and foreign capital. Foreign capital has been assisted by the state not only when it enters but also after it enters the market in Tamil Nadu. For example, the state has helped the foreign investors continue investment activities through various incentives and labour control although labour disputes have sometimes occurred in the foreign firms.

A suggestion from the previous chapter stresses that the industrial setting of Tamil Nadu challenges the 'local strongmen' point of view that has been highlighted by social scientists working on the agrarian societal structure of Tamil Nadu.[2] The local strongmen perspective underlines the role of a tripartite alliance between the state, agricultural elites, and bureaucrats in restructuring economic institutions in Tamil Nadu. Interestingly, however, findings from HMI and MI imply that foreign investors are powerful as much as the local agricultural elites, namely, the local strongmen, in the tripartite alliance formation. A discussion here will show how the industrial environment challenges the conventional understanding of the political economy of Tamil Nadu.

Also, it will point out that foreign firms tend to moderate social cleavages, such as caste and religion among Indian domestic workers employed by the companies. In the process of FDI inflows to the state of Tamil Nadu, the role of foreign investors has been critical not only in mediating social conflicts between different caste and religious groups but also in transforming its agrarian society into an industrial one. They have had significant roles in creating jobs in industry and contributing to economic growth through the export of their products from Tamil Nadu. For achieving the two fundamental aims, employment and economic growth, in short, the key state leaders and bureaucrats in Tamil Nadu encouraged the participation of foreign investors in its industry.

This chapter consists of two parts. In the first part, the relationships between foreign capital, domestic labour, and the state are examined through the case of HMI. For this, interviews were carried out with the South Korean management of HMI, Indian domestic workers on the shop floor of HMI, leaders and members of several trade unions, social activists, political leaders, and bureaucrats in the state of Tamil Nadu. The discussion in this section will show how the consistent ideas of chief ministers from different political parties in the state could successfully pursue the FDI projects particularly in the automobile industry by inviting foreign investors including Hyundai Motor Company (HMC). It implies that such

---

[2] See Bouton (1985); Harriss-White (2003); Harriss (2006; 2010).

consistent ideas have been a fundamental source of making progress in garnering FDI inflows in the process of industrialisation in the state. The state's strong support of foreign capital has also influenced the nature of the relationship between the foreign management and domestic labour. The discussion in this part includes conflicts between the two sides and the strategies of the state in mediating the struggles. It will demonstrate how the state could effectively intervene a strained relationship between the foreign investors and domestic workers.

Map 4.1: Fieldwork Sites in Tamil Nadu

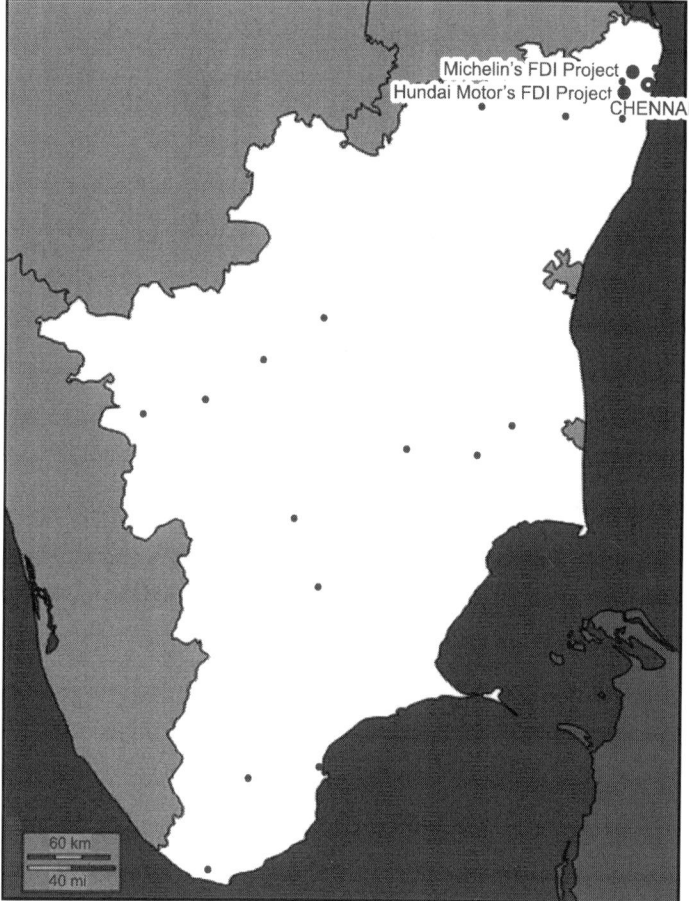

Source: Based on D-maps, accessed 5 September 2017, www.d-maps.com.

In the second part, the relationships between the state, bureaucrats, and foreign capital in Tamil Nadu are discussed. By exploring an FDI project embarked by MI in the village of Thervoy Kandigai and anti-Michelin protests deployed by villagers and activists, the discussion also supports the strong ability of the state in dealing with the strained relationship between foreign capital and its opposition in the society. It will present how the Government of Tamil Nadu forced foreign capital to bargain with the anti-FDI groups and how citizens responded to FDI inflows. For collecting data, interviews were conducted with the French management of MI, villagers, activists, and political elites in Tamil Nadu.

Political Economy of FDI by HMI

Close state–foreign capital relationship in HMI

The Government of Tamil Nadu's strong support of foreign capital is an extension of ideas embraced by key state elites about promoting the private sector. The nature of state–foreign capital nexus in Tamil Nadu can be described as an 'effective' relationship. In a cross-state study about state–business relations, Cali and Sen (2011) defined that effective state–business relations are a set of highly institutionalised, responsive, and public interactions between the state and the business sector.[3] Cali and Sen presented a strong causal relationship between the state–business linkage and economic growth from 1985 to 2006 by comparing states in India. They found that Tamil Nadu spent over an average of 25 per cent of its budget on economic services for commitment to the private sector. The state–business relationship index of Tamil Nadu and Karnataka was higher than that of many other states, which contributed to wealth of the states.

In a similar context, Sen (2009) also underlined the significant increase in employment in the manufacturing sector in Tamil Nadu. The manufacturing sector-oriented production structure that Tamil Nadu has developed in the process of industrialisation also promoted the rapid growth of FDI inflows. He argued that Tamil Nadu and Andhra Pradesh created conducive environments for developing the manufacturing sector like the automobile industry and utilising it to generate employment. However, it seemed difficult for him to indicate exact sources of the regional disparities of states in India in doing so. The discussion in this section and subsequent part of the chapter demonstrates how the ideas of key policy-makers in Tamil Nadu about employment generation have evolved in the process FDI inflows by illustrating two FDI projects on the ground. The contribution of this chapter would be in explaining the sources of regional disparities in presenting the dissimilar state–capital relations.

Hyundai is one of the South Korean *chaebŏl* [conglomerate] enterprises that were strongly patronised by the South Korean state during its industrialisation.

---

[3] Cali and Sen (2011), 1542.

Hyundai, like the other chaebŏl companies, was able to expand its business with 'a high degree of vertical and horizontal integration within a diversified business structure that ranges across a variety of industrial boundaries'.[4] In the process of globalisation of production, HMC established HMI as one of the global branches in 1998. HMI is a Wholly Owned Subsidiary having its sales office in New Delhi and two production factories at Sriperumbudur in Kanchipuram district in Tamil Nadu – Chennai is better known rather than Sriperumbudur as the location city of HMI since both cities are contiguous (Map 4.1[A]). HMI equipped two plants that were applying the Complete Knock Down (CKD) system of production. The CKD is a production system that exports components and assembles them in a destination with a low labour cost in host economies for obtaining benefits from tariff incentives.[5] HMI's plants were comprehensive automobile factories independently embarking on the Research and Development (R&D), test, production, and sales. After completing the second factory in 2008, both factories in Tamil Nadu had a production capacity of 600 thousand cars per year.[6]

Illustration 4.1: HMI in Chennai (27–28 December 2011)

[A] Cars Produced for Export   [B] Advertisement of Hyundai Motor at Chennai International Airport

Key policy-makers in Tamil Nadu considered potential employment in the automobile components industries significant when the Dravida Munnetra Kazhagam (DMK) government invited HMC for an investment in the mid-1990s.

---

[4] Kwon and O'Donnell (2001), 4.

[5] The idea of CKD production in the emerging markets aims to secure financial resource for new investment and to reduce marketing costs for the new markets.

[6] These two factories are the production bases in producing compact cars, such as i10 and i20 and exporting them to 120 countries in the world (Illustration 4.1 [A]). In addition, it has an R&D centre in Hyderabad in Andhra Pradesh. This technical research institute has a role in developing new products that are suitable in India and actively supporting the areas of design and analysis within the company.

Karunanidhi from DMK, who served as the Chief Minister of Tamil Nadu from 1996 to 2001 and again from 2006 to 2011 after the economic reforms of 1991, opined:

> The Hyundai car factory, with a production capacity of 120 thousand cars per annum, will commence production in October 1998. 2,800 persons will get direct employment in this factory and 9,750 persons in the ancillary industries.[7]

Also, it is important to note that the idea of creating employment through FDI inflows has been coherently pursued by both the DMK and All India Anna Dravida Munnetra Kazhagam (AIADMK) governments, as discussed in detail in the preceding chapter of this book. Such coherent ideas of key political leaders made Chennai as the 'hometown of Hyundai' (see Illustration 4.1[B]). In an interview, C. Ponnaiyan, who served as the Finance Minister of Tamil Nadu in the AIADMK government, mentioned the significance of foreign investments to key industries in the state:

> The primary reasons why we (AIADMK government) have encouraged the automobile industry (regarding FDI inflows) are employment and export. When a foreign car company enters our market, hundreds of ancillary companies need to be created. The hundreds of car component companies create plentiful jobs. Furthermore, we encourage them to export their product abroad. This export growth results in our economic growth.[8]

HMI produced 615 thousand cars in 2011 and exported 40 per cent of total production to other countries in the world. Maruti Suzuki occupies 43.3 per cent of domestic market share while HMI accounts for 19.2 per cent having 320 dealers in the year 2011 basis.[9] However, HMI exports more cars than Maruti Suzuki does by indicating 49.3 per cent of all export in the automobile sector. HMI's target in the India's automobile market is to maintain the second market share by producing the cars of good quality where fourteen strong global brands, such as Volkswagen, Ford, and General Motors are competing. For providing quality at reasonable prices, many subcontractors of HMI have also entered the market to provide automobile parts to HMI. Han-Woo Park, the former CEO of HMI, remarked on the increased competition saying, 'the automobile market in India has become a battleground that used to be a playground'.[10]

---

[7] GOTN (1998), 17.

[8] Interview at his residence in Chennai on 31 January 2012.

[9] HMI internal data, accessed 16 December 2011.

[10] Interview at HMI in New Delhi on 21 December 2011.

The reasons why HMC decided to enter the market in Tamil Nadu were closely related to cooperation from the Government of Tamil Nadu. Moon Sug Choi who served as the general manager of HMI in New Delhi explained:

> The failed experiences, when we could not sell 80 thousand cars in Canada in the early 1990s, led us to seek for new markets. Turkey, China, and India were discussed as the new markets at that time. Turkey offered an advantage in terms of a low rate of import duty for the CKD while India levied a high rate of import duty for the CKD. So we decided to establish a manufacturing factory in Turkey and founded a corporate body there in 1995 in order to secure a production base in the European market. Meanwhile India was discussed as a competitive market in the long-term perspective compared to China despite the high rate of CKD. And then we explored which state would be the best location within India. The state leaders and bureaucrats in Tamil Nadu were very cooperative towards the investment project. We thus decided to open a branch office at Irrungattukottai in Sriperumbudur in Tamil Nadu in May 1996.[11]

HMI appreciated the state's cooperation in dealing with several administrative problems as well as market requirements, such as incentives, labour costs, the supply of components, trade union, transportation costs, export, domestic market, and investment costs while deciding its location. For HMI, Tamil Nadu was the best option for investing quickly. As observed in many other states in India, foreign investors have usually encountered opposition in the process of acquiring lands and spent substantial time in negotiating with the protest groups. T. M. Kumar, a lawyer who has been working for HMI for a past couple of decades, underlined the effective governance of the state. He said:

> There was no land issue with HMI. There were some villagers when the government acquired lands for HMI, but the number (of villagers) was quite marginal. Even if there are some problems (in the process of land acquisition), yes, bureaucrats in Tamil Nadu are efficient at making progress.[12]

In an interview, Ponnaiyan also pointed out the aggressive and efficient role of the State Industries Promotion Corporation of Tamil Nadu (SIPCOT), a state agency that acquires lands for large-scale investment projects. He put it, 'I think our state does not need to worry about the land acquisition for next fifteen years as we have already acquired enough lands for building various industrial complexes that foreign investors can enter'.[13]

---

[11] Interview in New Delhi on 16 December 2011.
[12] Interview in New Delhi on 22 July 2013.
[13] Interview on 31 January 2012, *op.cit.*

The ideas of political leaders about industrialisation and education have helped foreign investors choose the market in Tamil Nadu as an investment destination. The trained workers and well-equipped infrastructure have helped them decide their investment location. Byeungwan Ryu who served as an executive director of HMI in the Chennai office also stressed the competitiveness of Tamil Nadu.[14] According to Ryu, first, geographical proximity with ports is beneficial to export. After Gujarat, Tamil Nadu has the second longest coastline, which is 1,076km, with three major ports and seventeen non-major ports. Second, the low labour cost made it competitive. Ryu indicated that the labour cost of Noida industrial complex in the state of Uttar Pradesh was much higher than that of states located in South India in the mid-1990s when HMI considered India as an investment destination. Furthermore, Ryu also commented that the nature of labour in Tamil Nadu seemed milder and more diligent compared with that in North India. Third, Tamil Nadu was supportive in providing attractive incentives than other states, such as in the areas of power supply, water supply, and railway connection. Fourth, the state retained many technical institutes that could supply skilled work force to industry. Byung-Suk Chang, trade commissioner of the Korea Business Centre in Chennai, put it:

> Chennai is quite good in terms of location. It offers the lowest logistic costs and has a manpower assistance system which is easily supported by hundreds of technical institutions which are based in this city.[15]

Ponnaiyan, former Finance Minister of Tamil Nadu, also mentioned the strong ability of the state in supplying skilled work force:

> Tamil Nadu has the largest number of engineering colleges in India. There are 520 engineering colleges having five-year programmes and 380 polytechnic colleges having three-year programmes out of around 2,000 engineering colleges in India. Every year, around 70,000 skilled engineers are produced.[16]

As such, the ideas of key state leaders in Tamil Nadu favouring FDI inflows have been pursued through various incentives and support of foreign capital.

Strong foreign capital and weak domestic labour in HMI

The Government of Tamil Nadu has supported foreign investors when the foreign firms encounter conflicts with Indian domestic workers. It may explain how the

---

[14] Interview at HMI's factory in Tamil Nadu on 23 December 2011.
[15] Interview in Chennai on 6 January 2012.
[16] Interview in Chennai on 31 January 2012.

state of Tamil Nadu could garner considerable FDI inflows despite occasional protests from society against foreign capital. Existing literature does not particularly pay attention to foreign capital as an actor in looking at the transformation of labour process in firm-based studies. For example, Burawoy (1985) discussed the changes of labour process at the shop floor level in an American multinational company producing a wide range of agricultural equipment under monopoly capitalism from 1945 to 1975. Defining the concept of labour process as 'a corresponding set of relations (in production)' into which workers transform raw materials into objects of their imagination, Burawoy explored the source of changes in the process.[17] The source of changes includes external factors, such as war and recession as well as internal factors, such as increased individualism, organisation change, managerial strategies, and internal labour market. He argued that these factors had important roles in changing the labour process by obscuring and securing surplus value which is continuously reproduced.

In a similar fashion, Krishnaswami (1989) also explored the labour process of knitting industry in Tamil Nadu. Through a case study of knitting factories in the state, he found that the nature of the capitalist mode of production was decided by management to a greater extent rather than by workers' resistance. He argued that the management was able to extract surplus value efficiently by changing the organisation of labour process. For example, expanding subcontracts is one of the changes that are used to reduce collective resistance from workers in organised trade unions. For the management of companies, expanding subcontracts is used as a means of creating competition between regular workers and casual or temporary workers. Harriss-White (2003) also observed such tendency in India's industry. Her work pointed out that the corporate sector in India had been influential in limiting the rights of labour and increasing the instances of outsourcing and subcontracting since the 1980s.

A puzzle is the significance of foreign capital in transforming the labour process in foreign firms in FDI host economies. How do the domestic labour–foreign management relations develop? How was it in the case of HMI plant? First, HMI was highly depending on the contractualisation of workers like many other foreign automobile companies did in Tamil Nadu.[18] For example, there were four ranks for non-regular workers in HMI. The ranks consisted of one apprentice level and three different levels of trainee stages. The level of apprentice was for workers who joined HMI after the completion of secondary schools or technological institutes. Workers who underwent the four stages in four years could become

---

[17] Burawoy (1985), 15.
[18] Based on interview with Samyuel Park at HMI in Tamil Nadu on 28 December 2011 and internal data of HMI.

regular workers with a one-year additional training. A worker in HMI explained other ranks, such as H3, H4, H5, H6, J level (a manager or a team leader level) for regular workers in HMI.[19] The worker said that the contract year would increase at higher ranks. For example, a three-year contract is a norm for H3, H4, and H5. However, a four-year contract is suggested above H5 level. HMI's practice for managing workers is not an exception of industrial trend that the number of permanent workers in the automobile sector has substantially decreased while that of temporary workers has rapidly increased. The tendency of 'contractualisation' and 'casualisation' of workers has a relationship with not only the automation in factories but also with the strategies of management in organising work spaces.[20] The contractualisation and casualisation make it difficult for workers to participate in trade union activities because many of the workers under contract would be in the daily labour market.

Second, another conventional understanding of labour–capital relationship is that management is influential in workers' trade union activities in industrial circumstances. Interestingly, the Government of India is likely to be in favour of capital in the relationship. The management of firms can decide trade unions with their will. Like many other states, the Government of Tamil Nadu has encouraged management to choose a representative trade union in firms. In HMI, for example, there were largely three groups of workers that insisted on the recognition for trade unions. One was the United Union of Hyundai Employees (UUHE) with 1,280 members out of 2,000 workers. Another union was Hyundai Motor India Employees Union (HMIEU) that was affiliated with a communist party, Communist Party of India (Marxist) [CPI(M)]. The third one was Anna Thozhir Sangam Peravai (ATSP), a trade union wing of AIADMK. The ATSP had just begun mobilising workers especially in Multinational Corporations of Tamil Nadu, such as HMI and FOXCONN.[21] HMI's management recognised only UUHE as HMI's trade union by arguing that only UUHE had no political affiliation. Samyuel Park, a former manager in the department of labour union management in HMI by putting it, 'There are "agreeable" trade unions and "disagreeable" ones. We (HMI's management) cannot accept trade unions that have political affiliation with any kind of political parties. What are trade unions? They should not represent political parties but utterly workers'.[22] About the nature of India's trade union activities, Patil (1976) clearly pointed out the politically oriented motive of workers:

---

[19] Interview with a worker of HMI in Tamil Nadu on 30 January 2012.
[20] Annavajhula and Pratap (2012), 53.
[21] FOXCONN is a Taiwanese multinational electronics company.
[22] Interview in Tamil Nadu on 28 December 2011.

Indian trade unionism is an arena of different central federations committed to different political ideologies. Every political party gathering its strength from the toiling masses has a trade union wing and a labour policy. Each trade union federation strives to organise the workers in each sector of the economy and in each industrial establishment of a considerable size, particularly in the public sector. Such a politically-oriented motive, namely to gain control over the state-owned undertakings, of the trade union federations has been responsible for the multiplicity of trade unions in Indian industries. Similarly, each trade union is interested in gathering strength mainly through political affiliation. As a matter of fact, even industrial disputes are not settled without the involvement of political party leaders. Therefore, it is rather difficult to find a purely economic union.[23]

The failure in recognising trade unions by the foreign management has often triggered conflicts between labour and management in foreign firms. In HMI, the groups of workers especially HMIEU, which was not recognised by the management of the company, created labour disputes several times. From 20 April to 7 May 2009, more than 1,300 workers participated in the strikes with demands on recognition of HMIEU and some other issues including wages, working conditions, and reinstatement of dismissed workers. HMI's management officially refused to recognise the HMIEU, which has a close relation with the Centre of Indian Trade Unions (CITU) supported by CPI(M) with an ostensible reason of 'non-majority' group. According to a note issued from SIPCOT that replied to a HMIEU's strike against HMI's management,

> The majority of the workmen had in the year 2011 chosen to form United Union of Hyundai Employees (UUHE) and sought for recognition of the management. The latter having been satisfied about their majority, which is obvious from the check off system, whereby each member of that union had given a letter of authorisation to the management to deduct the subscription for that union from their salary and to remit the same to the UUHE. Thus, the majority membership of UUHE remains unassailable. ... On this ground alone, action on the strike notice may be dropped, giving suitable advice to the HMIEU.[24]

The strikes settled down temporarily, yet HMIEU continuously demanded on the recognition.

HMI's management applied strict disciplines, such as disincentives for promotion, transfer, and dismissal, in dealing with the strikes. Foreign capital in India's industry has often announced such regulations to domestic workers in

---

[23] Patil (1976), 480–481.
[24] Kanagaraj (2011), 2–3.

pacifying labour disputes. Foreign capital's control of the workers has triggered further conflicts between the domestic labour and the foreign management.

Strong state and weak labour in Tamil Nadu

When labour disputes become severe and management fails to pacify the conflicts, the state finally intervenes to mediate between labour and management. In fact, the vast majority of industrial disputes are handled by the provincial states although the Indian Constitution grants concurrent power to the central government and the states to enact labour legislation and administer labour laws. Every state in India has the Department of Labour for conciliating the disputes that is headed by a Labour Commissioner who is often drawn from the Indian Administrative Service. The conciliation process, however, tends to drag for several months. Some states, such as Gujarat and Maharashtra have officially fixed the time limit at three months, yet many others have not set up such measure against administrative procrastination.

Similarly, the strikes of workers also occurred in the production factory of Maruti Suzuki located in Manesar in the state of Haryana from 7 to 21 October in 2011 for two weeks. More than 1,500 workers demanded on the reinstatement of their dismissed colleagues and the recognition of trade unions. Even though Maruti Suzuki suffered 400 million-dollar worth of loss by the strikes, it managed to settle the unrest through the three-party talks between the state, labour, and management.

In the three-party talks, the Government of Tamil Nadu has tended to be in favour of management rather than labour. Ramaswamy (1984) discussed state regulation in dealing with conciliation issues between labour and management in India's industry through two cases of domestic frims in Tamil Nadu. He argued that the system of state intervention in labour disputes reflects the preeminence of the state power which is influential in drawing the consequences of labour-management conciliation. Ramaswamy put it:

> Power is as significant in a system of state regulation as in collective bargaining, but with a difference. In collective bargaining the outcome of a conflict depends on the power labour and management wield over each other. Under state regulation, the power each of them has over the state is of far greater significance ... The complexity of the political calculus is such that the state cannot confer all the favours on one side and extract the full price from the other. But there can be no doubt that *substantial favours can be and are conferred by the state on its chosen favorites* (emphasis added) ... The occupancy of a position of pre-eminence by the state has important consequences for labour and management which are party to the industrial relationship as well as for the wider society which has a vital stake in this relationship.[25]

---

[25] Ramaswamy (1984), 189–90.

Thus, either labour or management, 'those who have the greatest access to political power gain the most'.[26]

The state of Tamil Nadu has been quite strong in controlling trade unions. Hence, the power of trade unions in the relationship with management in many industries in Tamil Nadu has been substantially weak even though Madras (former name of Chennai) was one of the cities in India having sizeable members of affiliated unions from the early 1920s. For example, Ramaswamy (1988) compared trade unions in four industrial cities, namely, Bombay, Madras, Bangalore, and Calcutta, in India. He found that there was no dominant force in trade unionism in Madras due to its political fragmentation supported by mass politics in Tamil Nadu, even though Madras was considered as the home of Indian labour movements.[27] He elaborated the reasons why trade unionism had weakened in the state as follows: (1) there was no difference in methods and aims between the trade unions; (2) trade union members in two dominant regional parties, DMK and AIADMK, split along their own factions; and (3) the state of Tamil Nadu under DMK's leadership was vindictive in controlling trade unions. Interestingly, both DMK and AIADMK have shown similar strategies in approaching trade unions and supporting capital rather than labour in its industrial relationship. Ponnaiyan, former Finance Minister of Tamil Nadu from AIADMK and, Elangovan, Spokesperson in DMK, also agreed with the perspective on the greater role of the state in regulating trade unionism in Tamil Nadu.[28]

Another noteworthy finding in Ramaswamy's work is the role of regional political leaders and industrialists who also substantially contributed to the weakening of trade unionism in the state. The DMK government led by Karunanidhi who served as the Chief Minister of Tamil Nadu strongly encouraged its trade union wing, Labour Progressive Front (LPF), to destabilise the trade union wing of Congress (INTUC) that had been supported by influential political leaders in Congress Party, such as R. Venkatraman and Gurumurthy in the earlier developmental stage of trade unionism in Tamil Nadu. The aggressive approach from DMK leadership in dismantling INTUC was encouraged by DMK's anti-Brahmin ideology that was developed in the late-1960s. In addition, the domestic industrialists in the state also helped the DMK leadership replace power struggle between two trade unions, LPF and INTUC, by quickly changing their party allegiances from the Congress Party to DMK. In short, Ramaswamy's observations provide a powerful tool for understanding the roles of different groups in the state including political leaders and India's domestic capital.

---

[26] Ibid., 189.
[27] Ramaswamy (1988), 79–80.
[28] Interview with C. Ponnaiyan, *op.cit.*; interview with T. K. S. Elangovan at the DMK office in Chennai on 1 February 2012.

On the other hand, another perspective paid attention to the societal and industrial structures of the state as factors that have contributed to weakening trade unionism in Tamil Nadu. Bagchi (1972), for example, stressed the significance of such societal structure in withering trade union movements in Tamil Nadu by putting it:

> Madras had led the trade union movements with the organisation of the workers into the Madras Labour Union but the movements could not really flourish in a region with abundant labour, slow industrial growth, and employers who were determined not to make any concession to labour organisations. In the growth of the trade union movements and in the frequency or intensity of industrial disputes, political factors – including in the phrase the national, or rather racial, character of the employers, the degree of homogeneity among the workers, the relation of the workers to the other people in the industrial centre and the ideology of the leaders of the labour organisations – inevitably played a large role.[29]

Interestingly, some of the findings collected from the HMI factories also emphasise the role of societal and industrial structures of the state in weakening trade unionism in foreign companies. First, recruitment system in the state mobilising work force via intermediaries seems ineffective.[30] The recruitment system hinders the growth of a permanent labour class because intermediaries tend to support the casualisation of workers to get profit by linking casual workers and foreign companies in the process of recruitment. For example, TVS, one of the largest domestic two-wheeler manufacturers in India, now more intensively does business as an intermediary supplying the domestic work force to foreign companies in the automobile industry in Tamil Nadu. There are other domestic companies besides TVS that have supplied temporary workers to foreign automobile companies in the state.[31] Second, the lack of homogeneity and class solidarity among workers in Tamil Nadu has been a chronic challenge for trade unions. It is aggravated not only by the growth of migrant workers in Chennai but also by those who easily shift to different companies within the state. Workers having different caste and using different language could not be committed to trade union activities. In an interview, a contract worker in HMI, also mentioned, 'The majority (of current workers) are Tamil, but there are many migrant workers from Northern India in HMI factories. The migrant workers from other states have a significant problem in communicating with the Tamil workers in factories'.[32]

---

[29] Bagchi (1972), 141.
[30] See Mathur and Mathur (1957), 82.
[31] Internal source of TVS, accessed 1 February 2012.
[32] Interview in Tamil Nadu on 12 February 2012.

Provided that the societal structure is also influential in the relationship between foreign capital and domestic labour in the state as discussed above, one may then raise a question about the role of caste and religious cleavages that significantly compose the structure of the society in India. According to findings collected from the HMI plant, religious conflicts among workers in the firm have rarely been observed. However, caste conflicts among workers have been an important issue not only in the case of HMI but also in many other trade unions in India's industry. Many South Korean employers in India's industry have found that most of the conflicts among the Indian domestic workers in both office and factories of their firms occurred due to the discordance of hierarchy between their societal caste and vocational position.[33] According to South Korean employers' observations, for example, the Indian domestic workers tend to accept mistakes made by their superiors socially positioned as higher castes. They are however more likely to create problems when their superiors as lower castes make mistakes. To resist the superiors belonging to lower castes, the workers who have complaints usually mobilise other workers within higher caste groups of their trade unions. Similarly, Maruthakutti, Kaliappan, and Reddy (1991) found that the trade union consciousness could moderate the class consciousness of workers within trade unions, but it failed to moderate their caste consciousness. Through a quantitative research on textile workers in Coimbatore in Tamil Nadu, Maruthakutti et al. concluded that 'caste free trade unionism cannot be visualised' in India's industry.[34]

Unlike such general observations, the caste cleavage among workers in HMI did not seem strong enough to create labour unrest within the company. The moderated caste cleavage was observed in HMI factories and offices. R. Sridhar, who had served as the General Secretary of HMIEU, and other workers in HMI agreed to it. Sridhar said, 'We did not have any labour dispute that resulted from caste conflicts. Within trade unions, we do not have much problem with caste'.[35] The tendency of moderated caste cleavage seems to have a close relationship with the high level of urbanisation and globalisation. In a study on the automobile industry of urbanised Bombay, Sharma (1970) found that the caste was not a significant factor, but other factors, such as occupational status, seniority, wages, and marital status were more important for workers to participate in unionism. On the basis of his earlier observation and findings from HMI, one would argue that the caste cleavage has a marginal role in triggering conflicts among workers in a place where industrialisation has progressed. Upon considering that Tamil Nadu is one of the urbanised states in India, the argument may be persuasive.[36]

---

[33] CII-KOTRA Forum at New Delhi in India on 20 December 2011.
[34] Maruthakutti et al. (1991), 390.
[35] Interview in Chennai on 30 January 2012.
[36] See also Vijayabaskar et al. (2004).

In the similar context, some studies have suggested that the high level of industrialisation has a positive relationship with the weakness of trade unionism in India. For example, Ratnam (2007) argued that trade union movements in India are overall becoming less powerful because of both internal and external factors. He underlined the role of market force, the relations of trade unions with the state, management, and other communities in civil society as external factors. In addition, he stressed some powerful internal factors, such as low membership, poor finance, weak organisation, and strong leadership, which were not democratic enough. He asserted that trade unionism in India needs to make alliances with other stakeholders in wider society and cooperate in work place institutions like works committees. By pointing an overall transition of trade unionism in India, Ghosh (2008) focused on the role of economic reforms as a factor. He argued that trade unions today are defensive, more pragmatic, and less militant compared with those before the economic reform of 1991. As one of the significant reasons behind the change, he highlighted the Trade Unions (Amendments) Act that was implemented in 2001 'in an attempt to stop the mushrooming of unions as well as to reduce the number of outsiders into any union'.[37] Ghosh's perspective is supported by Nair (2009). Nair found that the strategies of the trade union were responsive to the interaction with the state and industrialists through a case study of central Indian labour organisation of contract workers based in the state of Chhattisgarh. Nair's findings from the labour organisation are similar to what Ghosh argued. Nair's observation stresses that the state is in favour of industrialists whose interest is more congenial to that of the state, even though the labour organisation's strategies were pointed at better bargaining.

Interestingly, many of Indian domestic workers in HMI also seem to be content with their company even though they sometimes mobilise other workers to pursue their demand towards foreign management. For them, the issues regarding the increase of wages and promotion including from non-regular to regular position are more significant than other issues, such as caste and religious cleavages.[38] For example, the monthly income of non-regular workers at the level of apprentices and trainees ranged from 3,900 to 6,957 Indian rupees. Another 10,000 Indian rupees of bonus would be given at the end of year for those who were at the trainee level. Regarding the issues of labour, Agarwala (2006; 2008; 2013) indicated that liberalisation had changed the state and labour relationship particularly between

---

[37] Ghosh (2008), 359–60.
[38] Interviews at HMI in Tamil Nadu on 28 December 2011. Interestingly, the tendency is also well described in Agarwala's (2013) work. Agarwala argued that the populist politics and the state's welfare concern favouring informal workers in Tamil Nadu made the informal workers protected with the same rights as formal workers.

the state and informal workers in India by altering the structure of production. Agarwala argued that the informal workers tended to force the state rather company management not only to decommodify their labour power but also to provide welfare needs. It is worth noting that Agarwala's argument underscores that the state has to be responsible for reproduction when poor workers do not meet the costs of their social reproduction.[39] It is applicable to the state of Tamil Nadu in a sense that it has substantially attempted to meet the needs of workers through direct bargaining, which Agarwala (2008) mentioned as an 'interdependent' relationship. This perspective can be supported by what several key activists advocating workers in Tamil Nadu have said. A. Sounderarajan, who served as a Member of Legislative Assembly and representing CPI(M) in Kanchipuram district of Tamil Nadu, put it, 'Our HMIEU strikes in HMI have aimed for better bargaining with management for better wages of workers and their welfare'.[40]

HMI's workers expressed their pride of being employed by a recognised foreign company, though they were unhappy with tight production schedule on the shop floor.[41] Workers in the sales department showed stronger support of their company.[42] Many of workers highlighted a better wage HMI provides than that offered by other domestic companies in the same industry. However, the issue of working hours in HMI seems to remain controversial between the domestic workers and foreign management. Similar to other foreign companies in the automobile industry in the state, HMI's first and second production plants were operating in a three-shift system. The factories worked at full capacity by supplying workers with eight-hour shifts for twenty-four hours for around three hundred days per year. For the twenty-four-hour operation of factories, power was continuously provided by the state. It was one of the terms in a Memorandum of Understanding agreed between HMI and the state of Tamil Nadu.[43]

For HMC's management, however, the change of working hours was difficult. The same issue was also raised in the Ulsan factory of HMC in South Korea on the shop floor. Its current day and night double-shift factory system has been a difficult task to bargain with labour for a past few decades. Each worker in this system in South Korea participates in the production process for ten hours a day. Workers believe that the double-shift system damages their health due to the extension of working hours and midnight work. In order to solve the problems, workers suggested the company management change its system into the consecutive

---

[39] Agarwala (2006), 440.
[40] Interview in Chennai on 11 January 2012.
[41] Based on interviews with workers of HMI in Chennai on 10 and 30 January 2012.
[42] Interviews with workers of HMI in Chennai on 10 and 30 January 2012.
[43] Internal source of HMI, accessed 16 December 2011.

daytime double-shift by shortening working hours. In the daytime consecutive double-shift system, each worker participates in the production process for eight hours per day without midnight work. In fact, the consecutive daytime system was suggested in HMC in 1998 as a means of overcoming an unemployment crisis influenced by the Asian financial crisis. However, it is quite difficult for the company to change its system as the issue is related to many other important issues, such as a production method, a wage system, intensity of labour, and facility investment.

Political Economy of FDI by MI

Close state–foreign capital relationship in MI

The MI is a world-famous French tyre company of which manufacturing plant was proposed to be built in the village of Thervoy Kandigai having more than 6,000 *dalit* [untouchable] villagers in Thiruvallur district in Tamil Nadu. The factory was expected to produce 3 million units per annum at the initial stage and extend its production capacity up to 20 million tyres every year. As Tamil Nadu was promoting FDI inflows in the automobile industry, key policy-makers thought the tyre industry would be necessary to sustain the growth of the automobile sector.

However, the state required MI to promise to generate a certain level of employment. MI's management proposed to the state that it would hire 1,500 Indian domestic employees and provide required training programmes to them.[44] The programmes include English language skills, computer skills, accounting, and vocational training. Interestingly, the state of Tamil Nadu seemed to consider the foreign company not only as an investor but also as an agency to train work force that would create a synergy effect in parallel with education schemes, which state leaders highlighted.

As discussed in the previous chapter in detail, Tamil Nadu has offered various inclusionary schemes, such as vocational education and employment to citizens especially to the marginalised groups of the society. The state's concerns about the marginalised citizens functioned efficiently to prohibit the citizens from being mobilised by non-Dravidian parties. In other words, the regional Dravidian parties, DMK and AIADMK, have had roles of distributing the state's wealth to citizens and taking care of the marginalised citizens, which are usually dealt by the communist parties in some other states.[45] The bipartisan politics and the

---

[44] Interview with Jawahar Michael, HR manager of MI, on 17 January 2012. In fact, a training programme was ongoing during my visit to MI's plant site.

[45] It should be noted that a communist party's role in West Bengal is quite remarkable in mobilising the broader strata of citizens by distributing the benefits of economic growth to them and implementing social justice schemes.

consistent ideas of political leaders in the two ruling parties about social inclusion have thus made citizens feel secure so that the citizens do not need to ally with other political parties to pursue their demand.

Similar to many other foreign investors, MI had also faced with considerable difficulties when it proposed an investment plan. In particular, SIPCOT had intense conflicts with local villagers in the process of land acquisition. The protest groups against the company, which were called as 'anti-Michelin' groups, were the most difficult challenge for the company to negotiate. Jean-Pierre Guibbert, a Vice President of MI, mentioned that the protests from the society hindered its investment that had been prepared for seven to eight years.[46]

When I visited MI's plant site in the village of Thervoy Kandigai in January 2012, construction was in progress. Sand and cement were piled nearby. The land was bulldosed and fenced following the boundary between the land development zone and non-development zone that SIPCOT had divided (Illustration 4.4 [A], [B], and [C]). In fact, SIPCOT designed to set up an industrial complex in the village by allocating eight hundred acres of lands. Construction work for making a new access road to MI's plant was in progress in the development zone, but forests were still being preserved in the non-development zone.

About the land of forests where SIPCOT secured for MI's investment plan, interestingly, activists were insisting it is *makkal purampokku* [grazing land for people] while the bureaucrats in SIPCOT and MI's foreign investors were highlighting it as just dry and public land.[47] In fact, the dispute between the MI and anti-Michelin groups began with the use of land rather than its ownership because people were using the land for private purposes though it was registered as public land. An employee in MI explained about the former forest environment of the plant site before the company began logging: 'Here, everything was forest before, and many villagers were staying in the forests. This factory construction began only a few months ago because of people's resistance'.[48] When asked about the anti-Michelin protest, the employee described that several protests were organised in a large scale mostly led by several activists from the communist parties.

Strangely, village's atmosphere was not so hostile to foreigners though activists insisted that the protests were still going on. The village seemed rather peaceful. Many villagers were kind enough to guide me to MI's plant site when they were queried. The friendly atmosphere was a complete opposite of the one I encountered in the state of Odisha while visiting two large-scale investment projects embarked

---

[46] Interview at the head office of MI in Chennai on 24 January 2012.
[47] Interviews with activists in Chennai on 4, 6, and 30 January 2012; interviews with bureaucrats at SIPCOT in Chennai on 2 February 2012.
[48] Interview on 12 February 2012.

by POSCO and TATA. In Thervoy Kandigai, female farmers working in the fields were even waving their hands when they found me (Illustration 4.4 [D]). Such reaction was a puzzle when considering that the villagers could have recognised me as part of the investment since I was a stranger to them. It was odder when I heard from an MI's employee that the female villagers waving hands to me and their children had participated in the anti-Michelin protests.[49]

**Illustration 4.4: MI's FDI Project in Thervoy Kandigai
(17 January and 12 February 2012)**

[A] Thervoy Kandigai bulldosed   [B] MI's construction site

[C] Boundaries divided by SIPCOT   [D] Female farmers in Thervoy Kandigai

I initially had two assumptions while observing the peaceful village: (1) if it is true what activists and the Indian domestic employee told me, the demands of anti-Michelin groups were satisfied to some extent by incentives and rehabilitation schemes; (2) the activists perhaps exaggerated the strength of their protests for

---

[49] Fieldwork findings present that the mode of protests against FDI inflows in Tamil Nadu was less violent compared to those of other states like in Odisha where left-wing parties and their militant group allied for the protests.

a larger mobilisation. I found that the two assumptions were somewhat right. First, the anti-Michelin groups were negotiating with MI for enhancing the infrastructure of the village and seeking their employment in the project. It was quite surprising to hear complaints from the protest groups that people who participated in the protests were unhappy with MI because they could not find job vacancies in the company. Second, the strength of protest groups was too weak to achieve consensus from other villagers not only because others had an apathetic attitude in allying with communist parties but also because the state tried to hide people's resistance from the public's gaze.

Strong state and weak opposition in Tamil Nadu

The protests against MI began in 2007 when its investment project with 40 billion Indian rupees of budget was announced to the public. On 30 January 2007, the Gram Panchayat of Thervoy Kandigai passed a resolution without any process for consent in *gram sabha* [village council] by stating that there was no objection to SIPCOT's land acquisition. Vani, who had a political affiliation with DMK that was a ruling party in the state from May 2006 to May 2011, was a woman panchayat president at that time. Against Vani and the gram sabha leaders, a large group of villagers was mobilised by several activists from the communist parties who did not reside in the village of Thervoy Kandigai.

However, another group of villagers did not join the protest group. Many villagers who did not join the protest group supported Vani and other eight members of the *ward* [small administrative unit at the village level of India] in the panchayat who usually decide either to accept or reject SIPCOT's land acquisition plan for MI. Vani's husband was working as a middleman supplying workers to MI.[50] As her family was one of the subcontractors of MI, she strongly supported the investment project from the initial stage without having any public meeting to collect consensus from villagers. Madhumitta Dutta who led the anti-Michelin protests as a leader of the anti-Special Economic Zone (SEZ) group said:

> The land (for MI's plant) was administered by the gram sabha, even though the government owned it. In the case of Thervoy Kandigai, we found that the gram sabha was highly political in the process of land acquisition.[51]

This episode underlined the needs for employment in the village, although one could say that the personal interest of a small group constituted a major cause of

---

[50] Interview with Mary's (president of Thervoy panchayat at that time) husband at Thervoy Kandigai on 12 February 2012.
[51] Interview in Chennai on 30 January 2012.

conflicts. The key activists had a close tie with CPI(M) although they belonged to various non-governmental organisations, such as the Dalit Mannurumai Kootamaipu, National Alliance of People's Movements (NAPM), anti-SEZs group, and some others. Medha Patkar in the NAPM who had an influential role in Narmada Bachao Andolan, a social movement in the 1980s against the Sardar Sarovar dam building project across the Narmada River in the state of Gujarat, was one of them. The anti-Michelin groups asserted their rights to protect forests which were considered as their livelihood by demanding the withdrawal of investment project from MI. Some of the villagers and activists tried to bargain with key bureaucrats who played a significant role in the investment process of MI, such as the Thiruvallur District Collector, District Revenue Officer, and Managing Director of SIPCOT. The state resisted against opposition and collective action from the protest groups. It strategised to pacify protests by persuading the anti-Michelin groups with a comprehensive compensation package, using the coercive power of police force, and controlling the local media.[52] It disabled communication about resistance.

The strategies of foreign capital in bargaining with the opposition groups were also supportive of the state strategies. MI used both persuasion and discrimination strategies towards villagers who opposed MI's FDI plan. In the process of pacifying protests, the officials in MI asked the MI support group to approach to the protest groups for conversation. Asked a question about the strategies of the company, Jean-Pierre Guibbert highlighted that it worked with other NGOs that were supporting MI's investment plan.[53] Guibbert remarked:

> The NGOs (that worked with the company) tried to visit every household in the village. They met people there and listened to them about what kind of problems they had with regard to our investment.

The Foundation for Rural Recovery and Development (FORRAD) was one of them.[54] The main objective of the NGOs was to persuade villagers by showing the interest of the company in social concerns. However, the company was strict on the issue of employment. Many job applicants who had engaged with anti-Michelin protests were excluded from the employment of the company.

---

[52] For the regulation strategy of this state, see also Thervoy Youth Women and People's Struggle Committee (2012). Interviews with activists in Chennai on 4, 6, and 30 January 2012. See also Bose (2012), accessed 20 August 2012, http://na.acjnewsline.org/Groupc/Wecpages/Adrija/Thervoy%20struggle.html. According to Bose, some activists pointed out that the state does not want any agitation to be more violent through the release of sources by the media.

[53] Interview on 24 January 2012, *op.cit.*

[54] Interview with Susan Abraham at FORRAD in New Delhi on 6 March 2012.

In many ways, the anti-Michelin groups were comparatively weaker than the MI support group. In fact, many villagers mentioned that they were not part of the protests simply because they did not feel the need for opposition activities. They understood the process of industrialisation which had been taking place elsewhere within the state and opportunities of employment. The MI support group in the village was expecting what the state and its agencies in Tamil Nadu strongly pursued.

The key policy-makers in the state considered the MI's FDI project for generating employment and making the village industrialised. A primary motive with which the state has been successful in acquiring lands for SEZs and industrialisation was inclusionary compensation that it offered to those who sold their private lands or lose public land and livelihood in the process.[55] The compensation included the higher prices of land than market prices and a job offer for those who sold their private lands; and substantial inclusionary packages, such as the offer of shelter and substitute land for those who lost their livelihood in public land especially for the economically and socially marginalised groups. In fact, the state was constructing a new house for the sixteen dalit villagers who were displaced in the process of FDI project and alternative free lands for their livelihood (llustration 4.5). Interestingly, fieldwork findings indicated that many villagers who initially opposed MI's FDI plan turned their mindset towards supporting the project after the state and MI negotiated with them.

Illustration 4.5: Rehabilitation for the Displaced Dalit Villagers in Thervoy Kandigai (12 February 2012)

[A] New houses for 16 displaced dalits   [B] After interview with the displaced dalits

It is worth noting that none of the political parties in Tamil Nadu representing dalits supported the anti-Michelin protests even though the village of Thervoy

---

[55] See also Vijayabaskar (2010).

Kandigai was dominated by dalit villagers. A dalit leader who led the anti-Michelin protests put it:

> Do not trust any dalit party in Tamil Nadu. They just mobilise people for sustaining their political life, doing nothing for dalits. Even many political leaders in these parties have close relations with higher castes (in the process of FDI inflows) for getting their own profits.[56]

The villagers of Thervoy Kandigai also mentioned that none from the dalit parties came to the village to support the anti-Michelin protests.[57] This observation may challenge the recent work on the active participation of dalit parties in the state of Tamil Nadu for the improvement of their marginalised status in the political, economic, and societal relations with other caste groups.[58]

The communist parties in Tamil Nadu also did not support the anti-Michelin protests. Unlike their active approach to the activities of a trade union in foreign companies in bargaining with management for the better economic position of workers, their participation in mobilising citizens to oppose FDI projects was quite weak. Senthil Babu, a CPI(M) activist who was devoting to labour movements in Tamil Nadu for more than fifteen years, commented,

> The longer the lower caste land workers stay in works that are connected with lands, the stronger they feel low caste identity. For them, one way to emancipate from such feeling is to cut off themselves from the lands.[59]

Babu's point of view implied the enhanced bondage between the lower castes and lands in the process of production that has usually been observed in the feudal societies. For the lower caste land workers, hence, industrialisation would be an opportunity to liberate them from the feudal bondage with the land. Upon considering that Tamil Nadu is one of the lower castes-dominated states in India, Babu's perspective may provide a strong clue to understanding why citizens of the state supported industrialisation. It also supports what Gudavarthy (2012) recently observed regarding the decrease of social protests, especially from the marginalised groups. Gudavarthy mentioned:

> Political strategies that are being adopted by the marginalised social groups in India, as part of the process of exerting pressure on the state to recognise their

---

[56] Interview in Chennai on 6 January 2012.
[57] I revisited the village with Ashik Bonofer in the University of Madras. I thank him for accompanying to Thervoy Kandigai and helping me to communicate with the villagers.
[58] For discussion on the rise of dalit parties, see Gorringe (2005) and Manikumar (1997).
[59] Interview in Chennai on 14 January 2012.

rightful demands, have been varied and complex. In addition, they demand a framework that can make sense of currents that sometimes run concurrently, and at other times, in mutually exclusive ways. Subalturn response has varied from patiently building mass protest movements ... that have raised rising issues such as the implementation of minimum wages to the more basic issue of 'land to the tiller'. Amidst these protest forms, one can also observe the trend of a generic decline in the mobilisational capacity of political organisations of all hues.[60]

Gudavarthy's observation appears more valid when looking at sporadic protests from society against FDI inflows in Tamil Nadu. As discussed above, not only political strategies adopted by the marginalised groups in Tamil Nadu have been varied and complex but also the communist parties have been hardly successful in mobilising marginalised groups. As presented through two FDI projects embarked by two foreign companies, villagers protesting against the MI's FDI project in Thervoy Kandigai used protests as a way of raising their economic compensation and securing employment in the process of bargaining with the state and foreign capital by changing their orientation towards foreign capital. Indian domestic workers in HMI's plants located in Sriperumbudur were too factionalised to create a united labour union. In the two cases, more importantly, the mobilisation capacity of communist parties in opposing foreign capital was markedly weak. Also, the upwards mobility of lower caste groups in both political and economic spheres of Tamil Nadu challenges the conventional understanding of rural societies in India like what some scholars have highlighted through a framework of local 'strongmen' as discussed in the preceding chapter.

Conclusion

The primary aim of this chapter was to discuss the close relationship between the state, society, and foreign capital that is involved in the process of FDI inflows in Tamil Nadu through the two cases of FDI projects embarked by HMI and MI. The discussion explored how a tripartite alliance between the state, bureaucrats, and foreign capital had promoted FDI inflows in Tamil Nadu. It was emphasised that the ideas of key policy-makers in the state about employment and economic growth had encouraged FDI inflows. The coherent ideas of key political leaders in different ruling parties on the utility of FDI inflows have had a significant role in encouraging the FDI projects in the process of industrialisation. The discussion also presented that developmental ideas had been the fundamental source of the close ties with foreign investors.

---

[60] Gudavarthy (2012), 6.

In addition, employment opportunities and inclusionary schemes like vocational education provided by the state have effectively prevented citizens especially the marginalised groups of society from being mobilised by the communist parties having an anti-capital orientation. In fact, it was found that many local villagers affected by FDI projects embarked by HMI and MI showed their expectations for job opportunities and industrialisation. It was also found that domestic industrialists in the state had supported its promoting FDI inflows, as many of them had worked with foreign companies. Several examples in the automobile industry in the state indicated that domestic industrialists had obtained economic benefits by supplying the domestic work force to the foreign firms. Even though the domestic workers in foreign firms sometimes organise strikes for pursuing their demand of better wages and promotion, they have been largely content with their companies.

Another aim of this chapter was to demonstrate that the state of Tamil Nadu had strongly supported foreign capital with not only various incentive schemes but also in the process of pacifying labour disputes in foreign companies. The state's support of foreign capital had often been observed in the cases of HMI and MI. First, Tamil Nadu has offered attractive incentives and many economic advantages compared with other states regarding geographical proximity with ports, low labour costs, and access to skilled labour. Second, the state has intervened conflicts between labour and management and has been in favour of the management in foreign companies. In addition, other societal and industrial structures of the state have also contributed to weakening trade unionism. The important role of societal and industrial structures includes the ineffective recruitment system dominated by intermediaries and the lack of homogeneity and class solidarity among workers. Furthermore, fieldwork findings highlighted that the caste cleavage among workers in the state does not seem strong enough to create labour unrest. Similarly, it was also worth noting that none of the political parties representing lower caste groups in the state supported protests against FDI inflows despite the demographical dominance of dalit villagers in the case of Thervoy Kandigai. Interestingly, the communist parties in Tamil Nadu were also absent from supporting the protests of society except for several individual activists from CPI(M).

Upon considering observations on the domestic workers in Tamil Nadu's industry, one may argue that the caste and religious cleavages are insignificant factors in the industrial relationship between the domestic labour and foreign management in Tamil Nadu. For them, the issues of wages and promotion were more important than caste or religious cleavages for their collective action. As more frequently found in recent years, such observation needs to be further discussed within the context of urbanisation, industrialisation, and globalisation, which are significant factors in affecting the overall weakening of trade unionism in India. In other words, the observation highlights a positive role of foreign capital in India's industry in moderating the caste and religious cleavages among domestic workers.

5

FDI Inflows in Odisha
Weakened Ideas, Strong Interests, and Unstable Institutional Change

> Direct foreign investments in the exploitation of raw materials have involved powerful societal actors and a wide range of governmental institutions and have touched upon issues of major importance to the state ... Central decision-makers may be frustrated not only by other states but also by *their inability to overcome resistance from within their own society* (emphasis added).[1]

Odisha is one of India's provincial states located on the eastern coast, having abundant resources, especially for the steel and mining industry. Because of its locational and market advantage, many of the Indian domestic and foreign firms have attempted to embark upon their business in the state's resource-extractive industries. Despite such industrial demand, Odisha has long remained as one of the most backward states in India.

However, the state's recent initiative in boosting economy through the private investments seems quite resolute. In 2015, the Government of Odisha issued the Industrial Policy Resolution (IPR) to create a conducive environment through an enabling policy and regulatory framework to drive sustainable industrial growth in the state. The new policy resolution stresses that the state is committed to simplifying the processes and clearances for the 'Ease of Doing Business' framework. In addition, the state promises to facilitate the investors through a dedicated 'facilitation cell' and 'escort officers' who will act as a single point of contact for the investors.

Beyond the new policy resolution, some other indicators present that Odisha may be in transition. According to UNICEF, Odisha has reduced its poverty ratio from 57 per cent in 2004–05 to 32 per cent in 2011–12. It is a remarkable performance, which many of the other backward 'BIMAROU' [sick] states in

---

[1] Krasner (1978), 10.

India could not achieve.[2] Odisha's recent improvement for human development indicators seems hopeful for development as well.[3]

However, scholarly literature has indicated that the economically backward states like Odisha would struggle to produce industrial development unless the state's intervention aims at catching up other industrially advanced states through its indigenous industrial strategies and institutional rearrangement.[4] The 'patron–client' type of vertical relations between political elites and citizens, politicised bureaucracy, diffuse political support, and rent-seeking behaviours of political leaders in Odisha rather pose a question: is not the state of Odisha close to a neo-patrimonial state?[5] If so, how do we define the current Biju Janata Dal (BJD) Government's initiative for industrial development? Does Odisha suggest a new model of industrial development? Otherwise, are the current observations for a change negligible?

This chapter aims at answering the questions by revisiting scholarly literature on the state and society of Odisha. Also, it attempts to discuss the chances and challenges of the state to attract foreign investments.

It consists of largely four parts. The first section explores the nature of the state and society of Odisha by reviewing the literature. It is followed by a discussion on the neo-patrimonial nature of the state of Odisha and the origin of an idea towards industrialisation that developed through the 1970s and the 1980s with little success. It is important to understand it because the idea favouring FDI inflows emerged during the process of industrial development. This part emphasises the year 1967 as a key turning point when the regional parties' coalition politics was born. However, the discussion will point out that none of the ruling parties in Odisha, including regional parties and Congress Party, were successful in implementing social inclusion policies like land reforms. It was largely because of a strong tie that existed between the rent-seeking bureaucrats and landlords. In other words, the state has lacked autonomy from the landed class for pursuing its goals and policies in the socio–economic sphere. The next part of this chapter presents how societal structure has enhanced the exclusionary nature of state–society relations in Odisha. In the final section, the discussion deals with the

---

[2] The original term 'BIMAROU' has been used to indicate economically backward states in India including Bihar, Madhya Pradesh, Rajasthan, and Uttar Pradesh. However, Montek Singh Ahluwalia, who served as the Deputy Chairman of the Planning Commission, argued that the concept should include Odisha and it has to be 'BIMAROU'.

[3] Baijayant Panda delivered a keynote speech about Odisha's recent improvement in economic performance at 10th ISAS International Conference on 28 October 2015 in Singapore.

[4] See Gerschenkron (1962); Acemoglu and Robinson (2006).

[5] See Kohli (2004; 2012). Kohli (2012) portrayed some provincial states in India, such as Bihar and Uttar Pradesh and sub-Saharan African states like Nigeria as neo-patrimonial states.

institutional arrangements structured by the BJD government under Naveen Patnaik's leadership for attracting FDI inflows. This part of discussion stresses that Naveen Patnaik's leadership has attempted to make the ideas favouring FDI inflows materialised through the institutional arrangements. It also presents that Biju Patnaik, Naveen Patnaik's father, could not realise the ideas of industrialising the state by actively inviting foreign investors in the 1970s during his tenure as the Chief Minister of Odisha.

Neo-Patrimonial State and Struggles for Industrial Development

Several studies with a society-centred perspective have underlined the influence of interest politics and societal structure on the transformation of Odisha's political economy. They paid particular attention to underdevelopment, poverty, and the identity of local tribal groups in Odisha with the focus on economic backwardness and tribal-dominant demography.[6]

The research focus has moved more recently to the issue of societal opposition to the state-led industrialisation. For example, Swain (2010) discussed the relationship between social networks and protest mobilisation in Odisha and Kerala. Swain found that social movements against industrialisation were successful in Kerala while those in Odisha were not, especially in its inland region. Swain's findings indicate that the vigorous associational life and extended group network of citizens strengthened the protest in Kerala. By contrast, the lack of social capital and civic engagement in Odisha contributed to the weak mobilisation of citizens in protesting against large-scale investments and development-induced displacement. He also showed that there was a regional disparity between the inland and the coastal areas, and the coastal region presented the success of several protests through active associational engagement.

From a society-centred perspective, Padel and Das (2010a; 2010b) and Levien (2013) also paid attention to the phenomena of development-induced displacement in Odisha.[7] Padel and Das focused on local *adivasis* [scheduled tribes] in the

---

[6] For a discussion on socio–political change and its impact on the caste identity of tribals in two different villages in Odisha, see Bailey (1960). See Jenamani (2005) for a discussion on the low level of development and poverty in Kalahandi. For a discussion on the origin of various tribal groups, tribal development programmes and rehabilitation policies, see Panda (2006). For a debate on the nature of social stratification and agricultural settings in Odisha established before Independence, see Pati (2000). See also Pati (2001) for a discussion on the conflicting identity of *adivasis* [scheduled tribes] in Odisha.

[7] I benefited from a discussion with Samarendra Das, the co-author of *Out of This Earth* and a documentary filmmaker, over the issue of displaced Dongria Kondh tribals in Odisha followed by a film screening on 'Wira Pdika [earthworm]' at the National University of Singapore on 24 October 2013.

state where various large-scale investment projects are undertaken especially in the steel and mining sectors. By looking at the global network of big businesses and foreign companies, international organisations, and NGOs, their research demonstrates how big businesses have exploited natural resources and forced local tribals to be displaced from their shelter and culture in the state. In addition, Padel and Das explained how international organisations, such as the World Bank and the International Monetary Fund were involved in such investment projects. They argued that the international organisations and NGOs support the investment projects through funds by advertising themselves as the crusade against poverty. Similarly, focusing on the displacement of tribals, Levien (2013) discussed the politics of dispossession and countermovement over the issue of land commodification. Levien's particular attention to Odisha addresses the significance of severe land struggles from marginalised citizens and the lack of welfare among displaced citizens.

On the other hand, several studies have addressed the neo-patrimonial nature of Odisha with a state-centred perspective. For example, Currie (2000) examined welfare and relief administration in Odisha by looking at the implementation of the natural calamity relief code in Kalahandi and Nawapada. He found that the government officers having an important role in implementing the relief code at the block office level did not seriously follow the district manual that provides procedural guidelines for the relief code in the field. Further, he indicated that there was rarely enforceable power to punish government officers who do not fulfill the duties specified in the relief code in the state.

Such lack of accountability for bureaucrats in Odisha was also described in Kumbhar (2005). By comparing four sub-districts of Odisha, namely, Kalahandi-Bolangir-Koraput (KBK) and Cuttack, Kumbhar found that the underdevelopment of KBK region stemmed from the widespread corruption and lack of accountability of political leaders and bureaucrats, although the region secured abundant resources. Kumbhar underlined that bad governance, old institutions, and lack of political will contributed to the poverty of this region, while Cuttack showed better performance for developing agricultural infrastructure, poverty reduction, and the literacy rate of citizens.

In a similar fashion, Patnaik (2005) presented that the ability of elected panchayat leaders in Odisha is low in delivering the interests of marginalised groups after observing four panchayats in the district of Dhenkanal for a study of governance. Patnaik argued that affirmative action had not ensured effective representation of marginalised groups in the state even though it had promoted their political participation. To quote Patnaik:

> The representatives had very little awareness about the existence of specific interests of any particular (marginalised) group. Even the SC and ST representatives talked

about wider interests such as road, water, and education. Mostly they were not able to identify group-specific interests and distinguish them from the general interests of constituency. However, this does not mean that disadvantaged groups did not have any interests which were specific to their group ... We could observe that this group suffered from problems like social restrictions, poor housing, lack of employment, lack of community halls ... [8]

In a similar context, Bussell (2012) paid attention to the rent-seeking behaviours of political leaders and discussed the relationship between corruption and performance in public service reforms. She showed the differing capacity of bureaucrats in India in implementing technology-based public service reforms through a cross-state comparison. She argued that political incentives and the degree of corruption, whether it is petty or grand, played a significant role in shaping and implementing such reforms. She also found that politicians having larger political incentives were more likely to improve public service and efficiently implemented reforms despite the diverse outcomes across states in India. She found that Odisha had a higher rate of petty corruption and substantial delay in policy adoption.[9]

The state-centred explanations provided by Currie, Khumbar, Patnaik, and Bussell remind us of the predatory nature of the state in Odisha, as Evans (1995) described through the absence of effective bureaucracy in the Zairian state in his prominent work *Embedded Autonomy*. Evans presented the structural differences between the predatory and the developmental states. By describing India as an intermediate state between predatory and developmental, Evans argued that the developmental states were equipped with effective bureaucracy that can assist the state not only to become embedded in its society to make dense links with industrial capital in particular but also to deliver the state goals autonomously prior to individual interests. On the other hand, predatory states are less capable of pursuing collective goals before seeking for individual incumbents' interests.

With a state-centred perspective, Kohli (2012) has discussed the nature of several states of India. According to Kohli's explanation, Odisha is close to a neo-patrimonial state, which tends to lack institutional moorings, lack public purpose, and struggle with sluggish development and persistent poverty. Kohli put his finger on Bihar and Uttar Pradesh to model neo-patrimonial states where the personal interests of ruling elites are influential in the policy-making process. In contrast, social–democratic states, such as Kerala and West Bengal or developmental states like Gujarat are concerned about the public good. Kohli's argument indicated not

---

[8] Patnaik (2005), 4759.

[9] Bussell indicated a strong association between the human development index and the timing of policy enactment. See Chapter 4 of Bussell's study.

only that the personalised nature of neo-patrimonial states had limitations for economic growth and redistribution but also that the lack of public intervention from society in pressurising the state was unhelpful for reducing poverty.

Taking the state- and society-centred approaches together, the consecutive parts of this chapter explain how the nature of exclusionary state–society relations in Odisha has blocked the pursuit of ideas towards industrial development. The discussion also deals with how such state–society relations have influenced the unstable institutional change in the area of FDI inflows. It will address the aborted ideas of political leaders on not only the need for foreign capital but also the citizenship-forming schemes in the process of industrialisation. It will offer an insight into the ideational evolution of key state leaders in Odisha favouring FDI inflows and the constraints of societal structure that blocked such ideational pursuit.

Exclusionary State–Society Relations and Obstacles to Pursuing Ideas Favouring Foreign Capital in the 1970s and the 1980s

Upper-middle-group base of party organisation and political fragmentation

I argue that the neo-patrimonial nature of Odisha and its exclusionary relations with the society in the 1970s and 1980s hindered not only industrial development but also ideational pursuit favouring foreign capital. In other words, the ideas of key state leaders favouring foreign capital could not be realised in the poor progress for industrialisation. The positive attitude of key state leaders towards the need for foreign capital in Odisha's industry needs to be understood by tracing the process of industrial development.

To advance the argument, the discussion in this part finds that the state legislative election in 1967 was a key turning point. A regional political party alliance between Swatantra Party and Jana Congress Party came to power for the first time in the state through the 1967 election by defeating Congress Party. However, the regional ruling parties did not utilise the chance to enhance state–society relations through the pursuit of inclusionary schemes and pro-poor policies. Similarly, the Congress governments that ruled Odisha for a long time did not concern themselves with building a close tie with citizens but kept changing coalition partners regardless of party ideologies. As such, no single ruling party in Odisha has attempted to shape inclusionary relations with the citizens.

The exclusionary nature of ruling parties in Odisha can be found in the upper-middle group base of party organisation. Neither the Congress Party, which ruled the state for a long time, nor regional parties, which occasionally came to power, have a strong connection with citizens belonging to the weaker sections of society. The weak cadre-based organisation of ruling parties has been a critical factor in the political instability in Odisha. For example, the failure of Congress Party in the election of 1967 was closely related to its weak tie with marginalised citizens. When a student movement was organised in Odisha in 1964 to oppose the excessive use of police force and corruption that Congress Party leaders were involved in, the party could not secure any strong support from the society. Only left-wing political parties such as the Communist Party of India (CPI) and Samyukta Socialist Party that have strong solidarity with students and marginalised groups in society could oppose the ruling party.[10] As the movement got broader support from other political parties, such as Swatantra Party and Bhartiya Jana Sangh, Congress Party failed to garner votes against the big opposition group and finally lost power in 1967.

The weak cadre-based organisation of ruling parties in Odisha and the weak support from the grassroot level easily allowed party leaders to create factions, as there was no strong system to monitor the leaders.[11] Frequent conflicts between political leaders within Congress Party at the union level and its factions made Odisha politics more unstable and unpredictable. Several ministers of the state government in the 1950s and 1960s were involved in corruption and maladministration.[12] However, there was no monitoring system and party cadres within the ruling Congress Party that could alert members for their leaders' corruption. Thus, it allowed Harekrushna Mahatab's leadership to bring corruption charges against the Governor of Odisha and other ministers who had led highly scandalous lives.[13] The Congress government consequently had to resign, and Odisha came under President's rule for four months in 1961. The circumstances remained more or less the same through the 1960s. Several key leaders of the Congress Party who served as Chief Ministers of Odisha in the 1960s, such as Biju Patnaik, Biren Mitra, and Sadashiva Tripathy also had to struggle against the intense factionalism and political opposition within the governments. Various government reports issued at that point observe the conflicts.[14]

Furthermore, the role of key political leaders in the ruling parties in Odisha was not professional enough to strengthen the party organisation. The state leaders did not consider interaction with citizens at the grassroots significant

---

[10] Das and Choudhury (1985), 341.

[11] In a comparative study on the powerful role of local elites in rural development in Gujarat and Odisha, Mitra (1992) also found that 'political parties represent the most visible link between the village power structure and the political arena at the higher level; both in Surat (in Gujarat) and Dhenkanal (in Odisha) more people from the higher castes are affiliated to political parties than from the lower social strata' (101).

[12] Misra (1985), 34–49.

[13] Ibid., 24–25.

[14] See GOI (1966; 1967a; 1967b; 1968).

for making a strong political support base. Not only could they break coalition partners at any time for their political ends, but they could also withdraw their party affiliation when required. For example, Biju Patnaik, who is considered by citizens in Odisha as one of the most charismatic and enterprising state leaders for the state's economic development, shifted his party affiliation several times from Congress Party to Utkal Congress and again to Janata Party.[15] It implies that regional parties in Odisha hardly had strong and professional leaders who could pursue their ideas on the state's development without interference from the opposition group. In fact, Biju Patnaik's defection from the Congress Party and his struggle with other state leaders subsequently brought Odisha under President's rule again in 1973. A letter from B. D. Jatti, the Governor of Odisha at that time, to V. V. Giri, the President of India, requesting President's rule in Odisha presents the intensity of the state's unstable politics. B. D. Jatti wrote:

> The Utkal Congress in their meeting held on 9 June 1972 passed unanimously a resolution to merge with the Congress … The Congress organisation, after examining the individual applications of the Utkal Congress members of the Legislative Assembly admitted only 28 of the members to the Congress Party, leaving behind Shri Biju Patnaik and 6 others (who were ministers in the erstwhile coalition ministry). Shri Biju Patnaik seemed to have been dissatisfied with the Congress organisation for not having been admitted to the Congress Party along with his colleagues and has been attempting consistently to oust the Congress government in this state … In view of the above facts, and after a careful consideration of the political situation in the state, I am satisfied that no party or parties with any substantial majority can form a stable government. … I therefore, recommended that the President takes over the administration of this state under Article 356 of the Constitution of India.[16]

---

[15] The coalition government was created by two regional parties – Swatantra Party and Jana Congress – centring on local leaders in Odisha. One of the state leaders was Biju Patnaik who left Congress Party and organised Utkal Congress during the election of 1967. At the next election in Odisha in 1971, Biju Patnaik's Utkal Congress again won in a coalition with United Front, Swatantra Party, and Jharkhand Party. However, Utkal Congress rejoined Congress Party soon after the election by breaking the coalition. The Congress Party was able to come to power again in Odisha in 1972 with the support of Biju Patnaik's leadership in Utkal Congress. However, leaders in Congress Party particularly at the union level did not support Biju Patnaik to become the Chief Minister of Odisha. Instead, due to opposition from other leaders within Congress Party, Nandini Satapathy, who served as the Congress Party poll manager and was considered as Indira Gandhi's right hand, became the Chief Minister of Odisha in June 1972. See Misra (1985), 46.
[16] Nanda (1979), 317–19.

Emergence of ideas favouring foreign capital in the 1970s

Biju Patnaik tried to stay away from Odisha politics after the conflicts with other leaders in Congress Party in 1972. He, however, did not give up building his ideas on industrialisation and economic development for the state. His idea of the need for foreign capital developed when he served as the Minister of Steel and Mines in the Janata Party Government at the union level under Morarji Desai's leadership. Biju Patnaik not only believed that the steel industry in India had a lot of potentials to grow but that it also needed foreign assistance for learning technology and securing financial resources. He remarked in an upper house meeting in Parliament in 1977:

> The development of metallurgical and mineral based industries involves very large investment. Since the availability of internal financial resources is limited, the possibilities are being explored, for taking loan from foreign countries, strictly on commercial basis. The intention is to repay the foreign capital with the help of partial exports of the semi-finished/finished products, so produced, over a period of time. The exploration work is of continuing nature and a decision may be taken after taking into account the expansion plans, the details of which are being worked out presently.[17]

The financial deficit in Odisha in the 1970s also supports the context in which Biju Patnaik took the decision. In fact, financial difficulties encouraged the Central government and other provincial states in India like Tamil Nadu to attract FDI inflows. Table 5.1 shows the gradual increase of permanent debt in Odisha in the 1970s.

Table 5.1: Permanent Debt in Odisha in the 1970s

Year	Permanent Debt (Million Indian Rupees)
1970–71	652
1971–72	702
1972–73	741
1973–74	805
1974–75	876
1975–76	1,021
1976–77	1,080
1977–78	1,161
1978–79	1,227
1979–80	1,311

Source: Orissa Budget: Some Facts and Charts, cited in Rath (1985), 411.

---

[17] GOI (1977a), 49–50. See also GOI (1977b).

After a year, Biju Patnaik insisted on the need for foreign capital in a meeting of Parliament. Biju Patnaik seemed quite excited about his achievement in attracting foreign investors and the expectation of foreign assistance. At a meeting of Parliament in 1978, Patnaik said:

> During my last visit abroad, the possibility of obtaining technical and financial assistance JCO-operation from USSR, Romania and Federal Republic of Germany for setting up new shore-based steel plants in India was discussed by me with the leaders of their government and industry. Their response was favourable and further dialogue and negotiation with these countries as well as with the UK and the representatives of the Japanese Steel Industry is continuing.[18]

However, the idea favouring foreign capital conceived by Biju Patnaik in the process of industrial development in Odisha could not evolve due to several socio-political reasons. First, the unstable politics and incoherent ruling governments were not helpful in consistently pursuing the idea. Odisha came under President's rule again in 1976, 1977, and 1980. Meanwhile, no single ruling party in the 1970s, whether it was Congress Party or Janata Party, was able to focus on the state's industrialisation.

Also, some state agencies that were established during the 1970s and playing an important role of making industrial progress also seemed to have had substantial limitations to develop through the 1970s and the 1980s for the similar reasons. For example, the Industrial Promotion and Investment Corporation of Odisha Limited (IPICOL), a state agency developing medium- and large-scale industries, was established in 1973. Its primary aim was focused on industrial development in the 1970s and extended to attract FDI inflows in the post-reform period after 1991. However, the state agency could not evolve much in the 1980s. At the same time, some inclusionary policies to support industrialisation were introduced. The Orissa Resettlement and Rehabilitation Policy (ORRP) that was made in 1977 was one of the examples. However, the inclusionary policies were not successful to prevent marginalised citizens effectively from being displaced from the large-scale investment projects undertaken in the state.[19]

In addition, the societal structure in Odisha also challenged the pursuit of ideas on industrial development and the need for foreign capital in the industry. It is discussed in detail in the next part of this chapter.

---

[18] GOI (1978c), 36.

[19] See Baviskar (1995); Dutta (2007); Sundar (1997) for discussions on the displacement issue.

Corrupt bureaucrats and the failure of land reforms, taxation, and rehabilitation

The failure of land reforms constitutes another good example to highlight how and why the neo-patrimonial nature of the state and its exclusionary relations with citizens have blocked the reform process and further industrial development in Odisha.

The Odisha Land Reforms Act was initially introduced in 1960 and revised in 1964. The reform attempts continued in the 1970s and 1980s and had positive consequences. Some of the surplus land was given for some scheduled castes and scheduled tribes through the Odisha Prevention of Land Encroachment Act enacted in 1972 and the Odisha Prevention of Land Encroachment Rules implemented in 1985.[20]

However, the attempts could not be successful due to opposition from the upper-middle group in society and its symbiotic tie with rent-seeking bureaucrats. The failure was intimately related to the inefficiency of bureaucrats positioned in the administrative organisations of the state. The problem with bureaucrats who took care of the land administration in Odisha was their strong tie with the landlord class. They seemed to abuse a *zamindari* tenure system, which has considerable variation in the quality of land records management due to the existence of multiple layers of intermediaries between individual landlords and officers collecting land revenue at the district level.[21] The strong tie between bureaucrats and landed farmers encouraged rent-seeking bureaucrats to exclude tenants in the process of land redistribution. A study on land reforms in Odisha issued by the World Bank reports:

> The proportion of total agricultural land they operate has remained substantially unchanged since the 1950s, although substantial gains in area accrued to the largest among them during the 1960s, thereby swelling the ranks of farm households with medium-sized holdings by the 1970s. The proportion of households operating no land, whose livelihoods are based principally on agricultural labour, increased substantially following the widespread eviction of tenants from erstwhile landlord estates, and by the early 1960s accounted for a third of all households. Since the 1960s, some have gained access to at least some land, but around a quarter of all households in Orissa still operate no land. Overall, in spite of land reforms,

---

[20] Srichandan (1993), 315–17. See also Dash (2001).

[21] Around 80 per cent of districts in Odisha had adopted a *zamindari* tenure system while only 20 per cent had maintained a *ryotwari* tenure system. Compared to the *zamindari* system, which has a lot of intermediaries in the process of collecting land revenue, the *ryotwari* system in which land revenue is collected by a chief villager directly without intermediaries is considered more efficient. See Mearns and Sinha (1999).

socio–economic and demographic change over the last half century, these trends suggest that formidable obstacles continue to prevent the rural poor from improving their access to private arable land ... In practice, the survey and settlement process provides widespread opportunities for rent-seeking on the part of the government officers involved, and it is not uncommon for poorer and less powerful landholders to 'lose' at least a proportion of their land in the official record. Land-grabbing by more powerful individuals, facilitated by exerting leverage over settlement officers, appears to be commonplace during survey and settlement operations. While the contested amounts of land are usually small, *the net effect is systematically to discriminate against the rural poor and the socially excluded* (emphasis added).[22]

The attempts at land reforms were strongly opposed by the landed class. The landed class argued that the Acts did 'not merely intend to bring about the betterment of tenants but *desired to kill the landlord* and the abolition of mutation fee would lead to the *extinction of middle class* (emphasis added)'.[23] The landed class tried to make an alliance with bureaucrats in charge of land administration to protect their interests against the land reforms. The rent-seeking behaviour of state bureaucrats strengthened its tie with the landed class in the processes of land survey and creating records of land ownership. The symbiotic tie between the rent-seeking bureaucrats, political leaders, and the landed class has consequently made the state of Odisha less autonomous from the strong landed class. The state is consequently more oppressive towards marginalised groups in the society. Opposition from the upper-middle group against land reforms and further economic reforms continued.[24]

The corrupt and weak administrative organisation of the state also had problems in accumulating capital for industrial development. For example, the municipal councils that handled the financial administration of the state at the local level in Odisha were inefficient.[25] Their basic roles involve financial administration by imposing taxes, assessing the method of taxation, and allotting expenditure of collected taxes under the approval of the state government. Taxes constitute the

---

[22] Mearns and Sinha (1999), iii–iv.
[23] Srichandan (1993), 235.
[24] When Biju Patnaik wanted to set up various industrial parks in the state, the local landed class who dominated Odisha politics and society opposed the plan. For discussions on land reforms in other states, see Herring (1980; 1991). In his works, Herring discussed the strategies of a communist party in Kerala that brought more successful radical agrarian reforms than in West Bengal. Herring argued that the abolition of landlordism in Kerala as a social system protects the most depressed class in the state. Herring emphasised that welfare concerns of the state towards the depressed class were deeply related with active political participation from the class and social mobilisation in the state.
[25] Das (1985) and Dash (1988).

financial resource that is invested in Odisha's industrial development.[26] However, tax collection in urban areas was rather dismal. It occurred because the tax rate levied in the urban areas in Odisha was much lower than that of other states in India, even though Odisha had the highest ceiling of maximum tax rate among provincial states in India.[27] The pattern of urban taxation in Odisha from its state-building period to the 1970s is well described in Dash's work. The study presents:

> The urban local bodies have obviously taken advantage of the lacuna in the Act. Unlike Acts of other states the minimum rate of taxation has not been prescribed in the Orissa Municipal Act, 1950. The municipal councils in Orissa have intentionally levied taxes at low rates.[28]

Also, every local body in Odisha levied a different tax rate. The incoherent taxation system suffered from the Odisha Municipal Act that did not provide a detailed list of functions for the municipal councils.[29] The tax collection from Councils located in the urban areas is used to promote not only industrial development but also the process of urbanisation. Given that, it is worth noting how the dearth of securing state revenue owing to the state's poor financial administration affected industrialisation and urbanisation in Odisha. This is a clear contrast with the state of Tamil Nadu where the landed class in the urban areas was levied a higher tax rate for land ownership than others in the rural areas.

In addition, the Congress government in the 1980s that was captured by a small group of corrupt ministers and leaders seem to have hardly concerned themselves with building an inclusionary relation with citizens. In the Congress government from 1980 to 1989 under Janaki Ballav Patnaik's leadership, for example, Odisha was meant to develop the oilseed industry with the support of the central government.[30] The central government nationalised *sal* seed trading

---

[26] Dash (1988), 52.

[27] For example, the maximum tax rate in Odisha was 45% while that of Andhra Pradesh (28%), Uttar Pradesh (25%), Maharashtra (17%), and other states was lower. See Dash (1988), 66.

[28] Dash (1988), 66.

[29] Das (1985), 234.

[30] The National Seeds Projects launched during the Fifth Plan period for developing the oilseed industry set up State Seeds Corporations in Odisha, Haryana, Punjab, Andhra Pradesh, Maharashtra, Bihar, Karnataka, Rajasthan, and Uttar Pradesh. The projects aimed at 'placing the seed industry on a scientific footing by reorganising the functions of various institutions in a systematic manner' and 'augmenting infrastructural facilities like setting up of processing plants, seed certification agencies, and seed testing laboratories' (GOI, 1981, Chapter 9). For the central government's support of oilseed development project in Odisha, see also GOI (1982).

in 1983 and needed support from the state governments. As the seed cultivation was particularly related to tribals' income source in Odisha,[31] the project for developing the oilseed industry through the nationalisation scheme was expected to provide tribals with a stable income. However, Janaki Ballav Patnaik, the Chief Minister of Odisha at that time, and several other political leaders who were in favour of industrialists did not pass the scheme in the state assembly.[32] Thus, the tribals seemed to severely suffer from exploitation in the process of collecting seeds by several units run by the industrialists. Janaki Ballav Patnaik's leadership in pursuing state goals was captured by corrupt ministers and factional leaders within the Congress Party.

Also, historical evidence presenting that Janaki Ballav Patnaik's leadership in the 1980s was successful either in pursuing industrial development or in accumulating foreign capital hardly exists.[33] Despite it, it is justifiable to argue that the nature of institutional change favouring FDI inflows to Odisha was unstable, which is discussed in the later part of this chapter, compared with that of Tamil Nadu.

The exclusionary nature of state–society relations in Odisha was also often observed during the process of rehabilitation of those who were displaced by natural disasters. For example, Banik (2007) discussed the relationship between democracy and famine by looking at the cases of Odisha and West Bengal. He focused on local politics and the roles of various institutions, such as political parties, judiciary, bureaucracy, media, and NGOs in dealing with natural calamity and starvation in two different sub-districts, namely, Kalahandi in Odisha and Purulia in West Bengal. In contrast to the case of Purulia, Banik indicated that the vernacular media in Kalahandi dealt with issues on the local calamity without verification. Furthermore, factionalised local politics in Kalahandi brought little change in tackling drought and starvation. He pointed out that 'no one (among the Members of Parliament from Odisha) spoke of measures to improve health services or the need to improve the low purchasing power of the residents of areas like Kalahandi' by examining records of the Parliament debate.[34] He emphasised

---

[31] For a discussion on the importance of *sal* seeds as an income source for tribals in Odisha, see a report issued by an NGO, Regional Centre for Development Cooperation, accessed 19 April 2014, http://www.banajata.org/pdf/case-studies/ORISSA.pdf.

[32] Bhuyan (2010), 92–95.

[33] Bhuyan (2011) indicated that Janaki Ballav Patnaik's leadership did not have the political will to embark on foreign investments (24–25). However, Patnaik changed his attitude favouring FDI inflows when he served as the Chief Minister of Odisha again from 1995 to 1999. For discussions on J. B. Patnaik's attitude towards industrialisation and investments during his second term as the Chief Minister of Odisha, See Sengupta (2001).

[34] Banik (2007), 155.

that the political ownership of vernacular media in Odisha was biased its point of view. It had a political motivation that had a negative impact on famine prevention in Odisha. By contrast, the widespread presence and relative efficiency of CPI(M) cadres at the block and district levels in West Bengal had an important role in providing early-warning information on crises, such as drought and food shortage to both the party leadership and the district level administration. Banik argued that the efficient prevention of starvation deaths in Purulia in West Bengal also resulted from the roles of cadres in the ruling party. Banik's observation, in turn, points to the poor performance of Odisha in the social inclusion issues that have been discussed so far.

Causes and Consequences of Neo-Patrimonial State

Divided citizens: strong upper-middle group and weak marginalised group

The discussion in this part presents the societal structure in Odisha that represents the powerful interests of the upper-middle group that oppresses the marginalised groups. It addresses two significant notions in the society that have hindered the state's industrial development: (1) the structural division that has divided citizens into the economically advanced coastal areas and the backward hilly areas, and (2) the notion of state insecurity involving threats by left-wing extremists, such as Naxalites and Maoists and their mobilisation of uneducated and unemployed citizens for opposing the state-led industrialisation. The notion of a societal division between citizens in the coastal areas and hilly areas has encouraged social conflicts between the upper-middle group and the marginalised groups in society.

The upper-middle group in Odisha emerged from landlord families and has had severe conflicts especially with the tribal population. Regarding the upper-middle group, Mohanty (1990) underlined its strong origin in *brahman-karan* (upper-middle class who migrated from the coastal areas into the hilly tribal areas, playing the role of intermediaries between the urban elite and tribal population) domination in the state and its strong Hindu identity. The hierarchical Brahmanical social order has oppressed marginalised groups in the society. For example, a student movement organised in Western Odisha against *marwaris* [traders from Rajasthan] in 1980 showed an increasing number of grievances by marginalised groups in the hilly areas against the upper-middle group. The movement began when *marwaris* at the Khetrajpur area in Sambalpur did not contribute to flood-relief funds collected by students in Sambalpur, one of the very backward sub-districts in Western Odisha. The movement initiated in the anti-*marwari* orientation aimed at opposing not only the *marwaris* and their strong alliance with local landlords but also the state government.[35] Citizens and students in the movement criticised the overall price rise, black marketers, profiteers, and hoarders of economic activities as well as the state's negligence of flood victims and lack of concern for students.[36]

The origin of the societal division of citizens between the coastal areas and the hilly areas can be traced back to the period of colonial state building. When the British ruled the princely states in Odisha, the loyalty of tribals towards their leaders was very high. Later, some of the leaders from the princely states joined Rajendra Narayan Singh Deo to establish a new political party, Ganatantra Parishad. The leader of the new regional party, Singh Deo, was also the last ruler of one of the princely states. The leaders in the party targeted tribals as a support base when Ganatantra Parishad competed with Congress Party in the state legislative assembly election in 1951.[37] Since then, tribals in the hilly areas have frequently been targeted for mobilisation by political parties to oppose Congress Party in the elections. Local political elites provoked the tribal voters by propagating that Congress Party leaders purposely discriminated against the tribal populations in the state during the process of resource distribution. Their propaganda has hardened the gap of societal division between the citizens in the state.

Interestingly, the notion of the societal division has frequently been used by protest groups in Odisha to mobilise marginalised groups against state-led industrialisation. For example, both the anti-Tata and the anti-POSCO protests that were involved in the land acquisition process mainly addressed this issue. Social activists, who are mostly based in left-wing parties, used this notion to mobilise citizens not only from Odisha but also from other provincial states and international organisations to oppose investment projects. They often insisted that investments by both Tata and POSCO encroached on the local tribals' lands. However, the case of POSCO was in fact irrelevant to the tribal issue, as the affected villages in the district of Jagatsinghpur did not have any single tribe. The discussion in the next chapter elaborates on it.

Left-wing extremists: mobilisation of uneducated and unemployed citizens

The Government of Odisha has often reported that the left-wing extremists threatened the security of the state. Their threats seem to have blocked the

---

[35] The *marwaris* and Gujaratis dominated the Kendu [Tendu] leaf and timber trade in particular and had a strong tie with the local landlords, who invested in them for business. See Das and Choudhury (1985).

[36] Das and Choudhury (1985), 347.

[37] See Misra (1985).

industrial progress as well through the mobilisation of uneducated and unemployed citizens. Various official reports have clearly reported that the state officials and citizens have been victims of their threats. The Government of Odisha has asked the central government to help it eradicate such threats. Several discussions in the upper house meetings of Parliament testify to this:

> Equipped with modern weapons and improved explosive devices, they (Naxalites) are targeting the local police and indulging in large scale looting of public distribution system rice from the godowns. Their unabated activities are posing a grave threat to the internal security of Orissa and India ... The state needs the support of the central government for strengthening coastal security.[38]

> The menace of Maoist and Naxalite violence has reared its head in Orissa also. According to reports, the extremist groups in Jharkhand, Chhattisgarh, and Andhra Pradesh are trying to open a corridor through the districts of Sundergarh, Deogarh, and Sambalpur for east passage. In some recent incidents, lives of innocent civilians and some villages of Sambalpur have been lost, including that of police personnel. As such, the Southern District of Malkangiri, Gajpati, and Raigarh are facing violent incidents of Naxalites for quite some time. Even the house of a former Minister of Orissa was blown up in Malkangiri district last month. There is a general perception that this is a law and order problem and should be handled by the respective state governments. But, it is not limited to that alone. *Economic deprivation, regional imbalance, lack of employment avenues, lack of purposeful engagement of the rural, and tribal youth are some of the causes for the young men joining ranks of the extremists* (emphasis added). I, therefore, urge upon the central government to approach this problem taking a consolidated view. The misguided youth can be brought to the mainstream of civil society by offering them opportunities for gainful employment. For this, cash-strapped states like Orissa, need more central help and funding to improve the rural infrastructure. This can be done through special grants and not through normal channels of funding. At the same time, to improve the law and order machinery and to supplement the state police force, additional resources and manpower are required. The Union Finance and Home Ministries may consider these aspects with urgent attention.[39]

Chakrabarty and Kujur (2010) also supported a strong correlation between the higher poverty rate of Odisha, which is related to the societal division of citizens mentioned above and the Maoist emergence. They wrote:

> Maoism has evolved as a strong political force mostly in the tribal dominated part of Odisha that is lacking in the basic amenities for human existence. There is no

---

[38] GOI (2003a), 232.
[39] GOI (2005a), 254.

doubt that the lack of economic development is a propelling factor and thus it is not surprising that Maoism has grown in strength in tribal districts while the coastal districts, which are politically more conscious, remained comparatively free.[40]

It is worth noting that the lack of employment and education among youth in the state has a strong correlation with their active participation in joining the activities of left-wing extremists. Table 5.2 shows a higher dropout rate of students from schools and a higher rate of unemployment and poverty in Odisha. As can be seen in the table, the substantial gap between two states, namely, Odisha and Tamil Nadu, in education and employment could be correlated to the change in poverty ratio. As discussed in previous chapters of this book, Tamil Nadu with a higher level of education could employ the educated youth in industry, and it may have impacted poverty reduction. On the contrary, Odisha's higher rate of school dropouts seems to have failed to mobilise the educated work force in its industry. The remarkably higher rates of rural and urban unemployment in Odisha can explain why the state has shown poor performance in poverty alleviation for the past several decades.

Table 5.2: Dropout from Schools, Unemployment, and Poverty of Tamil Nadu and Odisha

	Dropout Rates from Classes 2010–11[a] (Per cent)			*Unemployment Rates 2004–05[b] (Per cent)*		*Poverty Ratio[c] (Per cent)*			*Per Capita State Domestic Product at Current Prices 2013–14[d] (Indian Rupees)*
	Primary	Upper Primary	Secondary	Rural	Urban	1983–84	1993–94	2004–05	
Tamil Nadu	–	8	25.9	1.2	3.5	Rural			112,664
						54	33	23	
						Urban			
						47	40	22	
All India	27	40.6	49.3	1.7	4.5	Rural			74,380
						46	37	28	
						Urban			
						41	32	26	
Odisha	7	55	64	6.7	13.4	Rural			52,559
						68	50	47	
						Urban			
						49	42	44	

Sources: (a) Ministry of Higher Education and Statistics of School Education 2010–11; (b) National Sample Survey Organisation (NSSO); (c) Planning Commission; (d) National Institution for Transforming India (NITI Aayog).

---

[40] Chakrabarty and Kujur (2010), 109.

With regard to an alliance between left-wing extremists and the uneducated and unemployed youth, a Member of Parliament from Odisha mentioned:

> In the past one year, Naxalites have attacked many places ... and killed ten police personnel and innocent people. They have even snatched away four self-loading rifles from the police. Now, the Naxalites are threatening and kidnapping the local businessmen for extortion and demanding huge ransom. A few days back they had kidnapped three forest officers ... *Due to lack of employment and education, local youth are also joining the Naxalite groups* (emphasis added). The local police are not well-equipped; they don't have modern communication system or devices and modern equipment. They are not even trained to counter or assault Naxalites in the region.[41]

As such, citizens in the state seem to have been exposed to such violent environments for long due to the state agencies acting very poorly.

Late Development of Ideas and Institutional Change Favouring FDI Inflows after 1991

Limited institutional change in the 1990s

Biju Patnaik's ideas on industrialisation began developing gradually only after he became the Chief Minister of Odisha in 1990 during his second term as a Chief Minister. First, such ideas included the need for funds from international organisations to boost Odisha's economy, as several state leaders in Tamil Nadu realised in the 1970s for Tamil Nadu's urbanisation. Mukherji (2007) described how Biju Patnaik adopted the privatised regulation model in 1993 in the power sector by agreeing with the World Bank's participation in the process. According to Mukherji, the World Bank in the early 1990s tried to set itself as an important institution in the power sector of developing countries to protect various interest groups involved with the power sector by declaring that lending would be given to the only countries accepting its changing principles. The changing principles of the Bank addressed the need for an independent and transparent regulator. To achieve such aims, the Bank encouraged 'commercialisation and corporatisation of public sector assets and private sector participation' in the power sector of developing countries.[42]

When the Bank approached, Biju Patnaik thought that the Bank's participation would help with the impending bankruptcy of the state electricity board in Odisha.

---

[41] GOI (2006b), 400.
[42] Mukherji (2007), 317.

In addition, Biju Patnaik's ideas on the need for a close tie between the public and private sector for industrial development led the Odisha Electricity Regulatory Commission (OERC) established in 1996. This OERC was born following the Odisha State Electricity Reform Act of 1995, which was in the same line of the Bank's principles.[43] Regarding such ideas for state-led industrial development that Biju Patnaik conceived, Bhuyan (2010) also wrote:

> Ambitious and enterprising as he was in his boyhood, Biju Patnaik always cherished a dream to industrialise Odisha and turn himself into a top-flight industrialist by setting up large industries in his state ... and show to the people in Odisha that it was possible for them to take up big enterprises on their own.[44]

In the process of state-led industrialisation, Biju Patnaik invited POSCO, a South Korean steel company, to Odisha in 1990. He recognised the need for big businesses and foreign technology for development in Odisha's steel industry. He wanted to establish a steel plant in Paradip, which he considered as a good export location.[45] He seemed to be knowledgeable about the steel industry since he had served as the Minister of Steel and Mines at the central government from 1977 to 1980.[46] The central government agreed with Biju Patnaik's idea on the need for foreign capital in the steel industry in Odisha. According to an official debate in the upper house of Parliament, the central government sought the assistance of POSCO from South Korea for setting up a steel plant at Paradip.[47] The state of Odisha asked POSCO to study the feasibility of a port-based steel plant and its investment in the steel project in Paradip, but POSCO rejected the proposal for some reasons that will be discussed in the next chapter. Despite the failure to attract POSCO, Biju Patnaik continued his efforts to invite foreign investors for the steel project in Paradip. The investment request from Odisha reached Jindal, TATA, and the CAPARO group after POSCO's rejection.[48]

The economic reform of 1991 at the union level encouraged Odisha to initiate foreign investments. Despite such institutional arrangements, however, Biju Patnaik's dream for Odisha's industrialisation by developing the steel industry turned out to be less successful than desired due to the socio–political reasons. First, the industrial strategies his government designed could not be pursued by the subsequent government. His investment ideas were eclipsed when his Janata Dal

---

[43] Ibid., 318.
[44] Bhuyan (2010), 105.
[45] Ibid., 108.
[46] See GOI (1977c; 1978a; 1978b).
[47] GOI (1990).
[48] Bhuyan (2010), 107–10.

was defeated by Congress Party at the state legislative assembly election in 1995. In an interview with *India Today* just before the election in 1995, Biju Patnaik said:

> I am unhappy because of the inordinate delay in the execution of projects such as power and aluminium. All these delays are owing to the centre and the World Bank ... What people see today are the little roads, the schools and the hospitals that I have built for them. But the future is blank. I need major projects. But how can I go about it? Without power, I can't even smelt coal.[49]

At the same time, there were limitations in the industrial strategies designed by policy-makers in the state. For example, Odisha's industry depended heavily on natural resources rather than the manufacturing and service sectors. For example, the total extent of forest cover in Odisha is about 44 per cent, which is expected to bring prosperity to the state.[50] However, forest-related industries like mining and wood have suffered limited growth because of the lack of infrastructure, even though those industries have contributed to the state's revenue. Railway facilities, roads, and port systems were in a very poor condition. According to a report issued by the state of Odisha, '11 million people are dependent either directly or indirectly on the forests for employment as forest-based products provide livelihood to a large section of the population of the state'.[51] Such industrial strategies in Odisha were significantly different from those of Tamil Nadu, which were more focused on the manufacturing and service-based industries that could absorb the trained and educated work force, as underlined in the preceding chapters.

---

[49] *India Today*, 'The Future is Blank: Unemployment Is Not Unique to Orissa: Biju Patnaik,' 31 January 1995, accessed 29 March 2014. Although the central government's approach to POSCO was friendly to attract investment in Odisha in 1990, some key state leaders at the union level, who were involved in the political struggles against Biju Patnaik, did not like Patnaik's efforts. When Patnaik invited POSCO in 1990 for a steel project as a major partner along with Jindal Strips, the Steel Minister from the central government accused him of 'violating the protocol by approaching a foreign company at his own' (Bhuyan, 2010, 109). In fact, large-scale investments require political consent and administrative support from the central government. Due to the reason, a coalition government at the state level having a factionalised national party as a coalition partner may struggle against political intervention by the national party. An investment project for the Paradip Oil Refinery, which was scheduled to be completed by 2003 after the approval in 1998, was also suspended by the central government (see GOI, 2003a; 2003b). The POSCO steel plant project also involved in pending legislative and judicial clearances where the strong support of the central government was expected.

[50] Nanda (1979), 6.

[51] India Brand Equity Foundation (IBEF), 'Odisha March 2013: Scenic, Serene, Sublime,' accessed 3 July 2013, www.ibef.org/aboutus.aspx.

More importantly, the lack of accountability in the administrative organisation of Odisha was not conducive for boosting the state's industry. A discussion in the upper house meeting of Parliament reports that there are some sick industries in Odisha. At the meeting, Raman Singh, who served as the Minister of Commerce and Industry in the Bharatiya Janata Party government under Vajpayee's leadership, said:

> According to the RBI, the number of non-Small Scale Industries (SSI) sick/weak industrial units in the state of Orissa as at the end of March 2001 was 59 ... A number of causes, both internal and external, often operating in combination, have been responsible for industrial sickness. The main causes include deficiencies in 202 planning, management, marketing, etc.[52]

Interestingly, Kalinga Industries Limited, which Biju Patnaik and his family had substantial interests in, was in the list of weak industrial units.

Institutional change favouring FDI inflows in Naveen Patnaik's BJD Government in the 2000s

The idea of attracting foreign capital that Biju Patnaik conceived was realised by the current BJD government under Naveen Patnaik's leadership. The BJD government has been in power since 2000. The BJD government has considered foreign investment as a major means of absorbing the workforce in Odisha's industry.[53] Naveen Patnaik's attitude towards FDI inflows in the manufacturing sector was positive, although his opinion depends on the sector that is hosting foreign investments.[54] During his leadership, the process of FDI inflows to Odisha has been streamlined through several institutional arrangements. For example, the state implemented a single-window clearance system through the enactment of the Odisha Industries Facilitation Act in 2004. The enactment of this Act aimed at streamlining inspection of industries by different state agencies and authorities for the clearance of industrial projects in the state of Odisha.[55]

---

[52] GOI (2001), 86.

[53] Interview with Bijayant Panda, a Member of Parliament from BJD, at his residence in Bhubaneswar on 3 October 2012.

[54] Naveen Patnaik opposed to FDI inflows in the retail sector.

[55] The single window system is strongly encouraged at the district level within the state. District-level authority works under the chairmanship of the District Collector for investment projects up to 500 million Indian rupees. Beyond that, the Chief Secretary of Odisha is involved in investment projects between 500 million and 10 billion Indian

In addition, other state agencies have accelerated the process of attracting foreign investors under the BJD government. For example, 'Team Odisha' was introduced especially to attract large-scale investment projects including FDI inflows in the IPICOL. The state of Odisha reports,

> Team Odisha shall mean the broad institutional framework of the government that is engaged in industrial facilitation and investment promotion in all key areas of economic growth. The Chief Minister is the captain of Team Orissa and the principal goal of the Team is to provide necessary synergies and convergence of all government efforts to ensure Odisha's position at the vanguard of economic and social prosperity.[56]

IPICOL, which was created in 1973 to promote medium and large-scale industries in the state, now deals with FDI inflows as well. The Odisha Industrial Infrastructure Development Corporation (IDCO) has also played a significant role in attracting FDI inflows. The primary role of IDCO for foreign investors is to provide infrastructure, such as helping to acquire land. IDCO has a pivotal role in bringing in private capital for development of infrastructure projects in the state. However, IDCO has had frequent conflicts with local villagers who were to be displaced during land acquisition for industry. Many local villagers in Kalinga Nagar and Paradip have been involved in protests against the land acquisition process for the Tata and the POSCO projects. P. K. Jena, former Chairman-cum-Managing Director with IDCO, and T. Ramachandru, former Chairman-cum-Managing Director of Industrial Development Corporation Odisha Limited, also admitted the difficulties of acquiring land.[57] Jena and Ramachandru underlined that their state agencies need to improve efficiency for the speedy process of land acquisition as well as provide the amicable settlement of disputes with the local villagers.

Furthermore, policies encouraging FDI inflows have been introduced in the current BJD government. The ORRP (2006), the Orissa Public Private Partnership (PPP) policy (2007), and the IPR (2007) are some examples. First, the ORRP

---

rupees through the state-level single window clearance authority, while the Chief Minister of Odisha examines investment proposals that have a scale of more than 10 billion Indian rupees. The multi-layered organisations for the single window system indicate that the effective implementation of the Act requires active and cooperative participation between key administrators at different levels in the state. See the official website of IDCO, accessed 19 April 2014, www.idco.in/2009/activitiestest.aspx?content=Industrial%20Promotion.

[56] GOOD (2007a), 8.
[57] Interviews at IDCO and IDCOL in Bhubaneswar on 4 October 2012.

was introduced in 2006 when the anti-TATA movements were intense.[58] The anti-Tata protests were deployed by various organisations and local villagers in Kalinga Nagar in the district of Jajpur, which will be discussed in detail in the next chapter of this book. It is worth noting here that increasing demands by the citizens for rehabilitation and welfare forced the state to implement the ORRP. In fact, the origin of this ORRP can be traced back to 1977 when the state embarked on the Rengali Dam project with World Bank funding.[59] A Government Order demanded that the state of Odisha should implement a rehabilitation package for pursuing the project.[60] But the state introduced the rehabilitation policy only in 1994, almost a couple of decades after the Government Order. Until then, many local villagers were displaced without adequate compensation or rehabilitation.[61]

Besides the Rengali project, several other dam and mining projects in Hirakud, Upper Kolab, Indravati, Gopalpur, Kashipur, and others also resulted in large displacement. Such displacement is described by Baviskar (1995) and Sundar (1997), where 'popular memories' of tribals towards the state's extractive development are discussed. The Department of Water Resources in the Government of Odisha formulated the 'Odisha Resettlement and Rehabilitation of Project Affected Persons Policy' in 1994. The policy, however, was not efficiently implemented due to the socio–political reasons discussed above.[62]

Second, the PPP policy was enacted to upgrade the infrastructure sector in the state for industrialisation. Regarding the objective of this policy, the Government of Odisha writes, 'the PPP approach is best suited for the infrastructure sector as it supplements scarce public resources, creates a more competitive environment,

---

[58] At the union level, the resettlement policy was introduced in 2003 for a better and more humane approach towards the victims of developmental decisions. See Dutta (2007), 115. See especially Chapter 3 of Dutta's study for a discussion on the evolution of Indian national policy on resettlement and rehabilitation. See also GOI (2006a) for the background on implementing ORRP in Odisha. The great influence of Naxalites on tribals was an important reason why the state of Odisha wanted to implement the scheme.

[59] Dutta (2007), 177.

[60] The Government Order Resolution was No.13169 (20 April 1977). See also Dutta (2007), 177.

[61] According to a study conducted by the Indian Council of Social Science Research (ICSSR), 546,794 people were displaced by various dam and mining projects in Odisha between 1951 and 1995. Quoted from Dutta (2007), 182. See also Mohanty (2005) and Mathur (2009).

[62] When ORRP was implemented in 2006 and BJD won in the state assembly election in 2009, inclusionary policy seemed to be welcomed. Pati (2009) mentioned that the 'human face' features of policy implementation would be primarily considered for BJD to be a political alternative in Odisha, which both Congress Party and BJP alliance failed to apply.

and helps to improve efficiencies and reduce costs'.[63] It also suggests the need for administrative support on issues, such as clearance at the union and state levels, rehabilitation and resettlement activities, and land acquisition. According to the Government of Odisha, some successful initiatives to promote PPP projects in infrastructure development include the Kalinga Nagar Industrial Complex where Tata has recently set up its steel factory despite protests from society, the promotion of Special Economic Zones (SEZs) at different locations, and many others.[64]

Third, the IPR was updated in 2007 by the Government of Odisha.[65] The IPR 2007 was originally introduced in 2001 to build an enabling environment for foreign as well as domestic investors rather than relying on fiscal subsidies and incentives.[66] Compared with IPR 2001, IPR 2007 seems stronger in dealing with issues, such as infrastructure development, environmental management, and rehabilitation in the process of investment. According to Team Odisha (2013), IPR 2007 aimed at 'reinforcing and further expanding the process of industrial promotion and investment facilitation in the state'.[67] The state of Odisha puts it:

> With a view to making the current industrialisation process sustainable, maximum emphasis shall be laid on sound environment management practices. With this objective in mind, the state government among other things is actively promoting investments in new cement plants based on blast furnace slag and fly ash, which would be available in abundance due to the large number of steel and power plants coming up in the state ... The state government has (also) made pioneering efforts in formulating a robust Rehabilitation and Resettlement Policy by adopting a holistic livelihood approach for rehabilitation and resettlement of project-affected families. Similarly, an appropriate policy dispensation has been put in place for industries to contribute towards periphery development as part of their corporate social responsibility.[68]

Also, significantly, the IPR of 2007 reflects the concerns of the state in generating employment through industrialisation. The state of Odisha indicates, 'As part of its strategy for employment generation and export promotion, the state

---

[63] GOOD (2007b), 1.
[64] GOOD (2007a), 243.
[65] GOOD (2007b).
[66] Team Odisha, 'Single Window System for Investment Promotion in Odisha,' accessed 4 July 2013, www.teamorissa.org/download.asp.
[67] Team Odisha, 243.
[68] GOOD (2007a), 2.

government shall create an enabling environment for the establishment of the SEZs at different locations'.[69]

To sum up, institutional arrangements were carried out actively only in the current BJD government under Naveen Patnaik's leadership, even though Biju Patnaik tried to invite foreign investors with his FDI-friendly orientation in the late 1970s. Ideas on the need for foreign capital for the state's economic development have existed as the apparent stability for the institutional change favouring FDI inflows, yet the state agencies and policies favouring FDI inflows could not evolve much throughout the 1970s and 1980s. The apparent stability has been strongly supported by the economic reforms of the central government favouring liberalisation since 1991.

Despite the lack of data about the development of such agencies and policies in the 1980s, it seems justifiable to argue that the institutional change favouring FDI inflows in Odisha was unstable compared with that of Tamil Nadu. On the contrary to Odisha, Tamil Nadu presented an incremental change by successfully building inclusionary relations with its citizens and utilising the relations to enhance the roles of state agencies favouring industrial development and FDI inflows throughout the 1970s and 1980s. It is worth noting that the origin of ORRP goes back to the year 1977, and it was revived to be implemented for those who are displaced in the process of industrialisation. The demands of the citizens for their welfare reached its peak in 2006 when protests against the Tata project were deployed. The marginalised groups, who suffered from the dearth of citizenship politics and exclusionary relations with the state, were the main protesters. Their intense protests and increased demands certainly played a role in building inclusionary relations with the state. However, it needs to be further observed whether or not the dramatic institutional reconfiguration will be sustainable.

Conclusion

This chapter discussed the reasons for the lower level of FDI inflows in Odisha and the process of the institutional change favouring FDI inflows. It took the exclusionary pattern of state–society relations in Odisha as a fundamental source that blocked state-led industrial development and the promotion of FDI inflows. The discussion argued that the exclusionary nature of state–society relations that stems from the neo-patrimonial nature of the state failed to shape citizenship politics. The failure to build citizenship politics has provoked citizens, the

---

[69] Team Odisha, 244.

uneducated, and the unemployed, in particular, into being mobilised by opposition groups against the state-led industrial development. Left-wing extremists, such as Naxalites and Maoists have targeted marginalised citizens and mobilised them to oppose large-scale investments embarked upon by the state in collaboration with capital. The marginalised citizens, who have suffered from the dearth of citizenship politics in Odisha, have been part of the opposition group, even though the mobilisation methods of the political extremists have been violent and plunderous. It was also found that strong ties between the upper-middle group, rent-seeking bureaucrats, and political leaders have substantially hampered inclusionary policies aiming at implementing redistribution. The discussion here found that the lack of autonomy caused by vested interest groups, the upper-middle caste, and the landed class constrained the state of Odisha from effectively intervening in the economic sphere and pursuing its goals.

Like Tamil Nadu, the ideational evolution favouring FDI inflows in Odisha needs to be understood in parallel with the process of industrialisation. In this context, the discussion here addressed the state legislative assembly election in 1967 through which the coalition government of regional parties was formulated. The key turning point, however, failed to help the ideational pursuit of state leaders towards citizenship politics. Compared to Tamil Nadu, it was also found that the industrial strategies pursued in Odisha have been heavily focused on resource extractive industries, such as the mining and steel sectors.

6

Making FDI Work in Odisha?

> Government participation in the emergence of an industry can be explained politically by the existence of masses that were mobilised without effective employment having been created to absorb them. This caused a dangerous situation for those who held power.[1]

This chapter discusses how the state of Odisha has garnered a low level of FDI inflows by paying attention to the social conflicts between the supporters and opponents of large-scale investments at the village level. Data collected from two locations in the field where Pohang Iron and Steel Company (POSCO hereafter) and Tata Steel Limited (TATA hereafter) embarked on their investment projects strongly support the argument underlined in the preceding chapter – that the exclusionary nature of state–society relations has blocked large-scale investments to Odisha. As discussed in detail in the preceding chapter, citizens who have been provoked by the dearth of citizenship politics especially in the marginalised groups of the society have opposed the state-led industrialisation. The central argument in this chapter points to the weak relationship between the state and capital, which seems to be recently evolving towards a close tie, and the divided citizens of society in Odisha that have hindered the state-led industrial development.

This chapter aims to understand the weak tie between the state and capital in Odisha in bargaining with protesters against large-scale investment projects. For this, it pays attention to the relations between the state, society, and capital, particularly in the process of land acquisition for industrial development. It examines two investment projects embarked on the manufacturing sector in two different districts of Odisha. One is POSCO's steel plant project undertaken in the district of Jagatsinghpur, and the other one is TATA's steel plant project placed in the district of Jajpur (Map 6.1).

Data were collected through a short visit to Odisha in February 2012, a four-month stay in Odisha and Delhi from September to December 2012, and another two-week brief visit to Odisha in December 2015. Intensive interviews were

---

[1] Cardoso and Faletto (1979), 140.

conducted with political leaders, bureaucrats, activists, villagers, India's domestic investors, and foreign investors through several visits to POSCO's FDI project site and TATA's manufacturing plant. Findings from the multiple instances of fieldwork also support the argument presented in the preceding chapter – the neo-patrimonial nature of the state has encouraged citizens in the marginalised groups to be easily mobilised by left-wing parties and extremists, who highly politicise the issue of development-induced displacement to oppose the state-led industrialisation. Their strong resistance has revealed not only against the state but also against both foreign and India's domestic capital in the state.

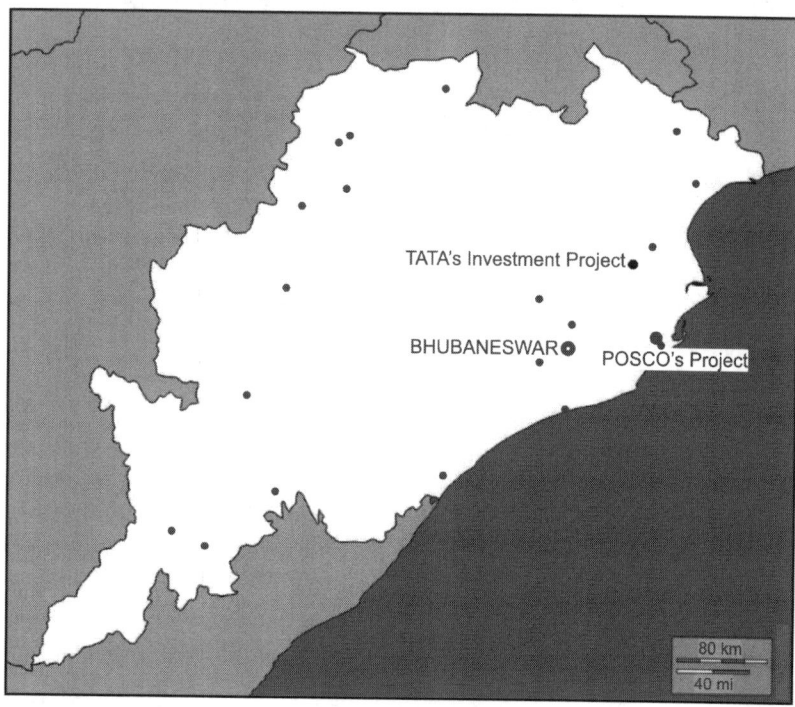

Map 6.1: Fieldwork Sites in Odisha

Sources: Based on D-maps, accessed 5 September 2017, www.d-maps.com.

The preceding chapter stressed that state strategies of Odisha for industrialisation had heavily focused on resource-based industries including mining and steel making, which frequently show an extractive nature, such as resource extraction and deforestation. Another aim of the discussion here is to present how the conflicts between the state and protesters in the process of such extractive industrial development have become highly politicised. This point of view challenges what Kale (2013) observed through the TATA and POSCO investments. Kale argued that even though 'social' opposition was frequently organised in Odisha, it was not yet successfully transformed into 'political' protest. However, her work does not detail the *political* means of protest. Contrary to her observation, this chapter will explain how the protests against the large-scale investments have been politicised and become more political while the state and society are involved in conflicts.[2] In the second part, the relationships between the state, India's domestic capital, and citizens, especially in the marginalised groups of Odisha, are discussed at the village level. For this, interviews were conducted with state leaders, bureaucrats, investors from TATA, and villagers in Kalinga Nagar *tehsil* affected by the TATA project. The discussion in the section presents the state's recent attempt to implement better rehabilitation packages to the citizens displaced by the TATA project by forcing the investor to cooperate in bargaining with the citizens and the increasing number of citizens who support the investment despite the remarkable contrast of divided groups supporting and opposing the project.

Political Economy of FDI by POSCO

Political leaders in India want POSCO

POSCO is the world's fourth largest steel producer from South Korea, which signed an MOU with the Government of Odisha on 22 June 2005 for its FDI project.[3] The project was proposed to establish an integrated steel plant that has a total capacity of 12 million tons per annum (MTPA) at Paradip in Jagatsinghpur district of Odisha with an investment of US$12 billion.[4] POSCO-India, the local subsidiary of POSCO in India, was incorporated on 25 August 2005 to embark on the steel project. As India's economy has huge potential for growth among emerging markets, executives in POSCO thought that India would be a better location regarding the market potential in the long run compared with other emerging markets.[5]

---

[2] The notion *political* in this chapter indicates the considerable participation of political actors and institutions like political leaders and parties in such issues to pursue their specific aims and interests in the realm of politics.

[3] GOI (2012); POSCO (2013).

[4] GOI (2010a; 2010b; 2010c; 2010d; 2012).

[5] Interview with a Vice-President of POSCO, who has been involved in the project since 2004, in Seoul on 14 June 2011. He mentioned that POSCO chose India as an alternative market of China as productive capacity of the Chinese domestic steel companies became high and overflowed in China.

In fact, several key political leaders in Odisha favouring large-scale investments were eager for the POSCO project. Interestingly, their ideas on Odisha's industrialisation were extremely focused on the resource-extractive industries like steel and mines. Biju Patnaik, the former Chief Minister of Odisha, was one of them. A newspaper source reports, 'He (Biju Patnaik) has gradually worn down the opposition of many of his party members of the legislative assembly to reform and has begun to sell off chunks of the public sector to private – and even foreign – investors'.[6] Naveen Patnaik, the current Chief Minister of Odisha from Biju Janata Dal (BJD) and Biju Patnaik's son, also supports such projects in the state. Bijayant Jay Panda, a Member of Parliament from BJD, remarked:

> We need investment and we need industrialisation. I am in favour of big investment projects including the POSCO project. We cannot bring our people from poverty without investments and economic growth. We have a lot of poor people. In recent years, fortunately, we have had investments. That has been leading to industrial growth, which is very high. In fact, we have the same level of industrial growth as Gujarat. And it has been the source of revenue of government for poverty alleviation programmes. So we are now subsidising food; we are helping pregnant women; we are improving our social measures quite a lot. For example, Odisha has shown the maximum poverty reduction in the entire country, according to the Planning Commission. Odisha has had the maximum improvement in child malnutrition and infantile mortality. All these are possible only because there are economic growth and investments.[7]

A significant reason why state leaders supported FDI projects as large-scale investments was to generate employment. In fact, the POSCO project was also expected to create substantial employment and contribute to economic growth in this state. According to the National Council of Applied Economic Research:

> POSCO's iron ore project would create an additional employment of 50,000 people annually for the next 30 years. This translates into 20 billion rupees of additional output for Odisha. In terms of value addition, the iron ore project would contribute 1.3 per cent to Odisha's State Gross Domestic Product by 2016-17 ... If POSCO puts up the steel project to utilise the entire iron ore mined in the state, the impact on the economy would be much greater – 870,000 people of additional employment each year over the next 30 years. This translates into 298 billion rupees of additional output for Odisha. In terms of value addition, the steel project would contribute 11.5 per cent to Odisha's SDP by 2016-17.[8]

---

[6] Prem Shankar Jha, 'A Bandwagon Everyone Just Has to Get On,' *The Business Times*, 16 February 1995, accessed 31 March 2013.

[7] Interview in Bhubaneswar on 3 October 2012.

[8] NCAER (2007).

The state of Odisha also clearly indicates its expectation of economic growth through the enhancement of steel production including the POSCO project. The *Economic Survey* issued by the state reports:

> Odisha has been receiving heavy investments in the industrial sector in recent years. There are new potential entrants, such as Vedanta, Jindal, and POSCO into this sector in Odisha. If and when these investments fully materialise, the steel producing capacity of the state will improve substantially and Odisha will grow at a much faster rate.[9]

The central government of India also showed an interest in attracting POSCO's investment for Odisha's industrial development from 1990, before the economic reform was carried out in 1991 at the union level. A debate in the upper house of Parliament reports that the central government sought the assistance of POSCO from South Korea for setting up a steel plant at Paradip in Odisha.[10] In the debate, the central government even considered the second option in case POSCO refuses to invest. It means that the government of Odisha needed not only large-scale investments but also foreign assistance for the state's steel industry.

Low commitment and opposition groups to investments in Odisha

Despite the interest in POSCO's investment that both the central government and the state of Odisha have long had, key political leaders in the BJD government did not seem to give the commitment to make the investment project take place when POSCO agreed to embark on the project in 2005. An executive of POSCO expressed their regret for the delay in embarking on the project and said, 'This is our eighth year. We trusted the state government and its initial promises for giving us licenses'.[11] For example, the Mining Leases (ML) and Prospecting Licenses (PL) are what the state government concerns. POSCO expected the state of Odisha to provide substantial support and institutional incentives, such as tax cuts in return for securing natural resources within the state. However, it took almost nine years for POSCO to hear news on the progress of the required licenses. Another executive of POSCO mentioned:

> Biju Patnaik invited us in 1990 for an investment to his state, but we refused the proposal as we thought it was not the right time. Many people say that we might not have had the problems and opposition you see now if we had entered

---

[9] GOOD (2012).
[10] GOI (1990).
[11] Informal conversation in Bhubaneswar on 2 March 2012.

the India's market then. However, we now know that we would have had similar kinds of administrative problems and delay in Odisha even if our investment had taken place in 1990.[12]

Odisha's weak state–business relation may explain why the level of FDI inflows to Odisha is low. It implies that the state of Odisha has not had close ties with either domestic private capital or foreign private capital. Table 1 presents the state–business relation ranks over the period from 1985 to 2005 suggested by Cali et al. (2013). Table 6.1 presents the state–business relation ranks among states in India from 1985 to 2005. The state–business relation in Odisha loosened more than in other states in India during the period, though the data for more recent years is not updated. It is not difficult to assume that ideas on the need for the private sector were hardly pursued in the state during the period. In other words, there was a substantial lack of commitment from the state, whether it stems from the dearth of political will or it results from the low capacity of bureaucrats to implement policies favouring the private sector investments.

Table 6.1: State–Business Relation Ranks among States in India, 1985–2005

Rank	1985	1995	2000	2005
1	Gujarat	Tamil Nadu	Tamil Nadu	Tamil Nadu
2	Madhya Pradesh	Andhra Pradesh	Rajasthan	Karnataka
3	Tamil Nadu	Gujarat	Andhra Pradesh	Andhra Pradesh
~	~	~	~	~
10	Odisha	Maharashtra	West Bengal	West Bengal
~	~	~	~	~
14	Punjab	Odisha	Assam	Uttar Pradesh
15	Assam	Assam	Odisha	Odisha

Source: Based on Cali, Mitra, and Purohit (2013), 47.

At the same time, several political leaders from opposition parties, both at the union and the state levels, opposed the POSCO project. The conflicts between the state leaders in Odisha and their incoherent ideas on FDI inflows have substantially challenged not only the state-led industrialisation but also the attempts to build close ties with foreign capital in the process of industrial development.

The first group of opposition in the state legislative assembly of Odisha was led by Congress Party and the communist parties.[13] For example, Bhupinder

---

[12] Interview in Seoul on 14 June 2011.

[13] Findings collected from the ground report that such strong resistance of left-wing parties in Odisha against the state-led industrialisation is the reverse of the left-wing parties'

Singh from Odisha Congress Party asked the Chief Minister to understand the 'magnitude of protest' by the locals and said, 'A government meant for the welfare of people should never play with their livelihood; industrialisation should not take place at the cost of agriculture and must go along with the wishes of people'.[14] And the opposition group in Odisha Congress Party and left-wing political parties was strongly supported by its head offices at the central government level and many non-governmental organisations (NGOs).

The second group of opposition, interestingly, was led by some leaders within the BJD party. Pyarimohan Mohapatra, a Member of Parliament formerly from BJD but currently from Odisha Jan Morcha, is well known to citizens in Odisha as the 'enemy of the Chief Minister', Naveen Patnaik. Regarding POSCO's project, there have been frequent conflicts between Pyarimohan Mohapatra and the Chief Minister. Mohapatra once accused Patnaik by saying, 'He (Naveen Patnaik) had suppressed all democratic movements including agitation against POSCO steel project by use of force in most inhuman manner'.[15]

The weak relationship between the state and foreign capital has also been considerably influenced by strong opposition from the society, especially citizens who have allied with the opposition parties against the state-led industrialisation. The next part of this chapter discusses the influence of societal resistance on the state and its weak capacity in dealing with the intense protests, by paying attention to a bifurcated society and the violent mobilisation by the left-wing extremists.

Divided Citizens and Weak State in Kujang

Field notes from Kujang on divided citizens

In October 2012, during my second visit, villagers were clearly divided into two groups – supporters and opponents – in three villages – Nuagaon, Gobindpur,

---

experiences in West Bengal. The contradictory strategies of the parties – supporting and opposing land acquisition for industrialisation – may be misleading scholars. For example, Levien (2013) discusses the land acquisition politics using the concept of 'Accumulation by Dispossession'. However, Levien's work does not distinguish between the two different types of CPI(M) strategies over the issue of land acquisition in states of India. It should be clearly noted that the CPI(M) and its militant group volunteered to support villagers' resistance against the investment projects in Odisha while the CPI(M) as a ruling party strongly supported the TATA's Nano project in West Bengal by allowing TATA to take over substantial farmland in 2006.

[14] *Times of India*, 'Stop Acquisition of Land, Cong Leader Tells CM,' 2 July 2011, accessed 31 May 2013.

[15] *Times of India*, 'Naveen Snubs Cong Concern Over Project,' 17 November 2011, accessed 31 May 2013.

and Dhinkia – in Kujang *tehsil*, where considerable *pan* [betel] vine was expected to be deforested in the process of land acquisition for POSCO's steel project. As *pan* cultivation was the primary source of income for the villagers, the issue of land acquisition for the project had long been a problem. The conflicts were becoming more severe between the two groups of villagers. The majority of villagers in Nuagaon and Gobindpur supported the project, while some in Dhinkia opposed it. Mamta Nayak, a female *sarpanch* [chairperson of panchayat] of Dhinkia *panchayat* [self-governing statutory institution at the village level] from 2009 and a protester of the project, remarked:

> Our conflicts have become more intense. For us, three things are critical for living: *pan*, *mina* [fish in Odia], and *dhan* [paddy in Odia]. This is our livelihood. We cannot live without it (Illustration 6.1 [A]).[16]

Villagers in Dhinkia who were leading the anti-POSCO protests set up barricades at the entrance to their village, which shares its border with Gobindpur. After the barricades had been installed, not only visitors but even neighbouring villagers from Gobinpur were strictly restricted from entering Dhinkia. The villagers were quite hostile when they found me in the village and asked whether I came to cover their stories for newspapers. Initially, they did not cooperate for interviews, and it took several days to make the villagers trust my identity and research. Later I came to know that some other researchers had attempted to visit the villages affected by POSCO's steel project to conduct interviews with the villagers but they failed. A couple of fieldwork strategies helped me access to them. First, I had built a reliable connection with political leaders in the communist parties from Delhi and Bhubaneswar for some time before I visited villages in Jagatsingpur. As the villagers protesting against POSCO were closely connected with the communist parties, my network assured the villagers that they could cooperate with my work. Second, I travelled the villages with local people from Odisha. I visited the villages with an Odia researcher in February 2012 and two other Odia activists from Bhubaneswar in October 2012.

When the villagers agreed to be interviewed, I was surprised to find that the number of villagers opposing POSCO's steel project was just around 35 out of the thousands in Kujang, and they all resided in Dhinkia. I later came to know through intensive interviews with villagers that the small size of the protest group resulted from the absence of a leader who can lead the protest group. Villagers in the protest group, in fact, had strong ties with POSCO Pratirodh Sangam

---

[16] Interview on 6 October 2012. I would like to thank Abijit Panda for helping me communicate with the villagers in Odia.

Illustration 6.1: Villages and Villagers in Kujang Tehsil

[A] Pan Vine in Dhinkia (29 February 2012)

[B] After Interview with Protesters in PPSS (29 February 2012)

[C] POSCO-India Transit Camp in Nuagaon (29 February 2012)

[D] After Interview with a Family in Nuagaon POSCO-India Transit Camp (29 February 2012)

[E] IDCO's advertisement for POSCO Project at Nuagaon–Gobindpur Border (29 February 2012)

[F] After Interview with a Group of Female Villagers in Gobindpur (7 October 2012)

[G] Paradip Port Advertisement (6 October 2012)

[H] Villagers in Gobindpur Threatened by PPSS and its Militant Group (7 October 2012)

Samiti (PPSS) [POSCO protest battle committee]. The PPSS was organised and led by Abhay Sahu, a Communist Party of India cadre (Illustration 6.1 [B]). At that point of my second visit, Abhay Sahu was in jail in Cuttack on charges of violence against villagers because he led a militant group during protests against the project.[17] Despite the larger number in the supporting group, the opposition group had occupied all the *pan* cultivation lands. The opposition group of villagers made an alliance with a militant group led by the PPSS and evicted neighbours who were supporting the POSCO project from their homes and lands. Many of the evicted villagers (preferably called 'displaced' villagers), who were staying in a transit camp in Nuagaon built by POSCO (Illustration 6.1 [C] and [D]), said that they could not imagine that their homes and livelihood had been taken by their neighbours with whom they had long cultivated *pan* together. A villager in the transit camp said, 'Many of the villagers were supporting the project, and we wanted to get economic compensation at the initial stage when we heard POSCO would come to our village'.[18] He meant that there was a substantially large group of villagers who willingly wanted to sell their lands for the project, which challenges previous observations on land struggles.

The PPSS led by Abhay Sahu and its militant group began mobilising villagers to oppose POSCO's steel project when the plan was announced in 2005. In particular, Gobindpur and Dhinkia, two villages where the anti-POSCO protests were intense, played an important role as a base camp for PPSS and its nexus with militant group.[19] Prashant Paikaray, the spokesperson of PPSS, put it: 'People have rights for their lands and water. They have rights to democratic fights for displacement'.[20] When asked about the influence of Naxalites on such protests in Odisha, Paikaray alleged that the state and POSCO instigated the violence.[21] Some other activists from PPSS also insisted that POSCO

---

[17] Abhay Sahu was in jail from 25 November 2012 to March 2013. He was again arrested on 11 May 2013 under the charge of murder, criminal conspiracy, and causing explosion which was likely to endanger life.

[18] Interviews in the POSCO-India transit camp on 29 February 2012; interviews in Dhinkia and Gobindpur on 6 October 2012. Several villagers said that PPSS had a close connection with left-wing extremists like Maoists and Naxalites.

[19] Abhay Sahu's son, Bapi Sahu was also with the PPSS group staying in Gobindpur. Interview on 29 February 2012. In October 2012, I tried to meet Bapi Sahu again at the Paradip port. However, he did not appear on the appointment date.

[20] Interview in Bhubaneswar on 3 October 2012.

[21] According to villagers in Gobindpur and Nuagaon, there was firing by the police from which an activist died in PPSS. It happened when a local construction company led by Bapi Sarkhel was building roads at the entrance to Nuagaon village. The road building was part of the FDI project in order to establish infrastructure before the process of land acquisition.

intentionally encouraged conflicts between the two groups of villagers in Kujang.[22] One of them said, 'POSCO has used the strategy of "divide and rule" in the villages by recognising the villagers as either supporters or opponents'.[23] However, the activist could not articulate how the divide and rule strategy worked for the citizens.

Their mobilisation seemed quite strong when other NGOs supported the protests, but it dwindled after a while. During my first visit to the three villages in February 2012, most of the Gobindpur villagers as well as Dhinkia villagers were hostile towards the project. Since then, the villagers in Gobindpur had slowly changed their minds to support the project. Many of them mentioned two reasons for the change: the violent nature of the mobilisation by PPSS and its nexus with a militant group, and a substantial compensation package offered by POSCO. The militant group kept forcing villagers to join its anti-POSCO protests. Most of the villagers who did not join the protests were threatened, and some of them were severely injured. The threatened villagers slowly changed their minds when Abhay Sahu was put in jail. A displaced villager said, 'The *goonda* [militant group] committed terrible outrage to villagers and sexual assault to some female villagers. My daughter was also about to be a victim. I feel indignation whenever I am reminded of the day (Illustration 6.1 [F])'.[24] Several other injured villagers in Gobindpur also told me about dreadful experiences with the militant group.[25] A villager said:

> Now, how much our village would develop through this POSCO project does little matter for us who were suffering enough from the *goonda*. We were fighting against them and their exploitation. The *goonda* collected 5,000 Indian rupees from each of the supporters of POSCO project in our village, as we were not joining his anti-POSCO protests (Illustration 6.1 [H]).

Meanwhile, land value has risen considerably. The anti-POSCO protest has prohibited land acquisition being pursued by the Industrial Infrastructure

---

However, people working for the local constructor were deterred by violent protests led by an anti-POSCO group from PPSS. A villager in Gobindpur, who saw a member of PPSS carrying bombs to deter the local constructor, called the police. The violent protests by PPSS and its militant group resulted in the police firing.

[22] Interview on 29 February 2012.

[23] I would like to thank Sarbeswar Sahoo in IIT Delhi for translating my conversation with activists into English.

[24] Interview on 29 February 2012. Regarding the sexual violence committed by the militant group, I had another group interview with female villagers in Gobindpur on 7 October 2012.

[25] Interviews on 6 and 7 October 2012.

Development Corporation (IDCO) (Illustration 6.1 [E]), a state agency that has a role in acquiring lands for industrial development in Odisha.

Weak state in bargaining with protesters

Despite the strong resistance by protesters, the discussion here raises a critical question on the role of the state: what did the state of Odisha do to pacify the social conflicts? The question addresses the state's weak ability in bargaining with the protesters. It substantially stems from the inefficient and less knowledgeable bureaucracy. The bureaucrats of state agencies in Odisha neglected procedures to request POSCO to acquire consent from the villagers in Kujang *tehsil* in the process of land acquisition.[26] According to an executive committee that conducted an inquiry into the status of the Forest Rights Act (FRA) for the POSCO project at the request of the Ministry of Environment and Forests:

> The district administration of Jagatsinghpur has not been fair and democratic in implementing the FRA in the project-affected villages perhaps for two reasons: (1) a number of villagers, specially of Dhinkia, have been opposing the setting up of the POSCO steel plant from the day (June 2005) when MOU was signed between Orissa government and POSCO and (2) the district administration wanted the project area to be free from such rights for smooth taking over … Odisha government must initiate implementation of the FRA process afresh in the project area in a transparent and democratic way and ensure the settling of individual and community rights as per the provisions of the Forest Rights Act and Rules made therein.[27]

Saila Suresh, a judge in the Madras High Court, agreed with this point of view by pointing that protests by society against the project resulted from the 'breakdown of law and order' approach by the state.[28]

Bureaucrats in the administration of land acquisition in Odisha did not seem to give enough commitment for making the project work. S. K. Mallick, Jagatsinghpur Collector, underlined the difficulties of negotiating with villagers in Kujang *tehsil* for the POSCO project.[29] By indicating the absence of bureaucratic professionalism and accountability in Odisha, P. K. Jena, former Chairman-

---

[26] See GOI (2010d); Pingle, Pandey, Suresh (2010).
[27] Pingle et al. (2010), 3–5. See also GOI (2010b).
[28] Interview in Chennai on 2 February 2012. Saila Suresh is the wife of V. Suresh, who was one of the three members that examined POSCO's steel plant project at the request of the MOEF.
[29] Phone interview on 16 October 2012.

cum-Managing Director in IDCO in charge of land acquisition for the POSCO project for a year, said how he developed strategies to make the investment projects work. He said:

> When I was appointed to this position, I was surprised to know that *no bureaucrat in IDCO tried to communicate with villagers* in Kujang (emphasis added). Twenty years back, I had the experience of displacing 25,000 people without using any single police force. I urged my deputy to use my own knowledge and experiences to solve the land acquisition problems regarding the POSCO project. And we opened up all issues to the public in the villages (of Kujang tehsil). Even if there is opposition, they must have some viewpoints. We talked with individuals and listened to them about their problems. We do not want to establish industry and do nothing. In four months after we talked to them, the number of protesters dramatically decreased.[30]

In a similar context of the negative impact of the unprofessional nature of state administration on industrial progress, Chandra (2008) explained the misconceived strategies of the state government led to the failure of investment project from TATA in Singur in West Bengal. Chandra mentioned that lack of scrutiny was observed on various matters in the process of land acquisition, such as fixing the land value and the compensation formula. A strong message implicated in Chandra's research was that such misconceived strategies ended up bringing pauperisation rather than industrialisation to Singur. In other words, like the failure of the TATA project in Singur, the slow progress of the POSCO project was influenced considerably by the inefficiency of bureaucrats and their misguidance.

The state of Odisha has shown weak capacity in dealing with international NGOs and local journalists that block the POSCO project. Several bureaucrats in state agencies and foreign investors from POSCO indicated in common as another challenge to overcome in the process of land acquisition. P. K. Jena in IDCO said, 'There is an international dimension with the perspective of NGOs regarding the POSCO project'.[31] In fact, many international NGOs were mobilised by local activists in India, and the mobilisation considerably influenced the delay in embarkation of the project. In May 2013, the challenge remained even though the judgement by the Supreme Court of India recommended that the central government should decide to grant POSCO India the PL for the Khandadhar

---

[30] Interview at IDCO in Bhubaneswar on 4 October 2012. P. K. Jena happened to be in a meeting with two officials from POSCO-India when I arrived at his office for an interview.

[31] Interview on 4 October 2012.

mines. When the judgement was announced in favour of POSCO, a Vice-President of POSCO put it, 'Now we have another challenge to overcome once more, which is the anti-POSCO protest from international NGOs that have a strong tie with activists in India'.[32] Prafula Samantrai, an activist based in Bhubaneswar who was involved with several NGOs for the anti-POSCO protests, said, 'We have opposed globalisation. Globalisation hurts the livelihood and culture of our tribals. We have deployed anti-globalisation campaigns in four countries. The FDI project by POSCO also needs to be understood in this context'.[33]

In addition, a journalist from OTV (Odisha TV) agreed that the reports from local journalists over the issue of anti-industrialisation protests in Odisha were lopsided and idle, saying, 'I agree with you. Regarding the POSCO issues, the local media is not presenting the facts on the ground. In large-scale investments like it, the local media might be in favour of the poor because many village labourers without skill and education are the most vulnerable and they are not able to get any compensation'.[34] Interestingly, the weak ability of Odisha in bargaining with the local media and the international NGOs is in remarkable contrast to that of Tamil Nadu discussed in a previous chapter of this book.

The findings collected from the POSCO project discussed above and the TATA project that will be dealt with in the next part of this chapter emphasise the negative intervention of political organisations that have not seized power and their role in the industrial progress of Odisha. Many of them have used the discourse of 'displacing *adivasis* [tribals]' in the context of 'development-induced displacement' in order to oppose investment projects including FDI inflows. For example, the anti-POSCO protest was misled by protesters who identified the POSCO project as the issue of displacing tribals. The POSCO project was, however, irrelevant to the tribal discourse because not a single tribal was affected by the investment.[35] This misleading discourse, in fact, is deeply associated with the division of citizens that was discussed in detail in the previous chapter. As observed by several researchers,[36] tribals have lost their shelter and livelihood in the process of industrialisation in Odisha.

The next part of this chapter discusses the recent struggles of Odisha in attempting to improve its strategies for bargaining with protesters through the case of TATA's investment project in Kalinga Nagar.

---

[32] Phone interview on 23 May 2013.
[33] Interview at his residence in Bhubaneswar on 16 October 2012.
[34] Email correspondence on 26 October 2012.
[35] See GOI (2010c; 2010d; 2011c).
[36] Chatterji (2009); Nayak (2010); Padel (2010a; 2010b).

Political Economy of a Large-Scale Investment by TATA
State struggles to build close ties with capital and citizens in Kalinga Nagar

TATA, formerly the Tata Iron and Steel Company, was registered in Bombay in August 1907 under J. N. Tata's business leadership. As one of the world's most geographically-diversified steel producers, it has operations in twenty-six countries and a commercial presence in over fifty countries. In 2004, TATA signed an MOU with the government of Odisha to establish a 6 MTPA integrated steel plan in the Kalinga Nagar Industrial Complex.

However, TATA, like POSCO, also had difficulties in embarking on its investment project due to strong protests from the society. The villagers, mostly Munda tribals whose livelihood and shelter were affected in the process of land acquisition for the project, opposed TATA's steel project. During the protests that were at a peak in January 2006, a dozen of villagers were killed by police firing, and protests became more intense after the incident. The protests involved Maoist organisations as well as several other social activists from all over India.[37] The Maoists' violence and threats targeted bureaucrats and political elites of Odisha in order to block the TATA project. Medha Patkar, a well-known activist who led the Narmada Bachao Andolan (Narmada rescue movement), also visited Kalinga Nagar to support the anti-TATA protests. She said:

> The tribals are the rightful owners of the land and they cannot be displaced ... The government must put in place a proper rehabilitation and resettlement policy that would be acceptable to all sections of society before allowing industrialisation to take place in tribal areas.[38]

Prashant Paikaray, spokesperson for PPSS, also strongly supported the protests of villagers by putting it:

> Government is trying to exercise compelling power, state violence. But the result is people are suffering. See, killing of tribals in Kalinga Nagar was also by the police force. But there was no inquiry about the firing. We will be responsible for finding whose fault it was.[39]

---

[37] *Hindustan Times*, 'Maoist Torch Vehicles in Orissa's Mining Belt,' 13 September 2006; 'Orissa Kidnapped Officials Appeal to Patnaik,' 30 March 2006, 'Orissa Tribals Get Medha Patkar's Backing,' 12 February 2006, accessed 30 May 2013. See also Bisheshwar Mishra, 'Kalinga Nagar Tribals to Continue Agitation,' *The Times of India*, 24 April 2006, accessed 30 May 2013.
[38] *Hindustan Times*, 'Orissa Tribals,' ibid.
[39] Interview on 3 October 2012.

In fact, such tribal discourse developed while several investment projects to build dams and steel plants were embarked on the state. The Rourkela steel project is a well-known example. Meher (2004) stressed the tribal-dominated nature of the city of Rourkela where the first steel plant was embarked on by the state of Odisha in the late 1950s. In the study on the Rourkela steel project, Meher discussed what kinds of ecological, societal, and economic impacts the investment project had. Meher indicated that the project had both positive and negative effects by arguing that the project failed in the sense that the project was insensitive about poor and migrant workers as well as proper environmental auditing that resulted in negative impacts on the tribals. Meher also pointed out that the project played a large role in boosting urban industrial culture and the economic growth of the city. Interestingly, Meher's work clearly demonstrated that the growth of urban industrial culture 'reduced the social barriers and interaction patterns, cutting across caste, community, language and region', although the middlemen and contractors play an important role in recruiting labourers mainly based on caste affiliations and their social networks.[40] Like the Rourkela project, TATA's investment got attention on the issue of displacing tribals.

When I visited Kalinga Nagar in October 2012, the TATA project was being implemented after the seven years of persistent conflicts between protesters and supporters.[41] From Jajpur Road, which is connected to the TATA project site, I could see many other steel factories built by India's domestic investors like Jindal. The nearby area of Kalinga Nagar was, in fact, specially designed for developing the steel industry of the state by Biju Patnaik. Abhay, a twenty-one-year-old supervisor for daily workers in the TATA project, whom I met at one of the TATA transit camps and who volunteered to guide me to the construction site, had the job of checking the attendance of workers and distributing daily wages to them. Most of the daily workers were not only healthy men and women but also the old who had lost their lands or livelihood to the project. Several groups of female workers, 100 or so in total, were sitting under the trees near the construction site. When asked about their work on the investment project, a female worker said, 'We do not have any special work here. We just come here every day in the morning and go back our homes (in TATA transit camps) in the afternoon'.[42] Their work was a sort of human barricade that protected the construction site from strangers, by watching and surrounding it. As Abhay put it:

---

[40] Meher (2004), 217.
[41] I would like to thank Abhay and Murtyajaya. Murtyajaya helped me communicate with daily workers at the TATA project site in Kalinga Nagar and villagers in Chandia in Odia.
[42] Interview on 10 October 2012.

These female workers do not have special skills for the construction. But TATA pays them 130 Indian rupees per day if they come here and spend a few hours. The company buses pick them up in their villages, where TATA transit camps and *parivar* [family] colony which is a permanent house block for the displaced villagers are located, in the morning and drop them at the same place in the afternoon.[43]

Many of the daily workers seemed satisfied with the TATA project. The majority of them indicated a new shelter, economic compensation, and work provided by the company as critical factors for their satisfaction. The daily workers were from the TATA transit camps and its *parivar* colony that was located in villages Dandagadi and Trijanga at Jajpur Road. The displaced villagers were supposed to stay in the transit camps while permanent house blocks were being built in the *parivar* colonies. The majority of residents in the transit camps and colonies were Munda tribals who were displaced from their villages and forests where the TATA project took over their lands. Abhay was also staying in one of the transit camps in Dandagadi with his family. Abhay's mother seemed to be very proud of her son working for the project. His family brought me to his uncle's new house that was being built by TATA as part of the compensation for paddy fields they sold.[44] His uncle's family was content with their new house and the compensation package that TATA provided. His uncle mentioned, 'We too opposed TATA initially in 2006 like many of our neighbours. But we are now very happy (with what we have obtained as compensation) and we support TATA'.

Surprisingly, through intensive interviews with the displaced villagers, it was found that the majority of displaced villagers residing in another transit camp and the *parivar* colony seemed also content with TATA's compensation, even though some bargaining was still ongoing between the displaced villagers and TATA. The ongoing negotiations were about an increase in economic compensation and employment for those who had not been hired for the construction.[45] A displaced villager in Dandagadi said, 'Now my son and I have work to do in TATA. We are happy with our work even though we lost our forefather's land'.

The state of Odisha and TATA seemed to work more closely than earlier to make the project work and satisfy the displaced citizens.[46] In a transit camp in Dandagadi, for example, the management of TATA's rehabilitation package was

---

[43] Interview on 10 October 2012.

[44] I visited the two transit camps and one parivar colony (permanent house block) for interviews with displaced villagers from the TATA project on 9 October 2012.

[45] The compensation package TATA provided included compulsory employment (one person per household), economic compensation according to the size of sold lands, and housing (permanent joint house that costs 250 thousand Indian rupees per three joint unit).

[46] Interviews with the managers of TATA's transit camp in Dandagadi on 9 October 2012.

organised by cooperation between the state and the company. Three managers, who were hired by TATA, came to the camp every day to check for problems with the displaced villagers staying in the camp. It was surprising to learn that they knew the financial status of every individual in the camp. A female manager said:

> One of the displaced people here squandered the compensation money on gambling and drinking at once on the next day after he got the money. Most of the people here do not know how to save and use such big money. We discussed this issue with TATA and helped him to get additional compensation and extra care from us. We pay attention to the financial management of people here because we do not want these people to use up their compensation money in wrong ways.

In a small room of the transit camp, a training program was being conducted. Seven female villagers were learning how to use a sewing machine. When asked about the programme, a manager replied that it was one of the company's programmes for empowering women and helping them to become self-employed. Also, the state and the company needed to be allied in the process of pacifying the anti-TATA protests. First, Tata had to design a better compensation package than that given earlier by other companies to the displaced citizens, while the state of Odisha used compelling power over the protest groups.[47] This is interestingly similar to the strategies used by the state of Tamil Nadu to make the anti-Michelin protesters change their attitude towards supporting Michelin's FDI project, as discussed in a previous chapter of this book. Abhay Kujur, who was involved in the TATA project and rehabilitation programmes for displaced villagers in Kalinga Nagar as an industrial relations manager for TATA, put it:

> Land acquisition process usually takes a long time from one year to four or five years. It is thus important to take care of the displaced people for this long time. For our case, people those who have given their lands to us think themselves as part of progress (for development in this area). The majority of workers in our construction site are Odia, local people. Although they were opposing our project for long, now they are happy, thanks to our job offer and compensation. Not only the local Odias but also many others from other states like Bihar and West Bengal are also working here.[48]

The findings from TATA's investment project were confusing, as they described the nature of state–society relations as an inclusive one. It was a clear contrast of

---

[47] Interview with T. Ramachandru, serving as the chairman-cum-Managing Director of IDCOL, at IDCOL in Bhubaneswar on 4 October 2012. See also Senapati (2013).
[48] Interview at the Duburi office of TATA Steel in Jajpur on 10 October 2012.

that found in POSCO's steel project. Is the state of Odisha transforming? The Odisha Resettlement and Rehabilitation Policy (ORRP) was introduced in 2006 when the anti-TATA protests reached the climax after a dozen of tribals were victimised by a police firing.[49] According to the government of Odisha, the policy's primary objectives were 'to avoid displacement wherever possible and minimise it exercising available options otherwise; to recognise voices of displaced communities emphasising the needs of the indigenous communities and vulnerable sections; to ensure environmental sustainability through participatory and transparent process; and to help guiding the process of developing institutional mechanism for implementation, monitoring, conflict resolution, and grievance redress'.[50]

Divided citizens and their needs for employment in Odisha

Although TATA began building plants in acquired lands, Kalinga Nagar was still divided into two groups like those of Kujang *tehsil* where the POSCO project was proposed. In contrast to villagers who stayed in the transit camps and worked for the TATA project, there were some villagers in Kalinga Nagar who opposed the project. The majority of villagers in Chandia, mostly Munda tribals, were the anti-TATA group. Four to five other villages that opposed the project were located near the TATA construction site.[51] The hostility of the villagers towards strangers was quite strong. When I managed to talk with some villagers in Chandia and asked about whether the state of Odisha helped their protests, an angered villager said, 'This is not a fault of the government of Odisha but of globalisation which has ugly faces. It changes and destroys our tribal system'.[52] Other activists residing in Odisha, such as Mayadhar Nayak, the author of *Land to Let* (2010), and Sudhir Pattnaik, the editor of *Samadrusti* [equal sight in Odia], an Odia magazine on human rights, also highlighted the impact of industrialisation and globalisation on the agricultural system of tribals and nature.[53] Like many others who have discussed the social conflicts between the state and the displaced tribals, Sahu (2008) demonstrated how the government of Odisha's strong support of Vedanta's FDI project encroached on the livelihood of Dongria Kondh tribals and their culture in Niyamgiri hills.[54]

---

[49] See GOOD (2006). The ORRP was initially designed in November 2005 for villagers displaced by the Tata investment in Kalinga Nagar.
[50] Ibid.
[51] I visited Chandia and some other villages on 10 October 2012.
[52] Interviews on 10 October 2012.
[53] Interviews with Sudhir Pattnaik at the head office of Samadrusti at Bhubaneswar on 15 October and with Mayadhar Nayak in Bhubaneswar on 21 October 2012.
[54] See also Padel and Das (2010).

Despite the ongoing debate and conflicts between the supporters and protesters of the large-scale investment projects in Odisha, an increasing number of citizens encourage such projects, substantially due to the possibility of employment. For example, within the village of Chandia, there were some people who wanted to join the TATA project. A young man said, 'I really wanted to work and make money. I met TATA people but they did not accept me because I am from Chandia (where many landowners do not sell their lands to TATA as they strongly oppose the project)'.[55] The man's family living below poverty line was depending on 100 Indian rupees, which was their daily income from selling *handia* [traditional Odia liquor]. He mentioned that he was looking forward to another chance to join as a daily worker in the TATA project. A migrant worker from a village in Karanjia that is around 150 km from the construction site also presented his support of the project. He was renting a room in Chandia and lived with his wife and an infant while working for the TATA project. He said, 'My contract is for a month. I came here with all my family because I needed work to do. I am working every day and night without holidays to earn more money. I am happy now, but I want to work longer'.[56] He was getting 130 Indian rupees for 8 hours of work and an additional 20 rupees per hour for overtime.

To sum up, the observations from Kalinga Nagar are likely to suggest that citizens in Odisha, particularly those in the marginalised groups, are primarily concerned about their employment when they negotiate with the state and capital in the investment projects that affect their livelihood. The preceding chapter of this book has pointed to a close relation between the low level of employment and the active participation of the unemployed in opposing the state-led industrial development. In fact, Odisha is one of the low-income states with a high rate of unemployment. According to the Planning Commission (2003),

> The rate of open unemployment is the highest in Orissa among the low-income states; the degree of visible underemployment is again higher in Orissa than for other low-income states and all-India, and this is observed both for male and female workers and also in both rural and urban areas.[57]

One of the impending tasks for the Government of Odisha would be to tackle the unemployment problem, given that the unemployed and the uneducated have been easily mobilised by the political extremists for opposing state-led industrialisation.

---

[55] Interview on 10 October 2012.
[56] Interview on 10 October 2012.
[57] The Planning Commission (2001), iv–v.

Conclusion

The primary aim of this chapter was to discuss the weak ability of state in Odisha in making FDI work by addressing the relations between the state, society, and foreign capital at the village level in the process of large-scale investments. Findings collected from two cases – POSCO's and TATA's steel investment projects – strongly support the arguments underlined in the preceding chapter of this book. One of the main arguments highlighted here was that the exclusionary pattern of the state–society relations substantially contributed to the lower level of FDI inflows. The exclusionary relations were observed in the lack of commitment by the state in bargaining with protesters who oppose the state-led industrialisation. Even though the two projects examined in this chapter had an extractive nature of the investment, like many other projects embarked on for industrialisation in Odisha, the discussion here focused on inefficient and less knowledgeable bureaucrats in implementing industrial strategies.

Also, a dearth of commitment by the state was also observed in providing citizens with security and protecting them against the influence of communist parties and left-wing extremists and their violent mobilisation for opposing state-led industrialisation. It was an another aim of this chapter to present how the communist parties and their alliance with the militant group of political extremists politicised the issues of development-induced displacement and divided citizens. It was found that the land struggles between the state, society, and foreign capital in Odisha have been highly politicised by various interest groups. In particular, the exclusionary relations between the state and society of Odisha are in clear contrast with those of Tamil Nadu that were discussed in several preceding chapters.

Despite the severe protests, it was found that the number of citizens in Odisha who support large-scale investment projects seems to be increasing, substantially due to their expectation of not only economic compensation but also employment. The employment opportunities and recent efforts by the state to cooperate with the private sector in providing welfare schemes for people displaced by industrialisation tend to make protesters shift their attitudes towards favouring investments. It is yet unclear, however, whether the exclusionary pattern of the state–society relations in the state would change towards an inclusionary nature like that of Tamil Nadu.

7

Conclusion

This book began with an empirical puzzle of how some states in India have facilitated FDI inflows better than others. Building upon the empirical evidence, the book addressed the regional variations of FDI inflows across states in India as a central question. It sought to answer the question by examining the relationships between the state, society, and foreign capital in two select provincial states of India, namely, Tamil Nadu and Odisha. Following an interdisciplinary approach and analysing data collected through fieldwork, it examined the socio–political factors that shaped the disparate levels of FDI inflows into the states. In particular, it emphasised the causal role of differing state–society relations in the evolution of institutions facilitating and regulating FDI inflows in the two states. The primary objective of this book is to understand the significant roles of socio–political factors, such as the ideas and interests of actors in restructuring institutions favouring FDI inflows. Another aim was to explain the dissimilar patterns of such institutional change both at the union and state levels.

Not only at the central government but also in the two states, it was found that the ideas of key policy-makers on the need for foreign capital as important financial resources critically influenced the institutional changes favouring FDI inflows in the process of industrial development. It is worth noting that the year 1967 was a key turning point for Tamil Nadu and Odisha during which regional political parties won the state legislative assembly elections and had a chance to capitalise on citizenship politics. In both states, the financial difficulties of the 1970s helped the state leaders consider foreign investments as significant financial resources. However, such ideas were implemented with a great difference in the two states. In Tamil Nadu, the state agencies playing roles in promoting industrial development and inclusionary policies that were protecting the rights of marginalised citizens developed incrementally throughout the 1970s and 1980s. With regard to state agencies and policies that began involving FDI inflows actively during the post-reform period after 1991, the state of Tamil Nadu was much better prepared than many other states for institutional change favouring FDI inflows. This book highlighted that the nature of inclusionary state–society relationship was a critical source of producing a higher level of FDI inflows in Tamil Nadu. In Odisha, on the other hand, the neo-patrimonial nature of the state and higher level of social conflict acted as barriers to FDI inflows. Although Biju Patnaik as the Minister of Steel and Mines at the union level conceived ideas favouring FDI inflows and industrial development in Odisha's steel industry in the early 1970s, his ideas failed to be realised for several socio–political reasons. The details of highlights, significance, limitations, and recommendations made in the book are as follows.

First, the pattern of institutional change favouring FDI inflows at the union level in India was examined in Chapter 2. The discussion focused on the interplay between two socio–political variables – ideas of key policy-makers about economic reforms favouring FDI inflows and various interest groups not only from the society but also from the central government supporting and opposing reforms – and their roles in the institutional change. On the basis of policy regime, the discussion demarcated three different periods: anti-FDI (1969–75), selective FDI (1975–91), and pro-FDI (after 1991). It presented how Foreign Investment Promotion Board, a critical state agency promoting FDI inflows at the union level, was used by policy-makers in two key ministries as a means of political tussle. It was an innovative attempt to suggest the larger pattern of FDI inflows by tracing political events and analysing institutional arrangements.

Another significant finding was that the patterns of institutional change in Tamil Nadu and Odisha were not identical with that of the central government. The discussions in Chapters 3 and 5 found that the economic institutions favouring FDI inflows in both the states did not evolve through three phases of FDI regime change – anti-FDI, selective, and pro-FDI – similar to the case of the central government. For both Tamil Nadu and Odisha, the institutions developed after the economic reforms of the central government in 1991. In other words, there was no anti-FDI period which the central government underwent from 1969 to 1975. It was because there was no clear concept of foreign investments for provincial states since the central government had only the power to facilitate or regulate FDI inflows until the reforms of 1991. When the central government announced economic reforms in 1991, however, Tamil Nadu could more actively promote foreign investments than other states like Odisha. The discussions in this book addressed several causal factors that made Tamil Nadu do so. The comparison presented how provincial states of India responded differently to the economic reforms of the central government favouring FDI inflows.

Following the same method used for looking at the institutional change at the union level, the discussion in Chapter 3 paid attention to socio–political factors in restructuring institutions favouring FDI inflows in Tamil Nadu. It was found that the ideas of political leaders in the state on the need for foreign capital evolved after the year 1967 when the bipartisan politics was initiated by two regional Dravidian parties, Dravida Munnetra Kazhagam (DMK), and All India Anna

Dravida Munnetra Kazhagam (AIADMK). Key political leaders in the two parties could consistently pursue industrial development by securing financial resources substantially from foreign capital due to the politically alienated relations with the central government and its poor financial assistance.

Two different types of ideas affected the institutional change favouring FDI inflows in Tamil Nadu. One was for industrialisation and foreign capital. Another one was concerned about inclusion. Both the ideas were consistently pursued by different ruling parties in the process of industrialisation throughout the 1970s, 1980s, 1990s, and finally in the post-reform period. Under economic uncertainty and financial deficit at the central government in the 1970s, the state of Tamil Nadu welcomed financial aid from multilateral organisations like World Bank and International Monetary Fund. Such financial aid was very helpful for the state to pursue industrialisation and urbanisation in the 1980s. Ideas favouring foreign capital already existed, and also the state–society relations were conducive to the state-led industrialisation. Therefore, the state of Tamil Nadu obtained legitimacy from citizens to pursue its ideas favouring FDI. Even though there were some sporadic protests against the state-led industrialisation and FDI projects, such interests were muted by the inclusionary state–society relationship. I argued that the social inclusion, which has a significant role of managing social conflicts, could help the state garner legitimacy to pursue state goals for industrialisation. The social inclusion was found in land reforms, public distribution, education, health services, and employment that state leaders concerned. It pointed to the nature of developmental state that led Tamil Nadu to accumulate substantial private capital for its industrial development. These significant findings provided a causal link between the role of social inclusion and a higher level of FDI inflows to Tamil Nadu. Historical explanations about the lower caste base of the Dravidian parties also supported the link. The idea of political leaders favouring FDI inflows was continuously pursued by different ruling parties and state agencies that playing roles of promoting FDI inflows could evolve incrementally in Tamil Nadu.

Through the reform in 1991, various policies were set up regarding FDI in the state of Tamil Nadu, driven by the central government's liberalisation and inclusionary state–society relationship. Similar to the case of the central government, the 1991 reform brought further change to Tamil Nadu. First, the role of State Industries Promotion Corporation of Tamil Nadu was extended to acquire lands for foreign investors. Second, GUIDANCE was set up in 1993 to promote FDI. Third, Acquisition Lands for Industrial Purposes Act was introduced in 1997 for making land acquisition for the FDI easier. Therefore, the institutions were reproduced and adapted after 1991 in a way that existing ideas on industrialisation and private investment strongly drove the institutional change favouring FDI. The muted interests from the society in Tamil Nadu supported the change while the interest group against FDI inflows at the union level was quite strong. It made the institutional change incremental in Tamil Nadu.

The causal linkage between the inclusionary state–society relationship, strong state capacity, and a high level of FDI inflows in Tamil Nadu is shown in Figure 7.1. The inclusionary idea of political leaders promoted skill-oriented education. The skilled labour produced from the skill-oriented education sector could be easily absorbed into Tamil Nadu's industry. The labour absorption resulted in the lower rate of unemployment. In addition, the inclusionary idea produced the high literacy rate of 80.3 per cent as India's 2011 Census indicated. It also influenced the method of tax collection in Tamil Nadu. For example, urban land owners were imposed higher tax rates than the landless compared with other states. The inclusionary ideas of political leaders structured political parties on the basis of the marginalised groups. The grassroots-based parties could enhance the tight-knit party organisation. The grassroots-based parties could establish the legitimacy of pursuing investment-friendly ideas from different ruling parties, as citizens strongly supported such ideas for the state-led industrialisation.

Three significant factors supported the investment-friendly ideas (Figure 7.1). First, the nature of the developmental state in Tamil Nadu, which has a strong tie to its industry, was conducive to the investment-friendly institutional arrangements. Here, the inclusionary state–society relations helped the state bargain with interest groups in the society that were against the state-led industrialisation. Second, financial difficulties that substantially resulted from the weak centre–state relations made the key state leaders in Tamil Nadu encourage large-scale investments in the state. Third, the need for foreign technology for Tamil Nadu's industry pushed it to maintain investment-friendly ideas from different ruling parties. In addition, knowledgeable and efficient bureaucratic capacity had a role in pursuing coherent state strategies towards industrialisation. In the process of industrialisation, land reforms based on inclusionary ideas were relatively successful than those of Odisha. The land reforms helped the state pursue land acquisition efficiently. The efficient and speedy process of land acquisition, in turn, resulted in the high level of FDI inflows in Tamil Nadu.

As a supplementary research supporting the arguments listed above, this book also presented how the state of Tamil Nadu encouraged FDI inflows by looking at two investment projects embarked upon in the field. On the basis of empirical evidence collected from the two FDI projects initiated by Hyundai Motor India and Michelin India, the discussion in Chapter 4 showed how the tripartite alliance between the state, bureaucrats, and foreign capital contributed to the substantial growth of FDI inflows in Tamil Nadu, despite sporadic agitations from the society against the state-led industrialisation. Findings supported that the consistent ideas of state leaders on the need for foreign capital and social inclusion have made FDI inflows work in the state. Citizens supported the large-scale investments like FDI inflows when the state provided substantial employment and education in the process of industrialisation. This explanatory variable, the inclusionary pattern of state–society relationship, has helped citizens not to ally with opposition groups against FDI inflows that are usually based on the left-wing political parties. However, it was also found that the state of Tamil Nadu sometimes used its coercive power for pacifying protests from the society and labour disputes that occurred in foreign companies. Workers hired by foreign companies in the state not only seemed to be highly satisfied with their job but also presented support of their companies, though they sometimes tried to bargain with foreign management through strikes for higher wages and promotion. Furthermore, bureaucrats in the state agencies were found to be proficient in dealing with the protests from society against FDI inflows and acquiring lands for large-scale investments. The efficient, knowledgeable, and coherent administrative organisation of Tamil Nadu has been another critical source that enables it to intervene economic affairs autonomously and realise its goals.

Compared to Tamil Nadu, the new norm and belief on foreign investments were realised in Odisha at a much later stage. For example, Biju Patnaik wanted to invite foreign investments in the 1970s for boosting Odisha's steel industry. Biju Patnaik's ideas on industrialisation, private investments, and foreign investments were challenged by socio–political reasons. Despite the fiscal deficit in the 1970s in Odisha, policy-makers did not capitalise on the private-sector investment to overcome the economic crises. This was a stark difference between Tamil Nadu and Odisha. It was found that such ideas of political leaders in Odisha could not be realised due to several socio–political reasons as follows: (1) the failure of ruling parties in providing inclusionary schemes for citizens; (2) frequent regime change, political conflicts between key state leaders, and their factional politics; and (3) rent-seeking and inefficient bureaucrats that have allied with the upper-middle group of the society. In addition, this book addressed two significant societal structures that have aggravated poverty and hampered industrial development: (1) divided citizens between the coastal areas and hilly areas; and (2) social insecurity caused by the plunderous activities of left-wing extremists towards citizens. In the case of Odisha, the recent renewal of institutions was promoted by societal demands forged by left-wing parties and marginalised citizens insisting inclusionary state–society relations. The demands of the society have stressed inclusionary schemes that need to be implemented especially for those who are displaced from the process of large-scale investments embarked in the state.

Figure 7.1: Inclusionary State–Society Relations, Strong State Capacity, and High Level of FDI Inflows in Tamil Nadu

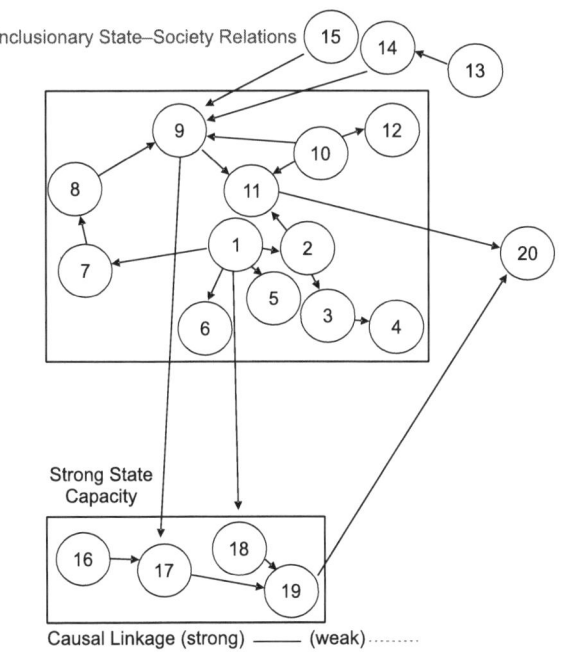

1: Inclusionary ideas. 2: Skill-oriented education (strong demand on employment). 3: Skilled labour absorption in the industry. 4: Employment rate (high). 5: Literacy rate (80.3%). 6: Tax collection (higher taxes to urban land owners). 7: Marginalised group-based political parties. 8: Tight-knit party organisation. 9: Investment-friendly ideas from different ruling parties (coherent). 10: Developmental state. 11: Investment-friendly institutional arrangements. 12: Controlled interests in the society. 13: Weak centre–state relations. 14: Financial difficulties in Tamil Nadu. 15: Need for foreign technology for Tamil Nadu's industry. 16: Bureaucratic capacity (knowledgeable and efficient). 17: State strategies towards industrialisation (coherent). 18: Land reforms (relatively successful). 19: Land acquisition for industrialisation (efficient). 20: High level of FDI inflows.

Source: Author.

Strong opposition against TATA's steel project in Kalinga Nagar was an example of the societal demands that forced the Odisha Resettlement and Rehabilitation Policy to be revised in 2006. In fact, the conflict between this state and society was at the peak in 2006 when a dozen of tribals were victimised during the anti-TATA protest that was deployed from 2000 to 2006. After the strong social protest, several institutions were introduced for smooth industrialisation. First, Odisha Resettlement and Rehabilitation Policy was revised in 2006. It promised alternative housing, livelihood, and employment to at least one member of a household displaced from the FDI process. Second, Odisha Public Private Partnership Policy was introduced in 2007 for boosting participation of the private sector in Odisha's industry. Third, Industrial Policy Resolution was made in 2007 for reducing administrative hassles and strengthening the infrastructure for foreign investments.

Figure 7.2: Exclusionary State–Society Relations, Weak State Capacity, and Low Level of FDI Inflows in Odisha

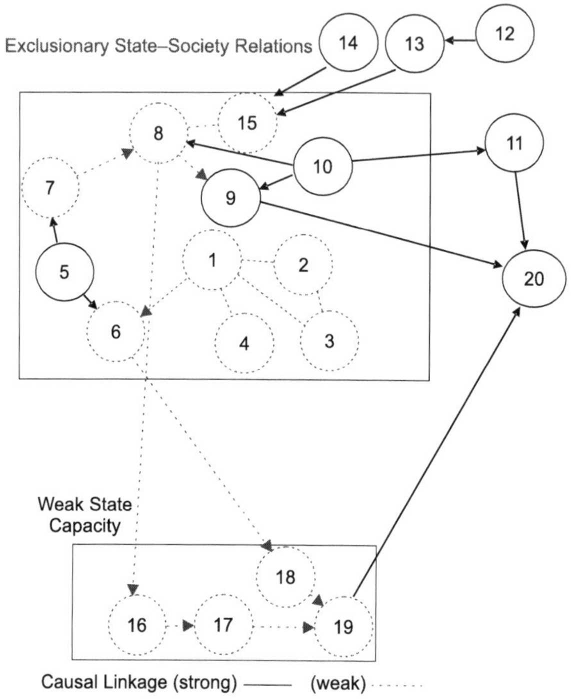

1: Inclusionary idea (absence). 2: Citizen's level of education (weak demand on employment). 3: Literacy rate (73.5%). 4: Employment rate (low). 5: Upper-middle-group–based political parties. 6: Tax collection (lower taxes to urban land owners). 7: Grassroots-level political participation and party organisation (weak). 8: Support for investment-friendly ideas from different ruling parties (weak demand on industrialisation). 9: Investment-friendly institutional arrangements (struggles). 10. Neo-patrimonial state. 11: Social opposition against the state-led industrialisation (strong tie between the left-wing parties and the marginalised groups). 12: Combative centre–state relations. 13: Financial difficulties in Odisha. 14: Need for foreign technology for Odisha's industry. 15: Pro-FDI orientation. 16: State strategies towards industrialisation (incoherent and extractive). 17: Bureaucratic capacity (knowledge-lacked, inefficient, and rent-seeking bureaucracy). 18: Land reforms (less successful). 19. Land acquisition for industrialisation (struggles). 20: Low level of FDI inflows.

Source: Author.

The causal linkage between the exclusionary state–society relationship, weak state capacity, and a low level of FDI inflows in Odisha is presented in Figure 7.2. On the contrary to the case of Tamil Nadu, the absence of inclusionary idea in Odisha generated the low level of education. The low level of education has close relations with the lower literacy rate and the higher unemployment rate than those of other states. According to the 68th round of National Sample Survey conducted from July 2011 to June 2012, the unemployment rate of Odisha was 8.7 per cent in rural areas and 5.7 per cent in urban areas. As one of the evidence of exclusionary state–society relationship, the upper-middle-group base of regional parties was also discussed. This nature influenced the method of tax collection. Unlike in Tamil Nadu, the urban land owners in Odisha were imposed the lower rate of taxes compared with those in the other states. The upper-middle-group base weakened party organisation in Odisha in which citizens of the grassroots level could hardly participate. The weak party organisation led state leaders to pay more attention to party fragmentation rather than pursuing investment-friendly ideas for the industrial development. With this lack of support, investment-friendly institutions could not develop. In addition, the nature of neo-patrimonial state provoked the marginalised groups in society, who had long been ignored regarding redistribution and rehabilitation from industrialisation. In particular, the citizens having a strong tie with the left-wing parties heavily opposed the state-led industrialisation. At the same time, the state of Odisha had combative centre–state relations especially in the late 1960s and the early 1970s when Biju Patnaik had ideas of developing Odisha's steel industry. The combative relations were not conducive to Odisha's steel industry at the incipient stage. It was because such relations influenced financial difficulties in Odisha since the financial assistance from the central government was insufficient to cover the permanent debt in Odisha in the 1970s.

Like in Tamil Nadu, in fact, the pro-FDI orientation of political leaders for Odisha's industry was substantially encouraged by the financial difficulties and need for foreign technology. It is interesting to find that the financial difficulties had an important role to promote norm and belief change favouring FDI inflows both in Tamil Nadu and Odisha. However, the two states responded very differently. In Tamil Nadu, inclusionary state–society relationship and strong state capacity accommodated FDI inflows. On the other hand, Odisha's exclusionary state–society relationship and weak state capacity acted as barriers to FDI inflows. Despite the existence of ideas favouring foreign investments, the lack of support for investment-friendly ideas from ruling parties was not helpful for industrialisation in Odisha. The state strategies for industrialisation were incoherent and extractive. The knowledge-lacked and inefficient bureaucratic capacity had limitations in pursuing land reforms successfully. Interestingly, the bureaucrats in Odisha tended to have a strong tie with the upper-middle group of the society. For example, they made land records in favour of the upper-middle group in the process of land reforms. Such process enhanced the neo-patrimonial nature of this state. Later, the unsuccessful land reforms were not helpful for industrialisation as well because the land reforms did not prioritise industrialisation and urbanisation like what Tamil Nadu did from the 1970s. It has to do with current struggles of the state from land acquisition for industrialisation. The struggles, in turn, contributed to the low level of FDI inflows in Odisha.

As a supplementary research supporting the arguments, the discussion in Chapter 6 presented how protests on the ground challenged the state of Odisha. On the basis of empirical evidence collected from two large investment projects embarked upon by POSCO and TATA, the discussion showed how and why the state of Odisha could not pursue such investments. Findings collected from the field supported that the failure of realising ideas of the state leaders on the need for industrialisation, foreign capital, and social inclusion have hindered investments in the state. It was also found that the citizens in the state were mobilised by left-wing parties and their alliance with the extremists, such as Naxalites and Maoists to oppose large-scale investments. However, the state has failed to provide the citizens security against the violent mobilisation. I argued that such failure encouraged citizens to ally with the left-wing parties and militant groups to oppose the state-led industrialisation. Historical evidence of the poor implementation of rehabilitation policies for the displaced people, who lost their livelihood and shelter in the process of industrialisation like dam building projects, supported the argument. Furthermore, it was also found that the inefficient, ill-informed, and incoherent administrative organisation substantively blocked the state from intervening economic affairs. The discussion demonstrated the explanatory variables that contributed to the lower level of FDI inflows in Odisha.

To sum up, commitment to industrialisation on the basis of ideas favouring industrial development and citizenship forming politics motivated the state of Tamil Nadu to promote the growth of FDI inflows. Tamil Nadu's exceptional autonomy from the labour class, opposition parties, and other anti-industrialisation groups in the society allowed it to dominate the formation of ties that bound capital and the state together. In Odisha, on the other hand, the lack of commitment made the state fail to accumulate FDI inflows. In addition, the lack of autonomy from the vested interest groups, the upper middle caste, and the landed class, made the state of Odisha fail to effectively intervene in the economic sphere and pursue its own goals. However, the aim of this study was not to argue that the difference of state autonomy between the two states in India generated the different levels of FDI inflows. The correlation of state autonomy with the state's ability to accumulate private capital has been already denied by Evans (1992).[1] This book affirms that view. In addition, it contrasted how the idea of state leaders favouring foreign capital produced different consequences for private capital accumulation after channelled through dissimilar societal structures. I agreed with Evans's understanding, which was that 'state structures and strategies (for industrial development) require complementary societal counterparts'.[2]

In Tamil Nadu, which was defined as the developmental state in this book, it was found that the state agencies showed extraordinary administrative capacities and played significant roles in attracting FDI.[3] Their capacities were strongly supported by the ideas of state leaders from different ruling parties as well as by the coherent and knowledgeable bureaucrats in the state agencies. Tamil Nadu had the power to selectively impose market force in the manufacturing sector, in the automobile industry in particular. In addition, it has equipped strategic necessities to make private investments as transformative projects. The strategic necessities have been realised through policies of social inclusion and ruling parties on the basis of the support of marginalised groups. The informal networks between party members, whether the party has a top-down approach (AIADMK) or a bottom-up approach (DMK) for strengthening its organisation, and tight-knit party organisation have assisted the state in consolidating citizenship politics.

In Odisha, which was defined as the neo-patrimonial state in this book, it was found that state agencies that are responsible for attracting FDI lacked administrative capacities. This lack of capacities was frequently observed in the process of land acquisition for industrial development. The informal networks have also been used by the citizens in Odisha to demand their interests. However,

---

[1] In his work *Embedded Autonomy*, Evans (1995) found that the Zairian 'predatory' state that has a patrimonial nature under Mobutu's regime had a greater autonomy from the aggregation of societal interests yet failed to enhance its capacity to pursue goals for industrial development. The state elites in Zaire not only showed rampant rent-seeking behaviours that undermined predictability of policies for private investments but also produced distorted incentives.

[2] Evans (1992), 181.

[3] This study concerns state capacity as a critical driver to lead a process of economic institutional changes to a certain result, since decisions that were made by governments should be carried through intervention that can implement the decisions in practice. Many political scientists seem to have agreed that the sources of state capacity are the efficient, knowledgeable, and coherent administrative organisation of governments in order to intervene autonomously and realise goals in the economic affairs (Skocpol 1982; Evans, Rueschmeyer, Skocpol, 1985). The discussion in this book thus also paid attention to the nature of administrative organisation of governments when comparing various levels of state capacity in intervening economic affairs and penetrating society in different provincial states of India.

informal networks in Odisha have had the nature of parochial geographic loyalties that stemmed from the patron–client relations. These informal networks did not advocate the welfare of marginalised groups. Admittedly, the organisation of political parties in Odisha has also been much weaker than that of the Dravidian parties in Tamil Nadu. Not only the Congress Party that ruled Odisha for decades but also the regional parties that could occasionally come to power struggled against intense factionalism. The ruling parties in Odisha neither had efficient cadres who can connect political leaders with the citizens nor had strong participation from the grassroots level. The absence of a concrete network did not allow the state of Odisha to assess, monitor, and shape the state leaders' responses to policy initiatives.

One key contribution of this book is that it is the first to explain economic institutional changes favouring FDI inflows in India focusing on the socio–political variables. The findings collected through in-depth fieldwork in India and South Korea are of crucial importance in providing insights on why different provincial states have shown differing patterns of FDI inflows from a comparative perspective. However, one limitation of this book is that it has given less attention to the economic variables that may also be affecting the dissimilar levels of FDI inflows among different states in India. Such economic factors were less weighed in this book. It has to be mentioned that any qualitative research could hardly consider both economic and socio–political variables, as dealing with such variables may be closely related to the methodological issues of research. However, it must be noted that economic variables drove large-scale investments in both the states. Thus, this constitutes a reasonable control for variation in economic factors. Future research is needed whether states other than Tamil Nadu and Odisha are also impacted by socio–political variables on institutional changes favouring FDI inflows. Such research could further support arguments advanced in this book. In addition, this book has provided a useful tool to look at other emerging market economies in the world that have garnered the differing levels of FDI inflows. This possible application to other emerging market economies will offer an in-depth insight to compare different relationships between the state, society, and foreign capital in the process of FDI inflows.

Bibliography

Acemoglu, Daron and James A. Robinson. 2006. 'Economic Backwardness in Political Perspective.' *American Political Science Review* 100 (1): 115-31.
Abegglen, James and Akio Etori. 1981. *The Secret of Japan's Economic Miracle*. Bombay: Centre for Monitoring Indian Economy.
Abramovitz, Moses. 1986. 'Catching Up, Forging Ahead, and Falling Behind.' *The Journal of Economic History* 46 (2): 385-406.
Agarwala, Rina. 2006. 'From Work to Welfare.' *Critical Asian Studies* 38 (4): 419-44.
———. 2008. 'Reshaping the Social Contract: Emerging Relations between the State and Informal Labor in India.' *Theory and Society* 37 (4): 375-408.
———. 2013. *Informal Labor, Formal Politics, and Dignified Discontent in India*. New York: Cambridge University Press.
Ahluwalia, Montek S. 1986. 'Balance-of-Payments Adjustment in India, 1970–71 to 1983–84.' *World Development* 14 (8): 937-62.
Amsden, Alice H. 1990. 'Third World Industrialization: "Global Fordism" or a New Model?' *New Left Review* 1 (182): 5-31.
Annavajhula, J. C. B. and Surendra Pratap. 2012. 'Workers Voices in an Auto Production Chain: Notes from the Pits of a Low Road – I.' *Economic and Political Weekly* 47 (33): 46-59.
Asiedu, Elizabeth. 2006. 'Foreign Direct Investment in Africa: The Role of Natural Resources, Market Size, Government Policy, Institutions and Political Instability.' *The World Economy* 29 (1): 63-77.
Bailey, Frederick G. 1960. *Tribe, Caste, and Nation*. Manchester: University of Manchester Press.
Banik, Dan. 2007. *Starvation and India's Democracy*. New York: Routledge.
Bardhan, Pranab. 1984. *The Political Economy of Development in India*. Delhi: Oxford University Press.
Barnett, Marguerite R. 1976. *The Politics of Cultural Nationalism in South India*. New Jersey: Princeton University Press.
Baviskar, Amita. 1995. *In the Belly of the River: Tribal Conflicts over Development in the Narmada Valley*. New Delhi: Oxford University Press.
Bernard, Mitchell and John Ravenhill. 1995. 'Beyond Product Cycles and Flying Geese: Regionalization, Hierarchy, and the Industrialization of East Asia.' *World Politics* 47 (2): 171-209.
Bhuyan, Dasarathi. 2010. *Orissa Politics from 1936 to Contemporary Politics*. Delhi: Manglam Publications.
Blyth, Mark. 2002. *Great Transformations: Economic Ideas and Institutional Change in the Twentieth Century*. New York: Cambridge University Press.

Borensztein, Eduardo, Jose De Gregorio, and Jong-Wha Lee. 1998. 'How Does Foreign Direct Investment Affect Economic Growth?' *Journal of International Economics* 45 (1): 115-35.

Bose, Prasenjit. 2010. *Maoism: A Critique from the Left*. New Delhi: LeftWord Books.

Bosworth, Barry P., Susan M. Collins, and Carmen M. Reinhart. 1999. 'Capital Flows to Developing Economies: Implications for Saving and Investment.' *Brookings Papers on Economic Activity* 1999 (1): 143-80.

Bouton, Marshall M. 1985. *Agrarian Radicalism in South India*. New Jersey: Princeton University Press.

Brunetti, Aymo and Beatrice Weder. 1998. 'Investment and Institutional Uncertainty: A Comparative Study of Different Uncertainty Measures.' *Weltwirtschftliches Archive* 134 (3): 513-33.

Bruton, Henry J. 1998. 'A Reconsideration of Import Substitution.' *Journal of Economic Literature* 36 (2): 903-36.

Burawoy, Michael. 1985. *The Politics of Production: Factory Regimes under Capitalism and Socialism*. London; New York: Verso.

Busse, Matthias and Carsten Hefeker. 2007. 'Political Risk, Institutions and Foreign Direct Investment.' *European Journal of Political Economy* 23 (2): 397-415.

Bussell, Jennifer. 2012. *Corruption and Reform in India: Public Services in the Digital Age*. Cambridge, New York: Cambridge University Press.

Büthe, Tim and Helen V. Milner. 2008. 'The Politics of Foreign Direct Investment into Developing Countries: Increasing FDI through International Trade Agreements?' *American Journal of Political Science* 52 (4): 741-62.

Cali, Kunal, Siddhartha Mitra, and Purnima Purohit. 2013. 'Measuring State-Business Relations in Indian States.' In *State-Business Relations and Economic Development in Africa and India*, edited by Kunal Sen, 35-54. New York: Routledge.

Calì, Massimiliano and Kunal Sen. 2011. 'Do Effective State Business Relations Matter for Economic Growth? Evidence from Indian States.' *World Development* 39 (9): 1542-57.

Capoccia, Giovanni and Daniel Keleman. 2007. 'The Study of Critical Junctures: Theory, Narrative, and Counterfactuals in Historical Institutionalism.' *World Politics* 59 (3): 341-69.

Cardoso, Fernando H. and Enzo Faletto. 1979. *Dependency and Development in Latin America*. Berkeley, California: University of California Press.

Chakrabarty, Bidyut and Rajut K. Kujur. 2010. *Maoism in India: Reincarnation of Ultra-Left Wing Extremism in the Twenty-First Century*. London; New York: Routledge.

Chand, Vikram K. 2010. *Public Service Delivery in India: Understanding the Reform Process*. New Delhi: Oxford University Press.

Chandra, Kanchan. 2004. *Why Ethnic Parties Succeed: Patronage and Ethnic Head Counts in India*. New York: Cambridge University Press.

Chang, Ha-Joon. 2007. *Institutional Change and Economic Development*. Tokyo; New York; Paris: United Nations University Press.

Chatterji, Angana P. 2009. *Violent Gods: Hindu Nationalism in India's Present, Narratives from Orissa*. Gurgaon: Three Essays Collective.

Chibber, Vivek. 2003. *Locked in Place: State-Building and Late Industrialization in India*. New Jersey: Princeton University Press.

Chidambaram, Palaniappan. 2007. *A View from Outside: Why Good Economics Works For Everyone*. New Delhi: Penguin.

Cohen, Stephen D. 2007. *Multinational Corporations and Foreign Direct Investment: Avoiding Simplicity, Embracing Complexity*. New York: Oxford University Press.
Cox, Ronald W. 1996. 'Explaining Business Support for Regional Trade Agreements.' In *Business and the State in International Relations*, edited by Ronald W. Cox, 109–27. Boulder: Westview Press.
Cumings, Bruce. 1984. 'The Origins and Development of the Northeast Asian Political Economy: Industrial Sectors, Product Cycles, and Political Consequences.' *International Organization* 38 (1): 1–40.
Currie, Bob. 2000. *The Politics of Hunger in India: A Study of Democracy, Governance, and Kalahandi's Poverty*. London; New York: Macmillan; St. Martin's Press.
Das, Hari H. and Bishnu C. Choudhury. 1985. 'Student Movements in Orissa: A Study of the Political Syndrome.' In *Indian State Politics: A Case Study of Orissa*, edited by A. P. Padhi, 333–50. Delhi: B. R. Publishing Corporation.
Dash, Gokulananda. 1988. *Municipal Finance in India: Based on Orissa*. New Delhi: Concept Publishing Company.
Dash, Susanta K. 2001. 'Odisha Prevention of Land Encroachment Manual.' Bhubaneswar: Odisha Law Reviews.
Dhar, P. N. 1990. *Constraints on Growth: Reflections on the Indian Experience*. Delhi: Oxford University Press.
Dutta, Ashirbani. 2007. *Development-Induced Displacement and Human Rights*. New Delhi: Deep and Deep Publications.
Encarnation, Dennis J. and Louis T. Wells Jr. 1986. 'Competition in Global Industries.' In *Competition in Global Industries*, edited by Michael E. Porter. Boston, MA: Harvard Business School Press.
Evans, Peter B. 1979. *Dependent Development: The Alliance of Multinational, State, and Local Capital in Brazil*. Princeton, NJ: Princeton University Press.
———. 1992. 'The State as Problem and Solution: Predation, Embedded Autonomy, and Structural Change.' In *The Politics of Economic Adjustment*, edited by Stephan Haggard and Robert R. Kaufman. Princeton, NJ: Princeton University Press.
———. 1995. *Embedded Autonomy: States and Industrial Transformation*. Princeton, NJ: Princeton University Press.
Evans, Peter, Dietrich Rueschemeyer, and Theda Skocpol. 1985. *Bringing the State Back In*. Cambridge; New York: Cambridge University Press.
Feng, Yi. 2001. 'Political Freedom, Political Instability, and Policy Uncertainty: A Study of Political Institutions and Private Investment in Developing Countries.' *International Studies Quarterly* 45 (2): 271–94.
FICCI (Federation of Indian Chambers of Commerce and Industry). 2010. *FICCI Foreign Direct Investment Survey 2010*. New Delhi: FICCI.
———. 2012. *Empowering India: Redesigning G2B Relations*. New Delhi: FICCI; Bain & Company.
Frank, Andre G. 1977. 'Emergency of Permanent Emergency in India.' *Economic and Political Weekly* 12 (11): 463–75.
Frank, Katherine. 2001. *Indira: The Life of Indira Nehru Gandhi*. London: Harper Collins Publishers.
Frankel, Francine. 2005. *India's Political Economy 1947–2004: The Gradual Revolution*. New Delhi: Oxford University Press.

Gandhi, Rajiv. 1998. 'Inaugural Address by the Prime Minister of India.' Paper presented at the National Conference Transformation of Indian Engineering Industry, Delhi, 19 April.

Ganguly, Sumit and Rahul Mukherji. 2011. *India since 1980*. Cambridge; New York: Cambridge University Press.

Gastanaga, Victor M., Jeffrey B. Nugent, and Bistra Pashamova. 1998. 'Host Country Reforms and FDI Inflows: How Much Difference Do They Make?' *World Development* 26 (7): 1299–314.

Gerschenkron, Alexander. 1962. *Economic Backwardness in Historical Perspective*. Cambridge, MA: Harvard University Press.

Ghosh, Biswajit. 2008. 'Economic Reforms and Trade Unionism in India—a Macro View.' *Indian Journal of Industrial Relations* 43 (3): 355–84.

Gorringe, Hugo. 2005. *Untouchable Citizens: Dalit Movements and Democratisation in Tamil Nadu*. Cultural Subordination and the Dalit Challenge. New Delhi: Thousand Oaks, California: Sage Publications.

Government of India (GOI). 1957. *The Mines and Minerals (Development and Regulation) Act*.

———. 1966. *Re Shri Biju Patnaik's Participation in the Chief Minister's Conference*, Rajya Sabha Secretariat. Accessed 7 July 2013.

———. 1967a. *Passport to Shri Biju Patnaik*, Ministry of External Affairs. Accessed 7 July 2013.

———. 1967b. *Reference to CBI Report about Shri Biju Patnaik*, Rajya Sabha Secretariat. Accessed 7 July 2013.

———. 1968. *Firms of Shri Biju Patnaik, Ex-Chief Minister of Orissa*, Rajya Sabha Secretariat. Accessed 7 July 2013.

———. 1969. *The 4th Five Year Plan*, The Planning Commission. Accessed 25 April 2012.

———. 1972. *Setting up of Rehabilitation Industries Corporation in Tamil Nadu*, Rajya Sabha Secretariat. Accessed 24 February 2013.

———. 1977a. *Foreign Investment in Metallurgical and Mineral Based Industries*, Rajya Sabha Secretariat. Accessed 7 July 2013.

———. 1977b. *Investment in the Metallurgical and Mineral Based Industries*, Rajya Sabha Secretariat. Accessed 7 July 2013.

———. 1977c. *Second Steel Plant in Orissa*, Rajya Sabha Secretariat. Accessed 6 July 2013.

Government of India (GOI). 1978a. *Report of the Committee on Import Export Policies and Procedures*. Accessed 22 April 2012.

———. 1978b. *Compensation for the Land Acquired for Setting up the Bokaro Steel Plant*, Rajya Sabha Secretariat. Accessed 6 July 2013.

———. 1978c. *Investment Plan for Steel Industry*, Rajya Sabha Secretariat. Accessed 6 July 2013.

———. 1978d. *Negotiations with Foreign Countries for Setting up of New Steel Plants in the Country*, Rajya Sabha Secretariat. Accessed 6 July 2013.

———. 1980. *Statement on Industrial Policy by Dr Charanjit Chanana*, Minister of State for Industry. Accessed 22 April 2012.

———. 1981. *Sixth Five Year Plan*, Planning Commission. Accessed 19 April 2014.

———. 1982. *Solvent Sal-seed Oil Extraction Plants*, Rajya Sabha Secretariat. Accessed 19 April 2014.

———. 1990. *Refusal by POSCO to Assist in Setting up Steel Plant in Orissa*, Rajya Sabha Secretariat. Accessed 14 September 2012.

———. 1991a. *Economic Survey 1990-91*, Ministry of Finance. Accessed 22 April 2012.
———. 1991b. *Lok Sabha Debates 1991.* Accessed 25 April 2012.
———. 1994. *Demand for Creating of Tamil Nadu Land Reforms Measure,* Rajya Sabha Secretariat. Accessed 24 February 2013.
———. 2001. *Sick Industries in Orissa,* Rajya Sabha Secretariat. Accessed 25 March 2014.
———. 2002. *Downstream Issues: Implementation and Operation*, Planning Commission. Accessed 22 April 2012.
———. 2003a. *Request for Central Help to Control Naxalite Activities on Orissa Coastal Belt*, Rajya Sabha Secretariat. Accessed 13 September 2012.
———. 2003b. *Demand for Immediate Completion of Paradeep Oil Refinery in Orissa*, Rajya Sabha Secretariat. Accessed 13 September 2012.
———. 2003c. *Need to Take Appropriate Steps to Implement the Paradeep Oil Refinery Project in Orissa*, Rajya Sabha Secretariat. Accessed 13 September 2012.
———. 2003d. *Request for Central Help to Control Naxalite Activities on Odisha Coastal Belt*, Rajya Sabha Secretariat. Accessed 13 September 2012.
———. 2005a. *Demand to Explore War and Means to Tackle Naxalite Menace in Orissa*, Rajya Sabha Secretariat. Accessed 13 September 2012.
———. 2005b. *Scheduled Tribes in Tamil Nadu,* Rajya Sabha Secretariat. Accessed 24 February 2013.
———. 2006a. *Displacement of Tribal People*, Rajya Sabha Secretariat. Accessed 7 July 2013.
———. 2006b. *Naxalite Problem in the Sambalpur District of Odisha*, Rajya Sabha Secretariat. Accessed 13 September 2012.
———. 2006c. *Tribals and Big Companies in Mineral Sector*, Rajya Sabha Secretariat. Accessed 7 July 2013.
———. 2010a. *2010 Review: Foreign Investment Promotion Board*, Department of Economic Affairs. Accessed 25 April 2012.
———. 2010b. *Clearance to POSCO Project*, Rajya Sabha Secretariat. Accessed 14 September 2012.
———. 2010c. *Environment Approval to POSCO Project*, Rajya Sabha Secretariat. Accessed 14 September 2012.
———. 2010d. *Environmental Clearance to POSCO Steel Project*, Rajya Sabha Secretariat. Accessed 13 September 2012.
———. 2010e. *Findings of Central Team on POSCO Site*, Rajya Sabha Secretariat. Accessed 14 September 2012.
———. 2010f. *Job Creation through Steel Project by POSCO*, Rajya Sabha Secretariat. Accessed 14 September 2012.
———. 2011a. *Clearance to POSCO's Steel Plant in Orissa*, Rajya Sabha Secretariat. Accessed 14 September 2012.
———. 2011b. *MOU with POSCO*, Rajya Sabha Secretariat. Accessed 13 September 2012.
———. 2011c. *Tribal Groups Affected by POSCO Project*, Rajya Sabha Secretariat. Accessed 13 September 2012.
———. 2012. *Report on Foreign Direct Investment*, Rajya Sabha Secretariat. Accessed 22 April 2012.
Government of Odisha (GOOD). 2005. *Biju Patnaik: A Tribute. Orissa Review.* Accessed 21 February 2014.

———. 2006. *Orissa Resettlement and Rehabilitation Policy*. Accessed 30 May 2013.
———. 2007a. *The Industrial Policy Resolution (IPR) of Orissa 2007*. Accessed 3 July 2013.
———. 2007b. *Orissa Public Private Partnership (PPP) Policy—2007*, Planning and Coordination Department. Accessed 3 July 2013.
———. 2012. *Economic Survey 2011–12*, Planning and Coordination Department. Accessed 13 September 2012.
Government of Tamil Nadu (GOTN). 1956. *Second Five-Year Plan (1956–61) Malabar District (Madras State)*. Madras: Government Press. Accessed 26 November 2012.
———. 1960. *Third Five-Year Plan Madras State Draft Outline*, Finance Department. Accessed 26 November 2012.
———. 1963. *The Third Plan Mid-term Appraisal*. Accessed 28 November 2012.
———. 1971. *Budget 1971-72 Speech of Thiru M Karunanidhi Chief Minister*. Accessed 26 November 2012.
———. 1973. *Draft Fifth Five-Year Plan Tamil Nadu: Memorandum to the Union Planning Commission*. Accessed 23 November 2012.
———. 1974. *The Perspective Plan for Tamil Nadu 1974-84: A Summary*, State Planning Commission. Accessed 26 November 2012.
———. 1975. *Budget 1975-76 Speech of Thiru M. Karunanidhi Chief Minister*. Accessed 26 November 2012.
———. 1979. *Budget 1979-80 Speech of Thiru V. R. Nedunchezhiyan Minister for Finance*, Ministry of Finance. Accessed 28 November 2012.
———. 1980. *Budget 1980-81 Speech of Thiru V. R. Nedunchezhiyan Minister for Finance*, Ministry of Finance. Accessed 28 November 2012.
———. 1981. *Budget 1981-82 Speech of Thiru V. R. Nedunchezhiyan Minister for Finance*, Ministry of Finance. Accessed 28 November 2012.
———. 1984. *Budget 1984-85 Speech of Thiru V. R. Nedunchezhiyan Minister for Finance*, Ministry of Finance. Accessed 28 November 2012.
———. 1986. *Budget 1986-87 Speech of Honourable Thiru V. R. Nedunchezhiyan Minister for Finance*. Accessed 28 November 2012.
———. 1989. *Budget 1989-90 Speech of Honourable Thiru M Karunanidhi Chief Minister*. Accessed 22 November 2012.
———. 1991. *Budget 1991-92 Speech of Honourable Thiru V. R. Nedunchezhiyan Minister for Finance*. Accessed 22 November 2012.
———. 1993. *Budget 1993-94 Speech of the Honourable Minister for Finance Thiru V. R. Nedunchezhiyan*. Accessed 22 November 2012.
———. 1997. *Ninth Five Year Plan Tamil Nadu 1997-2002: An Outline*, State Planning Commission. Accessed 23 November 2012.
———. 1998. *Budget 1998-99 Speech of Chief Minister Thiru M. Karunanidhi*, Legislative Assembly. Accessed 26 November 2012.
Greif, Avner and David D. Laitin. 2004. 'A Theory of Endogenous Institutional Change.' *American Political Science Review*, 98 (4): 633-52.
Grieco, Joseph M. 1986. *Investing in Development: New Roles for Private Capital?* New Brunswick, USA: Transaction Books.
Gudavarthy, Ajay. 2012. 'Introduction: Why Interrogate Political Society?' In *Re-framing Democracy and Agency in India*, edited by Ajay Gudavarthy. London; New York: Anthem Press.

Gupta, Dipankar. 2005. 'Whither the Indian Village: Culture and Agriculture in "Rural" India.' *Economic and Political Weekly* 40 (8): 751-58.

Haggard, Stephan. 1989. 'The Political Economy of Foreign Direct Investment in Latin America.' *Latin American Research Review* 24 (1): 184-208.

———. 1990. *Pathways from the Periphery: The Politics of Growth in the Newly Industrializing Countries.* Ithaca, NY: Cornell University Press.

Halperin, Morton H. and Priscilla A. Clapp. 2006. *Bureaucratic Politics and Foreign Policy.* Washington, DC: Brookings Institution Press.

Harriss, John, J. Jeyaranjan, and K. Nagaraj. 2010. 'Land, Labour and Caste Politics in Rural Tamil Nadu in the 20th Century: Iruvelpattu (1916-2008).' *Economic and Political Weekly* 45 (31): 47–61.

Harriss, John. 2006. *Power Matters: Essays on Institutions, Politics, and Society in India.* New York: Oxford University Press.

Harriss-White, Barbara. 2003. *India Working: Essays on Society and Economy.* New York: Cambridge University Press.

Henisz, Witold J. 2000. 'The Institutional Environment for Multinational Investment.' *The Journal of Law, Economics, and Organization* 16 (2): 334-64.

Henisz, Witold J. and Oliver E. Williamson. 1999. 'Comparative Economic Organization— Within and Between Countries.' *Business and Politics* 1 (3): 261-77.

Herring, Ronald J. 1980. *Abolition of Landlordism in Kerala: A Redistribution of Privilege.* 15 (26): A59-A61+A63-A69.

———. 1991. 'From Structural Conflict to Agrarian Stalemate: Agrarian Reforms in South India.' *Journal of Asian and African Studies* 26 (3-4): 169-88.

Hewitt, Vernon. 2008. *Political Mobilisation and Democracy in India: States of Emergency.* New York: Routledge.

Jenamani, Suvendra. 2005. *Poverty and Underdevelopment in Tribal Areas: A Geographical Analysis.* New Delhi: Concept Publishing Company.

Johnson, Chalmers A. 1982. *MITI and the Japanese Miracle: The Growth of Industrial Policy, 1925-1975.* Stanford: Stanford University Press.

———. 1999. 'The Developmental State: Odyssey of a Concept.' In *The Developmental State*, edited by Meredith Woo-Cumings, 32-60. New York: Cornell University Press.

Joshi, Vijay and I. M. D. Little. 1994. *India: Macroeconomics and Political Economy 1964-1991.* New Delhi: Oxford University Press.

Kale, Sunila. *Electrifying India: Regional Political Economies of Development.* Stanford, California: Stanford University Press.

Kanagaraj, B. R. S. 2011. *Strike Notices by Hyundai Motor India Employees Union (HMIEU)— Reply to the Notice Dated 16. 08. 2011.* Kanchipuram District: SIPCOT. Accessed 28 December 2011.

Kantha, Sharmila and Subhajyoti Ray. 2006. *Building India with Partnership: The Story of CII 1895-2005.* New Delhi: Portfolio.

Kaviraj, Sudipta. 1986. 'Indira Gandhi and Indian Politics.' *Economic and Political Weekly* 21 (38/39): 1697-708.

Kennedy, Loraine. 2004. 'The Political Determinants of Reform Packaging: Contrasting Responses to Economic Liberalisation in Andhra Pradesh and Tamil Nadu.' In *Regional Reflections: Comparing Politics Across India's States*, edited by Rob Jenkins, 29–65, New Delhi: Oxford University Press.

Keohane, Robert and Van D. Ooms. 1975. 'The Multinational Firm and International Regulation.' *International Organization* 29 (1): 169–209.

Kidron, Michael. 1965. *Foreign Investments in India*. London: Oxford University Press.

Knack, Stephen and Philip Keefer. 1995. 'Institutions and Economic Performance: Cross-Country Tests Using Alternative Institutional Measures.' *Economics & Politics* 7 (3): 207–27.

Kochanek, Stanley A. 1987. 'Briefcase Politics in India: The Congress Party and the Business Elite.' *Asian Survey* 27 (12): 1278–301.

———. 1995. 'The Transformation of Interest Politics in India.' *Pacific Affairs* 68 (4): 529–50.

Kohli, Atul. 1989. 'Politics of Economic Liberalization in India.' *World Development* 17 (3): 305–28.

———. 2004. *State-Directed Development: Political Power and Industrialization in the Global Periphery*. Cambridge, New York: Cambridge University Press.

———. 2012. *Poverty Amid Plenty in the New India*. New York: Cambridge University Press.

Kosalram, S. A. 1973. 'Political Economy of Agriculture in Tamil Nadu.' *Social Scientist* 1 (12): 3–21.

Krasner, Stephen D. 1978. *Defending the National Interest: Raw Materials Investments and U.S. Foreign Policy*. Princeton, NJ: Princeton University Press.

Krishnaswami, C. 1989. 'Dynamics of Capitalist Labour Process: Knitting Industry in Tamil Nadu.' *Economic and Political Weekly* 24 (24): 1353–59.

Krueger, Anne O. and Takatoshi Ito. 2000. *The Role of Foreign Direct Investment in East Asian Economic Development*. Chicago: University of Chicago Press.

Kumbhar, Sitaram. 2005. *The Politics of Poverty in Orissa: Comparing Kalahandi, Bolangir, Koraput (KBK) and Cuttack District*. MPhil dissertation, Centre for Political Studies, Jawaharlal Nehru University.

Kwon, Seung-Ho and Michael O'Donnell. 2001. *The Chaebol and Labour in Korea: The Development of Management Strategy in Hyundai*. New York: Routledge.

Lakshman, Narayan. 2011. *Patrons of the Poor: Caste Politics and Policymaking in India*. New Delhi: Oxford University Press.

Leftwich, Adrian. 1995. 'Bringing Politics Back In: Towards A Model of the Developmental State.' *Journal of Development Studies* 31 (3): 400–27.

Levien, Michael. 2013. 'The Politics of Dispossession: Theorizing India's Land Wars.' *Politics & Society* 41 (3): 351–94.

Lindberg, Staffan. 2011. 'Arduous yet Desirable? The Recent Social Transformation in Rural India.' Presented at the Indian Society of Labour Economics Annual Conference, Udaipur.

Lindberg, Staffan, V. Athreya, G. Djurfeldt, A. Rajagopal, and R. Vidyasagar. 2014. 'Progress over the Long Haul: Dynamics of Agrarian Change in the Kaveri Delta.' In *Persistence of Poverty in India*, edited by Nandini Gooptu and Jonathan Parry, 344–69. New Delhi: Social Science Press.

Mahoney, James and Kathleen Thelen. 2010. *Explaining Institutional Change: Ambiguity, Agency, and Power*. Cambridge; New York: Cambridge University Press.

Malhotra, Inder. 1989. *Indira Gandhi: A Personal and Political Biography*. London: Hodder and Stoughton.

Manikumar, K. A. 1997. Caste Clashes in South Tamil Nadu. *Economic and Political Weekly* 32 (36): 2242–243.

Maruthakutti, R., U. R. Kaliappan and T. Chandramohan Reddy. 1991. 'Caste, Class and Trade Unionism among Industrial Workers.' *Indian Journal of Industrial Relations* 26 (4): 384-94.
Mathur, A. S. and J. S. Mathur. 1957. *Trade Union Movement in India*. Allahabad: Chaitanya Publishing House.
Mathur, Hari M. 2009. 'Investor-Friendly Development Policies: Unsettling Consequences for the Tribal People of Orissa.' *The Asia Pacific Journal of Anthropology* 10 (4): 318-28.
Mearns, Robin and Saurabh Sinha. 1999. 'Social Exclusion and Land Administration in Orissa, India.' *Policy Research Working Paper*, 2124. South Asia Region, Rural Development Sector Unit: The World Bank.
Meher, Rajkishor. 2004. *Stealing the Environment: Social and Ecological Effects of Industrialization in Rourkela*. New Delhi: Manohar.
Melo, Marcus A., Njuguna Ng'ethe, and James Manor. 2012. *Against the Odds: Politicians, Institutions and the Struggle Against Poverty*. London: C. Hurst & Co.
Migdal, Joel S. 1988. *Strong Societies and Weak States: State-Society Relations and State Capabilities in the Third World*. Princeton, NJ: Princeton University Press.
———. 2001. *State in Society: Studying How States and Societies Transform and Constitute One Another*. Cambridge: Cambridge University Press.
Milner, Helen V. 1988. *Resisting Protectionism: Global Industries and the Politics of International Trade*. Princeton, NJ: Princeton University Press.
Milner, Helen V. and Keiko Kubota. 2005. 'Why the Move to Free Trade? Democracy and Trade Policy in the Developing Countries.' *International Organization* 59 (1): 107-43.
Mishra, P. K. 1979. *Political History of Orissa, 1900-1936*. Delhi: Oriental Publishers and Distributors.
Mishra, P. K. and D. D. Litt. 1985. 'Political Process in Orissa (1936-51).' In *Indian State Politics: A Case Study of Orissa*, edited by A. P. Padhi. Delhi: B. R. Publishing Corporation.
Misra, Surya N. 1985. 'Election and Political Development in Orissa.' In *Indian State Politics: A Case Study of Orissa*, edited by A. P. Padhi. Delhi: B. R. Publishing Corporation.
Mitra, Subrata K. 1992. *Power, Protest and Participation: Local Elites and the Politics of Development in India*. London; New York: Routledge.
———. 2006. *The Puzzle of India's Governance: Culture, Context, and Comparative Theory*. New York: Routledge.
Mohanty, Biswaranjan. 2005. 'Displacement and Rehabilitation of Tribals.' *Economic and Political Weekly*, 40 (13): 1318-320.
Mohanty, Manoranjan. 1990. 'Class, Caste, and Dominance in a Backward State: Orissa.' In *Dominance and State Power in Modern India: Decline of a Social Order*, edited by Francine R. Frankel and Madhugiri S. A. Rao, 321-66. Delhi; New York: Oxford University Press.
———. 2014. 'Persisting Dominance: Crisis of Democracy in a Resource-rich Region.' *Economic and Political Weekly*, 49 (14): 39-47.
Mooij, Jos. 2005. *The Politics of Economic Reforms in India*. New Delhi: Sage Publications.
Moore, Barrington. 1966. *Social Origins of Dictatorship and Democracy*. Boston: Beacon Press.
Moran, Theodore H. 1998. *Foreign Direct Investment and Development: The New Policy Agenda for Developing Countries and Economies in Transition*. Washington, DC: Institute for International Economics.
Mukherji, Rahul. 2000. 'India's Aborted Liberalization-1966.' *Pacific Affairs* 73 (3): 375-92.

———. 2007. *India's Economic Transition: The Politics of Reforms*. Oxford: Oxford University Press.

———. 2009. 'Interests, Wireless Technology, and Institutional Change: From Government Monopoly to Regulated Competition in Indian Telecommunications.' *The Journal of Asian Studies* 68 (2): 491–517.

———. 2013. 'Ideas, Intersts, and the Tipping Point: Economic Change in India.' *Review of International Political Economy* 20 (2): 363–89.

———. 2014. *Globalization and Deregulation: Ideas, Interests, and Institutional Change in India*. New Delhi: Oxford University Press.

Murali, Kanta. 2017. *Caste, Class and Capital: The Social and Political Origins of Economic Policy in India*. New York: Cambridge University Press.

Nair, Manjusha. 2009. 'Mixed Repertoire of an Indian Labor Movement, 1990-2006.' *Journal of Historical Sociology* 22 (2): 180–206.

Nanda, Chandi P. 2008. *Vocalising Silence: Political Protests in Orissa, 1930–42*. New Delhi: Sage.

Nanda, Sukadev. 1979. *Coalition Politics in Orissa*. New Delhi: Sterling Publishers.

NCAER (National Council of Applied Economic Research). 2007. *Social Cost Benefit Analysis of the POSCO Steel Project in Orissa*. New Delhi: NCAER.

Nayak, Bhabani S. 2007. 'Silenced Drums and Unquiet Woods: The Myth of Modernization and Development in Orissa.' *Journal of Comparative Social Welfare* 23 (1): 89–98.

Nayak, Mayadhar. 2010. *Land to Let*. Jajpur: Krusti Publications.

Nayar, Baldev R. 1971. 'Business Attitudes toward Economic Planning in India.' *Asian Survey* 11 (9): 850–65.

———. 2006. 'When Did the "Hindu" Rate of Growth End?' *Economic and Political Weekly* 41 (19): 1885–890.

———. 2007. 'The Limits of Economic Nationalism in India: Economic Reforms under the BJP-led Government, 1998-9.' In *India's Economic Transition: The Politics of Reforms*, edited by Rahul Mukherji, 202–30. New Delhi: Oxford University Press.

Nayar, Kuldip. 2006. *Scoop! Inside Stories from the Partition to the Present*. New Delhi: Harper Collins Publishers.

North Douglass C. 1990. *Institutions, Institutional Change, and Economic Performance*. New York: Cambridge University Press.

———. 1991. 'Institutions.' *The Journal of Economic Perspectives* 5 (1): 97–112.

Padel, Felix and Samarendra Das. 2010a. 'Cultural Genocide and the Rhetoric of Sustainable Mining in East India.' *Contemporary South Asia* 18 (3): 333–41.

———. 2010b. *Out of This Earth: East India Adivasis and the Aluminium Cartel*. New Delhi: Orient Black Swan.

Panagariya, Arvind. 2008. *India: The Emerging Giant*. New York: Oxford University Press.

Panda, Nishakar. 2006. *Policies, Programmes and Strategies for Tribal Development*. Delhi: Kalpaz Publications.

Patel, Indraprasad G. 2002. *Glimpses of Indian Economic Policy: An Insider's View*. New Delhi: Oxford University Press.

Pati, Biswamoy. 2000. 'Orissa Today: Fantasy and Reality.' *Economic and Political Weekly*, 35 (18): 1516–517.

———. 2001. 'Identity, Hegemony, Resistance: Conversions in Orissa, 1800-2000.' *Economic and Political Weekly* 36 (44): 4204–212.

―――――. 2007. 'The Order of Legitimacy: Princely Orissa, 1850–1947.' In *India's Princely States: People, Princes and Colonialism,* edited by Waltraud Ernst and Biswamoy Pati, 85–98. Abingdon; New York: Routledge.

―――――. 2009. 'Biju Janata Dal: Signal for Change.' *Economic and Political Weekly* 44 (9): 12–13.

Patil, B. R. 1976. 'A Study of Trade Unionism in Karnataka.' *Indian Journal of Industrial Relations,* 11 (4): 473–91.

Patkar, Medha. 1998. 'The People's Policy on Development, Displacement and Resettlement: Need to Link Displacement and Development.' *Economic and Political Weekly* 33 (38): 2432–433.

Patnaik, Pratyusna. 2005. 'Affirmative Action and Representation of Weaker Sections: Participation and Accountability in Orissa's Panchayats.' *Economic and Political Weekly* 40 (44/45): 4753–761.

Pattnaik, Binay K. 2013. 'Tribal Resistance Movements and the Politics of Development-Induced Displacement in Contemporary Orissa.' *Social Change* 43 (1): 53–78.

Pingle, Urmila, Devendra Pandey, and V. Suresh. 2010. *Majority Report of the POSCO Enquiry Committee, Executive Summary.* Delhi. Accessed 2 February 2012.

Planning Commission. 2001. *The Orissa State Development Report.* New Delhi: Government of India.

Polanyi, Karl. 2001. *The Great Transformation: The Political and Economic Origins of Our Time.* Boston, MA: Beacon Press.

Ponnuswami, K. P. 1982. *Anna 73 Souvenir.* Madras: Purasawakkam.

Prasad, Eswar S., Raghuram G. Rajan, and Arvind Subramanian. 2007. 'Foreign Capital and Economic Growth.' *Brookings Papers on Economic Activity* 2007 (1): 153–209.

Pushpendra. 1999. 'Dalit Assertion through Electoral Politics.' *Economic and Political Weekly* 34 (36): 2609–618.

Ramaswamy, E. A. 1984. *Power and Justice: The State in Industrial Relations.* Delhi; New York: Oxford University Press.

―――――. 1988. *Worker Consciousness and Trade Union Response.* Delhi; New York: Oxford University Press.

Rath, Sharada. 1985. 'Financial Relations between the Union and the States: With Special Reference to Orissa.' In *Indian State Politics: A Case Study of Orissa,* 391–433, edited by A. P. Padhi. Delhi: B. R. Publishing Corporation.

Ratnam, C. S. Venkata. 2007. 'Trade Unions and Wider Society.' *Indian Journal of Industrial Relations* 42 (4): 620–51.

RBI. 2000. *Foreign Exchange Management (Transfer or Issue of Security by a Person Resident Outside India) Regulations, 2000.* Mumbai: Reserve Bank of India.

―――――. 2003. *Report of the Committee on Compilation of Foreign Direct Investment in India.* Mumbai: Reserve Bank of India.

Rudolph, Lloyd I. and Susanne H. Rudolph. 2001. 'Iconisation of Chandrababu: Sharing Sovereignty in India's Federal Market Economy.' *Economic and Political Weekly* 36 (18): 1546–552.

Rudra, Ashok. 1989. 'Emergence of the Intelligentsia as a Ruling Class in India.' *Indian Economic Review* 24 (2): 155–83.

Sahoo, Radhamohan. 1985. 'The Formation of Orissa: A Political Backdrop.' In *Indian State Politics,* edited by A. P. Padhi. Delhi: B. R. Publishing Corporation.

Sahu, Geetanjoy. 2008. 'Mining in the Niyamgiri Hills and Tribal Rights.' *Economic and Political Weekly* 43 (15): 19-21.

Samal, J. K. and Pradip K. Nayak. 1996. *Makers of Modern Odisha*. New Delhi: Abhinav Publications.

Saraswathi, S. 1995. *Government, Politics, and People: Linkage Politics of Tamil Nadu*. Delhi: Manak Publications.

Sawhney, Dhruv. 1985. *Inaugural Address by Shri Dhruv Sawhney (Chairman-Export of AIEI)*. Paper presented at the National Conference on Engineering Exports, New Delhi, 22 March.

Sen, Amartya. 2000. 'Social Exclusion: Concept, Application, and Scrutiny.' *Social Development Papers*. Office of Environment and Social Development, Asian Development Bank.

Sen, Kunal. 2009. *Trade Policy, Inequality and Performance in Indian Manufacturing*. London; New York: Routledge.

Sengupta, Jayanta. 2001. 'State, Market, and Democracy in the 1990s: Liberalization and the Politics of Oriya Identity.' In *Democratic Governance in India: Challenges of Poverty, Development, and Identity*, edited by Niraja G. Jayal and Sudha Pai, 179-200. New Delhi: Sage Publications.

Shin, Jang-Sup. 1996. *The Economics of the Latecomers: Catching-up, Technology Transfer and Institutions in Germany, Japan and South Korea*. New York: Routledge.

———. 2005. 'Globalization and Challenges to the Developmental State: A Comparison between South Korea and Singapore.' *Global Economic Review* 34 (4): 379-95.

Shin, Sojin. 2016. 'Politics of Foreign Direct Investment in South Asia.' *Oxford Bibliographies*. DOI: 10.1093/OBO/9780199756223-0195.

Singh, Manmohan. 1991. *Budget 1991-92*. New Delhi: Ministry of Finance.

Singh, Vishwanath P. 1990a. *Inaugural Address by Shri Vishwanath Pratap Singh Prime Minister of India*. Paper presented at the 41st Meeting of the National Development Council, Delhi, 18 June.

———. 1990b. *Inaugural Address by the Prime Minister of India*. Paper presented at the National Meeting on India, 9 April.

Sinha, Aseema. 2005. *The Regional Roots of Developmental Politics in India: A Divided Leviathan*. Bloomington: Indiana University Press.

Sinha, Yashwant. 2007. *Yashwant Sinha: Confessions of a Swadeshi Reformer*. London: Penguin.

Skocpol, Theda. 1982. 'State Capacity and Economic Intervention in the Early New Deal.' *Political Science Quarterly* 97 (2): 255-78.

———. 1985. 'Bringing the State Back In: Strategies of Analysis in Current Research.' In *Bringing the State Back In*, edited by Peter Evans, Dietrich Rueschemeyer, and Theda Skocpol, 3-38. New York: Cambridge University Press.

Srichandan, G. K. 1993. 'Tribal Development and Welfare Legislation in Orissa.' *Prativa Prakashan*: Delhi.

Streeck, Wolfgang and Kathleen Thelen. 2005. 'Introduction: Institutional Change in Advanced Political Economies.' In *Beyond Continuity: Institutional Change in Advanced Political Economies*, edited by Wolfgang Streeck and Kathleen Thelen, 1-39, New York: Oxford University Press.

Subramanian, Narendra. 1999. *Ethnicity and Populist Mobilization: Political Parties, Citizens, and Democracy in South India*. Delhi: Oxford University Press.

———. 2002. 'Identity Politics and Social Pluralism: Political Sociology and Political Change in Tamil Nadu.' *Commonwealth & Comparative Politics*, 40 (3): 125–39.
Sundar, Nandini. 1997. *Subalterns and Sovereigns: An Anthropoligical History of Bastar, 1854–1996.* Delhi: Oxford University Press.
Tendulkar, Suresh D., and T. A. Bhavani. 2007. *Understanding Reforms: Post 1991 India.* New Delhi: Oxford University Press.
Thakurta, Paranjoy G. 2004. 'Ideological Contradictions in an Era of Coalitions: Economic Policy Confusion in the Vajpayee Government.' In *India-the Political Economy of Reforms*, edited by Bibek Debroy and Rahul Mukherji, 9–80, New Delhi: Bookwell.
Thelen, Kathleen. 1992. 'Historical Institutionalism in Comparative Politics.' In *Structuring Politics: Historical Institutionalism in Comparative Analysis,* edited by Sven Steinmo, 1–32. New York: Cambridge University Press.
Thun, Eric. 2014. 'The Globalization of Production.' In *Global Political Economy*, edited by John Ravenhill, 283–304. Oxford: Oxford University Press.
Tomlinson, B. R. 1978. 'Foreign Private Investment in India 1920–1950.' *Modern Asian Studies* 12 (4): 655–77.
Vaasanthi. 2006. *Cut-Outs, Caste, and Cine Stars: The World of Tamil Politics.* New Delhi: Penguin Books.
Vanaik, Achin. 1990. *The Painful Transition: Bourgeoisie Democracy in India.* Verso: London.
Varshney, Ashutosh. 1995. *Democracy, Development and the Countryside: Urban-Rural Struggles in India.* Cambridge: Cambridge University Press.
Verghese, Boobli G. 2010. *First Draft: Witness to the Making of Modern India.* New Delhi: Tranquebar.
Vernon, Raymond. 1966. 'International Investment and International Trade in the Product Cycle.' *The Quarterly Journal of Economics* 80 (2): 190–207.
Vijayabaskar, M., Padmini Swaminathan, S. Anandhi, and Gayatri Balagopal. 2004. 'Human Development in Tamil Nadu: Examining Linkages.' *Economic and Political Weekly* 39 (8): 797–802.
Wade, Robert. 1990. *Governing the Market: Economic Theory and the Role of Government in East Asian Industrialization.* Princeton, NJ: Princeton University Press.
Washbrook, D. A. 1976. *The Emergence of Provincial Politics: The Madras Presidency 1870–1920.* New York: Cambridge University Press.
Wells, Louis T. 2007. *Making Foreign Investment Safe: Property Rights and National Sovereignty.* New York: Oxford University Press.
Wyatt, Andrew. 2010. *Party System Change in South India: Political Entrepreneurs, Patterns and Processes.* New York: Routledge.
———. 2013. 'Combining Clientelist and Programmatic Politics in Tamil Nadu, South India.' *Commonwealth & Comparative Politics* 51 (1): 27–55.

Index

Andhra Pradesh, 3, 5n10, 41, 63, 82, 83n6, 118n30, 122, 138
administrative
  organisations, 14, 22, 90, 116–117, 127
  problems, 85, 138
  reform policies, 13, 67
All India Anna Dravida Munnetra Kazhagam (AIADMK), 51–52, 54, 57n17, 58–59, 62, 65–73, 73n79, 74–75, 84, 88, 91, 96, 156, 163
apprentice, 87, 94
Argentina, 8
Assam, 138
Associated Chambers of Commerce and Industry (ASSOCHAM), 37–38
autonomy, 14, 27, 45–46, 54, 61n29, 107, 110, 132, 162, 163n1

balance of payments (BOP), 6, 16, 26
bargain, 4, 8, 21, 28, 53, 82, 90, 94–95, 100, 102–103, 133, 135, 144–146, 149, 153, 157–158
barriers, 6, 8, 11, 32, 148, 155, 161
Bharatiya Janata Party (BJP), 29, 38, 45–47, 129n62
Bihar, 2–3, 26, 41, 76, 107n2, 110, 118n30, 150
Biju Janata Dal (BJD), 107–108, 127–128, 129n62, 131, 136–137, 139
BIMAR(O)U, 41
Bombay Club, 37–38
Brazil, 8
Budget, 35, 58, 60, 62, 69, 73, 82, 93
bureaucrat(s)/bureaucratic/bureaucracy, 2, 4, 9–12, 21, 24, 27–28, 30, 36, 38–39, 43, 45n75, 1, 48, 53, 68n61, 79–80, 85, 97, 100, 103, 107, 109–110, 116–117, 132, 134–135, 138, 144–145, 147, 153, 157–159, 161, 163
Burma, 58

Calcutta, 4, 38, 91
capital-intensive 4, 75
capital-labour/labour-capital relationship, 86–90
central government, 4, 10–11, 41, 46, 51–52, 55, 58–60, 60n27, 61, 66–67, 70, 73, 75, 77–78, 90, 114, 118, 118n30, 122, 125, 126n49, 131, 137, 139, 145, 154–156, 161
Centre of Indian Trade Unions (CITU), 72, 89
Ceylon, 58
Chief Minister(s), 11–12, 21, 34n43, 40–41, 45, 55, 57, 60, 62, 65–66, 68, 68nn61, 74, 80, 84, 91, 108, 112, 113n15, 119, 119n33, 124, 128, 136, 139
citizen(s)/citizenship, 2, 10–12, 15, 21–22, 40, 51, 54, 56–57, 64–68, 71–73, 75–77, 79, 82, 96–97, 102, 104, 107–109, 111–113, 115–116, 118, 120–122, 124, 129, 131–135, 139–144, 146–147, 149–154, 156–158, 160–164
coalition(s), 8, 12n21, 45–47, 107, 111, 113, 113n15, 126n49, 132
Communist Party of India (CPI), 39, 112, 142
Communist Party of India (Maoist) (CPI(Maoist)), 39
Communist Party of India (Marxist) (CPIM), 26, 39, 88
Confederation of Indian Industry (CII), 33, 37–38

conflict(s), 26, 37, 39, 45, 51, 53, 55, 58–59, 72, 74–75, 80–81, 86, 89–90, 93, 97, 100, 104, 112, 114, 120, 128, 133–135, 138–140, 143–144, 148, 151–152, 155–156, 158–159
Congress Party, 24–27, 33, 49, 54–56, 58, 91, 107, 111–115, 113n15, 119, 121, 126, 129n62, 138–139, 164
correlation, 6, 122–123, 162
corruption, 5n10, 7, 9, 27–28, 54, 109–110, 112
crisis/crises, 6, 11, 16, 25–26, 33, 35, 37, 42, 49, 59, 61, 66, 73, 96, 120, 158

decision-making, 12, 12n21, 26, 45n75, 46, 61
Delhi, 2–3, 63, 79, 83, 85, 133, 140
Desai, Morarji, 31–32, 114
developing countries, 6, 6n16, 33, 124
developmental state(s), 5, 5n10, 6, 6n15, 10–11, 12n21, 14, 14n27, 15, 21, 34n43, 50, 62, 62n37, 110, 156–157, 163
Department of Industrial Policy and Promotion (DIPP), 3n6, 17n31, 43, 48
domestic investments, 4–6, 50
double-shift, 95–96
Dravida Munnetra Kazhagam (DMK), 45, 51, 83, 155
Dravidar Kazhagam (DK), 56, 57n13
Dravidian movement, 4, 57n13
dropout, 2, 19–20, 123

economic growth, 3–6, 14n27, 19, 24, 35, 53, 55, 62, 71–73, 80, 82, 84, 96n45, 103, 111, 128, 136–137, 148
economic performance, 3, 3n8, 4–5, 10, 14, 17, 41
economic reform(s), 4, 11, 16, 23n3, 24, 29, 34–37, 39, 42–43, 46, 48, 51–52, 55, 61, 68n61, 70, 73, 78, 84, 94, 117, 125, 131, 137, 155
election, 4, 9–10, 25, 27, 51–52, 55–57, 65, 71–72, 111–112, 113n15, 121, 126, 129n62, 132, 154
emergency, 29–30
employment, 11, 19, 21, 50–53, 62–64, 66, 75, 77, 80, 82–84, 96, 99–101, 103–104, 110, 122–124, 126, 130, 133, 136, 149, 151–153, 156, 158–160
exclusion(ary), 5, 5n10, 12, 12n21, 21–22, 107, 111, 116, 119, 131, 133, 153, 160–161
export-oriented, 6n15
extractive, 2, 10, 106, 129, 132, 134, 136, 153, 160–161

financial aid, 26, 59, 156
financial resource, 6, 10, 25–27, 33, 41, 43–44, 51, 59, 61, 69, 73, 83n5, 114, 118, 154, 156
firm(s), 5n11, 8–9, 12, 16–17, 21, 28–29, 37–39, 53, 73, 80, 86–89, 93, 104, 106
Five-year Plan, 34, 58, 60
foreign capital, 6–8, 10, 20–21, 24–25, 29–32, 34–35, 37–40, 49, 51–52, 55, 60, 66, 68–70, 73n79, 79–82, 86, 88–90, 93, 100, 103–105, 111, 114–115, 119, 125, 127, 131, 138–139, 153, 154–158, 162–164
foreign currency, 28, 32, 42
Foreign Direct Investment (FDI), 2–3, 3n6, 5–6, 6n15, 7–8, 8n19, 9–13, 15–18, 20–24, 29–49, 51, 53, 60–61, 69–75, 77, 79–87, 96–100, 102–105, 107–108, 111, 114–115, 119, 119n33, 127–128, 131–138, 142n21, 146, 150–151, 153–164
foreign exchange, 25–26, 28, 31–32, 59
Foreign Exchange Management Act (FEMA), 13, 42
Foreign Exchange Regulation Act (FERA), 25
Foreign Investment Board (FIB), 29
Foreign Investment Promotion Board (FIPB), 21, 24, 45, 155
foreign investments, 2, 5, 6n15, 8, 10–11, 17, 21, 24–25, 29–30, 32–35, 37–38, 40, 47–49, 70, 84, 106–107, 119n33, 125, 127, 154–155, 158, 160–161
foreign investors, 2, 8–9, 18, 21, 34–35, 37, 38n58, 40–42, 42n72, 46, 53, 62, 71, 73, 75, 80–81, 85–86, 97, 103, 108, 115, 125, 128, 131, 134, 145, 156

Index

foreign management, 21, 81, 89–90, 94–95, 104, 158
foreign presence, 6
foreign reserve(s), 31–33
France, 16

Gandhi, Indira, 24–33, 37, 49, 55, 59, 113n15
Gandhi, Rajiv, 33–34, 67
Government of Odisha, 1, 1n2, 2, 106, 121–122, 129–130, 135, 137, 147, 151–152
Greenfield type of FDI, 17–18, 41
Gujarat, 2–5, 41, 62n37, 68n61, 86, 90, 100, 110, 112n11, 136, 138

hazard(s), 8–9, 9n20
historical institution, 12–17, 24
host countries, 5n11, 6–10
Human Development Indices (HDI), 18–19, 76
Hyundai Motor Company (HMC), 17–18, 80
Hyundai Motor India (HMI), 21, 73, 73n79, 75, 79, 88, 157

identity politics, 12n21
inclusion(ary), 10–12, 19–22, 51–52, 54–69, 72, 74–79, 96–97, 101, 104, 107, 111, 115, 118, 120, 129n62, 131–132, 153–154, 156–163
Indian Chambers of Commerce and Industry (FICCI), 37–38, 42n72
industrial development, 6, 6n15, 10–11, 14n27, 21, 28, 34n43, 51, 61–65, 71, 74, 107–111, 115–120, 125, 128, 131–134, 137–138, 144, 152, 154–156, 158, 161–163
industrial growth, 7, 32, 55, 70–71, 92, 106, 136
industrial organisation, 7–8
industrial progress, 115, 122, 145–146
industrial structure, 62
industrialisation, 4, 8, 10–12, 14, 14n27, 15, 19, 21–22, 23n2, 24, 26, 35, 39, 41, 45, 50–52, 55–56, 60–63, 65, 67–68, 70–71, 74–75, 77, 81–82, 86, 93–94, 101–104, 107–108, 111, 114–115, 118, 119n33, 120–121, 124–125, 129–134, 136, 138–139, 145–147, 151–153, 156–162

institution(s), 13n22, 124, 140
institutional change, 13n22, 14–15, 20–21, 24, 34, 42, 51–52, 60, 69–74, 111, 119, 124–131, 154–157
interest group(s), 11, 14n27, 157
International Monetary Fund (IMF), 26, 55, 73, 109, 156

Jammu & Kashmir, 3
Jana Congress Party, 111
Janata Dal, 34, 45, 107, 125–126, 136
Joint Venture, 9, 42n71
Justice Party, 56

Karnataka, 2–3, 63, 67, 82, 118n30, 138
Kerala, 26, 65, 108, 110, 117n24
knowledge, 10, 145, 160–161
Kujang, 1n2, 2, 139–146, 151

labour process, 87
Labour Progressive Front (LPF), 91
labour-intensive, 4, 17, 75
land acquisition, 1n4, 18–19, 50–51, 72, 74–75, 85, 97, 99, 121, 128, 130, 133, 138n13, 140, 142n21, 143–145, 147, 150, 156–157, 159–160, 162–163
land reform(s), 11, 13, 21, 51, 64, 70–71, 77, 79, 107, 116–120, 156–157, 159–162
large-scale investment(s), 2, 5, 12, 21–22, 75, 77, 85, 97, 108–109, 115, 126n49, 128, 132–133, 135–137, 146–152, 157–158, 162, 164
Latin America, 8
left-wing, 4–5, 11, 21–22, 25–27, 39, 48, 72, 98n49, 112, 120–124, 132, 134, 138n13, 139, 153, 158, 160–162
legitimacy, 19–21, 51, 156–157
Liberation Tigers of Tamil Eelam (LTTE), 67
lobby, 4, 34, 38, 49

macro-economic, 7, 39
Madhya Pradesh, 41, 107n2, 138
Madras, 51, 63–64, 69, 74, 91–92, 144
Maharashtra, 2–3, 5n10, 40, 90, 118n30, 138
manufacturing, 9, 11, 16–17, 41, 43, 50, 69, 72, 75, 79–80, 82, 85, 96, 126–127, 133–134, 163

marginalised, 10–11, 21, 49, 54–59, 65–66, 70, 76, 96, 101–104, 109, 112, 115, 117, 120–121, 131–135, 152, 154, 157–161, 163–164
market factors, 5, 7–8, 10
market(s), 5–11, 17, 23, 26, 28–30, 32, 34–35, 38–39, 49, 59, 66, 71, 73, 80, 83n5, 84–88, 94, 101, 106, 135, 138, 163–164
Memorandum of Understanding (MOU), 1, 79n73, 95
Mergers and Acquisition (M&A), 42n71
Mexico, 8
Michelin/Michelin India (MI), 21, 79, 97–102, 150, 157
Ministry of Commerce and Industry (MOCI), 12, 21, 43–46, 48–49
Ministry of Finance (MOF), 12, 21, 27
Ministry of International Trade and Industry (MITI), 14n27
MNCs, 6, 8–9, 16–17, 28, 32, 39–40
mobilisation, 53–54, 56, 99, 103, 108, 117n24, 120–124, 132, 139, 143, 145, 153, 162
Monopolies and Restrictive Trade Practices (MRTP), 30, 32
mortality rate, 19, 76

North American Free Trade Agreement (NAFTA), 17
National Democratic Alliance (NDA), 38
Nehru, Jawaharlal, 23n2, 24
neo-patrimonial states, 5, 11, 14–15, 14n27, 107, 107n5, 108–111, 116, 120–124, 134, 155, 160–163
NGOs, 100, 109, 119, 139, 143, 145–146
non-market factors, 7–8
Non-resident Indian(s), 32, 69

Odisha, 1, 1n2–3, 2–3, 5, 10–12, 17–22, 26, 40–41, 63, 77, 97, 106–108, 108n6, 109–113, 113n15, 114–116, 116n21, 117–118, 118n30, 119–129, 127n55, 129n61, 130–139, 142–154, 157–158, 160–164
Orissa Resettlement and Rehabilitation Policy (ORRP), 115, 128–129, 129n62, 131, 151

Parliament, 35, 114–115, 119, 122, 124–125, 127, 136–137, 139
party/parties, 5, 10–12, 21–22, 24–29, 31–33, 34n43, 37, 39, 45–49, 51–57, 57n17, 58, 65, 71–73, 73n79, 75–77, 80, 88, 91, 96–97, 99, 101–104, 107, 111–113, 113n15, 114–115, 117n24, 119–121, 126, 127, 129n62, 134, 138–139, 138n13, 139–140, 153, 154–164
policy-maker(s), 10–11, 15–16, 20–21, 23, 23n2, 26, 31–33, 35–36, 42, 45, 49, 51, 53, 55, 59, 63, 73, 77, 82–83, 96, 101, 103, 126, 154–155, 158
political economy, 3, 8–9, 12, 14, 23, 23n4, 47, 52, 80, 82–103, 108, 135–139, 147–152
political elite(s), 5, 51–52, 82, 107, 121, 147
political leader(s), 2, 4, 12, 15, 23n3, 24, 34n43, 39, 41, 45–47, 52, 54–56, 59–61, 63–64, 66–75, 77, 79–80, 84, 86, 91, 97, 102–103, 107, 109–112, 117, 119, 132, 134–138, 140, 155–158, 161, 164
politics, 4–5, 5n10, 7, 10–11, 12n21, 15–16, 23, 23n3, 42–48, 52, 54, 57–58, 66–67, 71, 77, 91, 94n38, 96, 107–109, 112–115, 117n24, 119, 131–133, 135n2, 138n13, 154–155, 158, 162–163
POSCO, 1, 1n2, 2, 5, 10, 17, 22, 40, 98, 121, 125, 126n49, 128, 133–147, 151, 153, 162
poverty, 4, 19–20, 27, 64, 73, 76–77, 106, 108, 108n6, 109–111, 122–123, 136, 152, 158
Prime Minister, 12, 24, 26, 27, 31–32, 34, 37–40, 43, 45–46, 49
Prime Minister's Office (PMO), 16, 25
private capital, 11–12, 21, 25–26, 32, 49, 128, 138, 156, 163
process of FDI flows, 8
Public Distribution System (PDS), 56, 122
public sector, 4, 30, 59, 75, 89, 124, 136
Punjab, 5n10, 118n30, 138

quantitative restrictions, 25

Index

Rajasthan, 41, 107n2, 118n30, 120, 138
Rashtriya Swayamsevak Sangh (RSS), 39
regime(s), 5n9, 7, 9, 11, 13n22, 14n27, 21, 24, 48, 155, 158, 163n1
research and development (R&D), 83
Reserve Bank of India (RBI), 3n6, 27, 75
right-wing, 39–40, 48
Rourkela Steel Plant, 1, 1n4
rule implementer(s), 12–13, 15
rule maker(s), 12–13, 13n22, 15
rural, 18–20, 67, 71–73, 76, 103, 112n11, 117–118, 122–123, 152, 161

Scheduled Caste(s) (SCs), 18, 57, 76, 116
Scheduled Tribe(s) (STs), 18, 57, 76, 108, 116
Shekar, Chandra, 34
Singapore, 6n15, 14n27, 74
social integration, 11
social structure, 8, 21–22, 51–52, 76, 80, 92–93, 107–108, 111, 115, 120, 158, 163
society-centred, 52, 108, 111
socio-economic, 1n3, 22, 107, 117
socio-political, 5, 7–11, 14, 14n27, 15, 18, 21, 23, 42, 48, 50–51, 108n6, 115, 125, 129, 154–155, 158, 164
South Korea, 1, 6n15, 14n27, 17, 32, 73, 80, 82, 93, 95, 125, 135, 137, 164
Special Economic Zone(s) (SEZs), 40, 50, 99, 130
state capacity, 3, 10, 22, 61n29, 157, 159–161, 163n3
State Planning Commission, 64
state-centred, 54, 109–110
state-society, 5, 5n9, 10–15, 21–2, 51, 61n29, 74, 77, 79, 107, 111, 119, 131, 133, 150, 153–154, 156–161
steel plant project(s), 10, 22, 126n49, 133, 144n28
subnational, 3
swadeshi, 26, 37–40, 46–47
Swadeshi Jagran Manch (SJM), 39

Swatantra Party, 111–112, 113n15

Tamil Nadu, 2, 3, 3n6, 4, 10–12, 17–21, 34n43, 40–41, 45–46, 50, 50n2, 51–55, 57–60, 61n29, 62–69, 71–77, 79–96, 99–104, 114, 118–119, 123–124, 131–132, 138, 146, 150, 153–159, 161–164
Tamil Nadu Congress Committee (TNCC), 55–57
TATA, 2, 22, 98, 121, 125, 128–131, 133–135, 138n13, 145–153, 159, 162
technology transfer, 6
tehsil, 68, 135, 140–141, 144–145, 151
the United Nations (UN), 28, 37
the United States, 16–17, 26, 73
tipping point, 16, 23, 42, 51, 77
trade, 8, 17, 24, 24, 34, 37, 39, 45, 72, 74, 80, 85–94, 102, 104–105
triple alliance, 8

unemployment, 19–20, 64, 96, 123, 152, 157, 161
United Nations Children's Fund (UNICEF), 61, 106
United Progressive Alliance (UPA), 47
upper-middle, 11, 21, 111–113, 116–117, 120–121, 132, 158, 160–162
urban/urbanisation, 18–20, 50n2, 51–52, 55, 60–64, 69–72, 74, 79, 93, 104, 118, 120, 123–124, 148, 152, 156–157, 159–160, 161–162
Utkal Congress, 113, 113n15
Uttar Pradesh, 3n6, 5, 26, 41, 76, 86, 107n2, 110, 118n27, 118n30, 138

Vajpayee, 37–39, 46–48, 127

West Bengal, 2–5, 26, 63, 72, 96n45, 110, 117n24, 119–120, 138, 145, 150
wholly-owned subsidiary, 42n71
World Bank, 26, 36, 52, 55, 61, 69, 73–75, 109, 116, 124, 126, 129, 156
World Trade Organization (WTO), 40